GET OUT THE VOTE

GET OUT
THE VOTE

HOW TO INCREASE VOTER TURNOUT

FOURTH EDITION

Donald P. Green
Alan S. Gerber

Brookings Institution Press
Washington, D.C.

The Brookings Institution is a private nonprofit organization devoted to research, education, and publication on important issues of domestic and foreign policy. Its principal purpose is to bring the highest quality independent research and analysis to bear on current and emerging policy problems. Interpretations or conclusions in Brookings publications should be understood to be solely those of the authors.

Library of Congress Cataloging-in-Publication Data
Names: Green, Donald P., 1961– author. | Gerber, Alan S., author.
Title: Get out the vote : how to increase voter turnout / Donald P.
    Green, Alan S. Gerber.
Description: Fourth Edition. | Washington, D.C. : Brookings
    Institution Press, [2019] | Includes bibliographical references and
    index.
Identifiers: LCCN 2019018089 (print) | LCCN 2019018862 (ebook)
    | ISBN 9780815736943 (epub) | ISBN 9780815736936 | ISBN
    9780815736936 (paper) | ISBN 9780815736943 (ebook)
Subjects: LCSH: Political campaigns—United States. | Campaign
    management—United States. | Voter turnout—United States.
Classification: LCC JK2281 (ebook) | LCC JK2281 .G74 2019 (print)
    | DDC 324.70973—dc23
LC record available at https://lccn.loc.gov/2019018089

9 8 7 6 5 4 3 2 1

Typeset in Life and Univers Condensed

Composition by Elliott Beard

Contents

Preface

What are the most cost-effective ways to increase voter turnout? Whether the ambition is to win elections, promote civic engagement in a community, or bolster the legitimacy of democratic institutions, this question is of enormous significance.

This book is a practical guide for managing get-out-the-vote (GOTV) drives, while at the same time pulling together all of the scientific evidence about the cost-effectiveness of face-to-face canvassing, direct mail, phone calls, and other tactics. In the years since our initial field experiment in New Haven in 1998, experimental research on voter mobilization has grown rapidly, furnishing a wealth of studies that encompass municipal, state, and federal contests; campaigns run by Democrats, Republicans, interest groups, and nonpartisan coalitions; campaigns targeting populations living in urban, rural, and suburban neighborhoods; and voter mobilization efforts directed at African Americans, Latinos, and Asian Americans. Although many questions remain unanswered, these studies have brought new scientific rigor to the study of campaigns. Unfortunately, most have been published in technical, academic journals, and many scientific reports have never been published at all. This book aims to bring this research to the attention of a broader audience.

We are deeply grateful to the many researchers, candidates, consultants, organizations, and campaign workers who made this line of research possible. Some of the studies reported here were conducted under our direction, but with each passing year, the network of scholars and groups who conduct this type of research grows larger and more diverse. The first edition of *Get Out the Vote* described a few dozen experiments and lamented that they were as "rare in politics as successful third party candidates"; this new edition summarizes hundreds of experiments.

Thanks go to the dozens of researchers from various universities and organizations who graciously shared their results with us. We are especially indebted to David Nickerson and Costas Panagopoulos, who played such a central role in the growth and development of field experimental studies of voter turnout, and to Peter Aronow, Daniel Biggers, David Broockman, Alex Coppock, Tiffany Davenport, Al Fang, Josh Kalla, Andrew Kapadia, Oliver McClellan, Mary McGrath, Melissa Michelson, Jenny Smith, Joe Sutherland, Amy White, and Adam Zelizer, whose work conducting, assembling, or analyzing experiments has made it possible for us to assess the effectiveness of various GOTV tactics. Special thanks go to Jose Gomez, who helped update the meta-analyses for this edition.

We are grateful to the campaigns and organizations that allowed us to study their voter mobilization efforts. Organizations such as Civic Nation, Look Ahead America, the National Association of Latino Elected Officials, MoveOn, Optimus, the Public Interest Research Group, Rock the Vote, Freedom Works, Service Employees International Union, Texans for Rick Perry, #VoteTogether, Vote.org, and several partisan campaigns that asked to remain anonymous deserve the gratitude of all those who will learn from their experiences. We are also grateful to firms that have been eager collaborators on experimental evaluations, such as TargetSmart (Senior Data Analyst Christopher Brill). They helped facilitate productive, public research partnerships with One Arizona (Executive Director Ian Danley) and Alliance for Climate Action (Deputy Director Leah Qusba).

Generous financial support for our research and for research conducted jointly with our collaborators has come from a variety of sources. The Smith Richardson Foundation funded our first studies in 1998. The Pew Charitable Trusts invited us to evaluate the Youth Vote campaign in 2000 and the New Voters Project in 2004. A grant from the Center for Information and Research on Civic Learning and Engagement made possible our 2001 and 2002 studies of Youth Vote and Votes for Students. The Carnegie Corporation funded research we conducted with Lynn Vavreck on the effects of Rock the Vote's 2004 television campaign. In 2006 and 2007, the James Irvine Foundation sponsored field experiments associated with its California Votes Initiative that Melissa Michelson and Lisa García Bedolla conducted with Donald Green. Working Assets funded a series of experiments that Donald Green conducted with Elizabeth Addonizio, James Glaser, and Costas Panagopoulos in 2006 that assessed the effects of Election Day festivals and radio advertisements publicizing mayoral and congressional elections. The Boston Foundation funded research conducted by Donald Green and Tiffany Davenport on the effects of canvassing during a 2007 municipal election. The Carnegie Corporation supported research conducted by Donald Green and Eline de Rooij on the effects of radio messages on voter turnout in 2008 and 2010. Research funding from Columbia University made possible several experiments conducted since 2011, and the Institution for Social and Policy Studies at Yale University has provided generous support since 1998. None of these funders, of course, bear any responsibility for the conclusions we draw.

Previous editions of *Get Out the Vote* have earned a spot on the bookshelves of people from across the political spectrum. From our frequent correspondence with readers, we know that this book is read closely and that important decisions are informed by its conclusions. We take very seriously the charge of evaluating the experimental literature and presenting it in an accessible and accurate manner. Although many of the conclusions from earlier editions are bolstered by the addition of dozens of new experiments, some need revision. Certain topics about which previous editions could only speculate are now addressed with hard evidence.

The fourth edition of *Get Out the Vote* features fresh updates of the research literature on an array of topics, especially outreach via social media, text messages, and Election Day festivals. Chapter 12, which discusses the relative efficiency of voter mobilization versus persuasion, brings to bear new evidence suggesting that mobilization is a better bet. In order to keep the book concise and current, we have trimmed many of the older studies that were described in previous editions. Finally, in an effort to make our quantitative summaries accessible and transparent, the data and open-source software used to generate the meta-analysis appendix chapters are available online at https://doi.org/10.7910/DVN/VE43O6.

CHAPTER ONE

Introduction:
Why Voter Mobilization Matters

The United States has the busiest election calendar on earth. Thanks to the many layers of federal, state, and local government, Americans have more opportunities to vote each decade than Britons, Germans, or Japanese have in their lifetimes. Thousands of Americans seek elective office each year, running for legislative, judicial, and administrative posts.

Given the frequency with which elections occur and the mundane quality of most of the contests, those who write about elections tend to focus exclusively on the high-visibility contests for president, senator, or governor. This focus gives a distorted impression of how election battles are typically waged. First, high-profile races often involve professionalized campaigns, staffed by a coterie of media consultants, pollsters, speechwriters, and event coordinators. Second, in order to reach large and geographically dispersed populations, these campaigns often place enormous emphasis on mass communications, such as television advertising. Third, the importance of these races calls press attention to the issues at stake and the attributes of the candidates.

The typical election, by contrast, tends to be waged on a smaller scale and at a more personal level. Few candidates for state representative or probate judge have access to the financial resources needed to produce and air television commercials. Even long-standing incumbents in state and municipal posts are often unknown to a majority of their constituents. The challenge that confronts candidates in low-salience elections is to target potential supporters and get them to the polls, while living within the constraints of a tight campaign budget.

A similar challenge confronts political and nonpartisan organizations that seek to mobilize voters for state and local elections. Making scarce campaign dollars go as far as possible requires those who manage these campaigns to think hard about the trade-offs. Is it best to assemble a local phone bank? Hire a telemarketing firm? Field a team of canvassers to contact voters door-to-door? Send direct mail and, if so, how many pieces?

This book offers a guide for campaigns and organizations that seek to formulate cost-effective strategies for mobilizing voters. For each type of voter mobilization tactic, we pose two basic questions: (1) What steps are needed to put it into place, and (2) How many votes will be produced for each dollar spent? After summarizing the "how to do it" aspects of each get-out-the-vote (GOTV) tactic, we provide a scientifically rigorous assessment of whether it has been shown to produce votes in a cost-effective manner. We discuss some high-tech campaign tactics, such as voter mobilization through social media, some low-tech tactics, such as door-to-door canvassing, and some high-priced tactics, such as television and radio. The concluding chapter discusses the uncharted frontiers of GOTV research and guides readers through the process of conducting their own experiments to evaluate the effectiveness of their campaigns.

Does Voter Mobilization Matter?

The sleepy quality of many state and local elections often conceals what is at stake politically. Take, for example, the 1998 Kansas State Board of Education election that created a six-to-four conservative majority. This election featured a well-organized campaign that used personal contact with voters to mobilize hundreds of churchgoers in low-turnout Republican primaries. This victory at the polls culminated a year later in a dramatic change in policy. In August 1999, the Kansas State Board of Education voted six to four to drop evolution from science education standards, letting localities decide whether to teach creationism in addition to or instead of evolution. The story of hard-fought campaigns for the Kansas State Board of Education does not end there. In 2000, moderates regained the majority and reinstated evolution into the science education standards. The 2002 election resulted in a five-five split between moderates and conservatives, and 2004 put conservatives back in control of the Kansas State Board of Education. The conservative majority approved the teaching of "intelligent design" as an alternative to evolution (which could now be taught as a theory but not a scientific fact). Power switched once again in 2006, and moderates repealed science guidelines questioning evolution. With an eight-to-two majority, moderates in 2013 adopted K–12 curriculum standards that treat evolution (and climate change) as fact.

These elections and their policy implications attracted national attention and renewed debates about science curricula and religious conviction. But what occurred in Kansas is a story not only about clashing ideologies, but also about how campaigns work to get voters to the polls. We suspect that very few Kansans changed their mind about the merits of evolution and creationism over the course of these election cycles. What changed over time was who showed up to vote.

As politics in the United States has grown more ideologically polarized, victories by one party or the other cause abrupt policy shifts. The narrow victories by Republican presidential candidates in 2000 and 2016 led to dramatic changes to the tax code a year later. An analysis of hundreds of close gubernatorial elections finds that Democrats who won close elections presided over increases in spending on education, health, and public safety.[1] A similar study of nearly 1,000 close mayoral elections reveals that narrowly-elected Democrats presided over a sizable increase in municipal spending.[2]

The ability to mobilize supporters can be decisive in close elections, and close elections are plentiful. In 2018, the margin of victory separating Democratic and Republican candidates for the House of Representatives was under 1 percent in nine districts and under 2 percent in ten more. Granted, many House constituencies are uncompetitive, but 89% of Americans live in jurisdictions where at least one close election for some federal or state office occurs over the course of six years.[3] This share grows even larger when we consider the many offices that are contested in primary or municipal elections, where the margin of victory is often less than 500 votes. Voter mobilization campaigns are sometimes derided as "field goal units," adding only a few percentage points to a candidate's vote share. Although few GOTV campaigns are capable of reversing the fortunes of an overmatched candidate, field goals do win close games.

Getting Advice on Getting Out the Vote

Campaigns vary enormously in their goals: some are partisan, some nonpartisan; some focus on name recognition, some on persuasion, and some on mobilizing their base of loyal voters. Some campaigns seek to educate citizens, some to register citizens, and some to motivate citizens. But varied as they are, campaigns have important and obvious commonalities. As Election Day approaches and campaigns move into GOTV mode, their aims become quite similar and their purposes very narrow. By the week before the election, they are all homing in on one simple task: to get their people to the polls. Each campaign struggles with the same basic challenge: how to allocate remaining resources in order to turn out the largest number of targeted voters.

Ask around and you will receive plenty of advice on the best way to mobilize voters in those final days or weeks. You may hear that it is one part mailings to three parts phone calls for an incumbent race. You may hear that, regardless of the office, you should build your campaign around phone calls and, if you can afford it, buy radio airtime. You may even hear that, for a nonpartisan GOTV campaign, you should try door-to-door canvassing but fall back on leafleting if you run short on campaign workers. Much of this advice is based on conjecture—conjecture drawn from experience, perhaps, but conjecture nonetheless.

What sets this book apart from the existing "how to win an election" canon is the quality of the research on which it relies. The studies reported in this book use *randomized experiments* to assess the effects of GOTV interventions. These experiments divide lists of potential voters into a *treatment group* that receives some kind of campaign intervention and a *control group* that does not. After the election is over, researchers examine public records to see who voted and then tabulate the results to determine whether those assigned to receive the GOTV treatment voted at higher rates than those assigned to the control group. Although these experiments still leave room for interpretation, their scientific rigor goes a long way toward replacing speculation with evidence.

Another aspect of our work that contributes to our objectivity is that we are not in the business of selling campaign services. In the past, scanning for truth about the effectiveness of various GOTV strategies was like having to consult with salespeople about whether to purchase the items they are selling. Many campaign consultants have financial interests in direct mail companies, phone banks, or media consultancy services. When they cite scientific evidence (such as the studies we have conducted), they do so selectively to portray what they are selling in a positive light. In this book, we make a concerted effort to incorporate the results of every experimental study of which we are aware.

GOTV Research and Larger Questions about Why People Do Not Vote

Political observers often turn to broad-gauge explanations for why so few Americans vote: alienation from public life, the lack of a proportional representation system, the failings of civic education, the geographic mobility of the population. Many books written by academics focus exclusively on these broad cultural or institutional explanations.

This book, in contrast, is concerned with factors that affect turnout over the course of a few days or weeks. We do not discuss the ways in which political participation is shaped by fundamental features of our political, social, and economic system, although we agree that structural and psychological barriers to voting are worthy of study and that certain reforms might raise turnout. In the concluding chapter, we describe research that might be useful to those interested in learning more about how voter turnout relates to these broader features of society. The focus of this book is quite different. Our aim is to look closely at how GOTV campaigns are structured and to figure out how various GOTV tactics affect voter participation. This close-to-the-ground approach is designed to provide campaigns with useful information about the effectiveness of common GOTV techniques. With six weeks until an election, even the most dedicated campaign team cannot reshape the country's culture, party system, or election laws. What a campaign can do, however, is make informed choices about its GOTV strategy, ensuring that its resources are being used efficiently to produce votes.

Evidence versus War Stories

Before delving into the research findings, we want to call attention to assumptions that often hinder informed GOTV decisionmaking. One such assumption is that experts know best. People who have worked with a lot of campaigns are assumed to know which tactics work and which do not. Campaign professionals often speak forcefully and authoritatively about what works. On the other end of the spectrum is the assumption that no one really knows what works because no one can adequately assess what works. There is no way to rerun an election using different GOTV methods, no parallel universe in which to watch the very same campaign focusing its efforts on mass mailings, then on phone banks, and then on television ads. A third assumption is that if everybody is doing it, it must be useful: thousands of campaigns can't be wrong about prerecorded calls! The following chapters respond to these misguided assumptions. In short,

✓ Experts, be they consultants, seasoned campaigners, or purveyors of GOTV technology, rarely measure effectiveness. Hal Malchow, one of the first campaign professionals to embrace experimentation, reports that his calls for rigorous evaluation often go unheeded, notwithstanding the large quantities of money at stake.[4]

✓ Experts frequently adduce dubious statistics purporting to show the effectiveness of their campaign efforts. People who manage campaigns and sell campaign services have a wealth of experience in deploying campaign resources, formulating campaign messages, and supervising campaign staff. But lacking a background in research design or statistical inference, they frequently misrepresent correlation as causation. They might claim, for instance, that a radio GOTV campaign is responsible for increasing the Latino vote in a particular media market. In support of this assertion, they might point to lower Latino turnout in a previous election or in a neighboring media market. But are the two successive elections truly comparable? Are the neighboring media markets truly comparable? If not, this style of proof-by-anecdote is potentially misleading.

✓ There is an accurate way to assess the effectiveness of GOTV techniques, namely, through experimental research. Randomly assigning a set of precincts or media markets to different campaign tactics makes meaningful and even-handed evaluation possible. This method has been used hundreds of times to evaluate GOTV campaigns.

✓ Our results may surprise you. Just because everybody is doing it does not necessarily mean that it works. Large sums of money are routinely wasted on ineffective GOTV tactics.

We will count ourselves successful if you not only learn from the experimental results we report, but also become more discerning when evaluating claims that rest on anecdotes and other nonexperimental evidence. The recurrent theme of this book is the importance of adopting a skeptical scientific attitude when evaluating campaign tactics.

Preview of Our Findings

The overarching conclusion that emerges from rigorous voter turnout research may be summarized as follows: the more personal the interaction between campaign and potential voter, the more it raises a person's chances of voting. Door-to-door canvassing by enthusiastic volunteers is the gold-standard mobilization tactic; chatty, unhurried phone calls seem to work well, too. Automatically dialed, prerecorded GOTV phone calls, by contrast, are utterly impersonal and rarely get people to vote.

Here is the trade-off confronting those who manage campaigns: the more personal the interaction, the harder it is to reproduce on a large scale. Canvassing door-to-door is therefore not the answer for every GOTV campaign. That is why we consider this book to be a "shoppers' guide." No candidate or campaign manager can read this book and, without considering his or her own circumstances, find the answer. The key is to assess your resources, goals, and political situation and then form a judgment about what tactics will produce the most votes at the lowest cost. What we do offer is a synopsis of scientifically rigorous evidence about how well various GOTV tactics worked in specific contexts. Thanks to our experience conducting experiments, as well as our immersion in the published and unpublished literature, we are better positioned than other authors of how-to books on campaigns to describe the experimental findings.

Structure of the Book

We begin the book by explaining why experimental evidence warrants special attention. Chapter 2 discusses the nuts and bolts of how randomized experiments are conducted and why they are better than other approaches to studying the effectiveness of GOTV tactics. Chapters 3 through 9 present our evaluations of GOTV mobilization techniques: door-to-door canvassing, literature and signage, mail, phone calls, e-mail, social media, events, and communication through the mass media. Chapter 10 assesses the vote-producing efficiency of registration drives, whether conducted in person or by mail. These chapters discuss the practical challenges of conducting these campaigns and provide a cost-benefit analysis of each GOTV tactic. To help readers make informed decisions about which kinds of messages to deploy, chapter 11 summarizes existing theory and evidence about various GOTV appeals. Chapter 12 wraps up by discussing some of the many unanswered questions in GOTV research. In the interest of helping you to customize research for your own purposes, the concluding chapter also gives some pointers about how to conduct experimental studies of voter turnout. Experimentation is not some special form of sorcery known only to college professors. Anyone can do it, and several innovative mobilization experiments have been conducted by readers of previous editions of this book.

CHAPTER TWO

Evidence versus Received Wisdom

I t is not hard to find advice about how to run an effective get-out-the-vote campaign. Every consultant or campaign manager has a story about the tactics he or she used in a recent election victory. The web pages of firms that specialize in phone calls offer testimonials about how their calls were decisive, while firms that specialize in direct mail or social media tout the special powers of those tactics. The litany of advice can easily be expanded to include digital advertising and door-to-door canvassing, as well as special combinations of these tactics that, when deployed together, are said to have synergistic effects.

Phone calls, direct mail, digital ads, and precinct walking all sound like good campaign tactics, and a campaign with an infinite supply of time and money would use them all. But here on planet earth, campaigns face budget constraints. So, the question is not, What are some helpful campaign tactics? but rather, What are the most cost-effective campaign tactics?

In order to know whether a campaign tactic is cost-effective, it is necessary to determine how many votes are produced for each dollar spent (see box 2-1). Most firms and organizations that offer campaign services or recommend campaign tactics have a clear idea about the costs involved. Those experienced in running campaigns know the approximate unit cost of each mailer or phone call, the hourly rates of canvassers and supervisors, and the setup costs of producing literature and supervising

---

Box 2-1. Thinking about Cost-Effectiveness

When thinking about the cost-effectiveness of a get-out-the-vote tactic, it is helpful to ask, How many dollars will it take to produce one additional vote? This yardstick will help you to compare the cost-effectiveness of various types of GOTV tactics. One tactic might produce votes at a rate of $40 per vote, another at $75 per vote.

Keep three things in mind as you read our assessments of cost-effectiveness. First, some tactics, such as e-mail, generate votes cheaply insofar as they give a tiny nudge to vast numbers of people. If your constituency does not have vast numbers of people, these tactics might be useless to you. Second, the costs and benefits we report in the chapters that follow are calculated based on the experiences of particular campaigns. A campaign that goes door-to-door to mobilize voters might successfully contact every fourth person and generate votes at a rate of $33 per vote. This finding says something about the efficiency of that type of campaign, but it might not provide an accurate assessment of what would happen if your canvassers returned repeatedly to each house in an effort to contact three out of four voters. Be cautious when extrapolating to campaigns that are very different from the ones we have studied. Finally, special considerations sometimes come into play when assessing campaign costs. Depending on the specific campaign finance laws under which you are operating, you might have special financial incentives to spend dollars on one campaign tactic rather than another. Or you might know someone in the printing or telemarketing business willing to offer you a great deal.

---

these campaign operations. Indeed, one of the reasons that campaign professionals are valuable is that they possess an immense amount of knowledge about what it takes to execute a campaign. Seasoned campaign veterans know a great deal about the inputs, but they seldom possess reliable information about the outputs: the number of votes that these tactics produce.

Campaign professionals and candidates frequently tell war stories about the mailers that Candidate X distributed before winning a big upset victory or how Candidate Y squandered her big lead in the polls by failing to mobilize her base. These anecdotes do not enable you to isolate the influence of any particular input. They simply encourage you to imagine a world in which the campaign behaved differently, while everything else about the campaign remained the same. The skeptic might well wonder, Was Candidate X's victory really due to mailers? Might something about Candidate Y have caused her campaign to run into trouble other than her alleged problems in mobilizing her core supporters?

The problem of drawing sound conclusions from anecdotes persists even when campaign veterans are equipped with many, many war stories and perhaps even a statistical analysis to boot. It is sometimes quipped that the word "data" is plural for "anecdote." Suppose that voter turnout rates tend to be higher in districts where campaigns spend unusually large sums on professional phone banks. What would this say about the influence of phone banks on voter turnout? Not a whole lot. It could be that the same forces that bring a lot of money into campaigns—such as a tight race for an important office—are the very things that attract voter interest. We might observe a strong correlation between turnout and expenditures on professional phone banks even if calls from phone banks have no effect whatsoever on voter turnout.

Even fancy statistical analysis of survey data or historical voting patterns cannot overcome the basic principle that correlation is not causation. Suppose that you ask survey respondents to describe whether they were called by a campaign and whether they voted. The correlation between these two reports may be quite misleading. First, to put it politely, respondents may "inaccurately recall" whether they were contacted and whether they voted. Those who wish to present themselves as politically involved may be more likely to indicate both that they were contacted and that they voted. Second, campaigns often target likely voters. Even if canvassing had no effect, your survey would still reveal higher voting rates among the folks who were contacted. That is *why* they were contacted.

Statistical fixes cannot resolve these problems without relying on untestable assumptions about response error and the targeting strategies used by campaigns. Complex statistical analysis creates a fog that is too often regarded as authoritative. When confronted with reams of impressive sounding numbers, it is easy to lose sight of the weak research design that produced them. A weak design can be used to prove things that are patently false. For example, calls that simply encourage voters to "buckle up for safety when driving" appear to produce huge increases in turnout. This statistical illusion grows out of the fact that people who are likely to answer calls (regardless of the message) tend to vote at higher rates than those who do not answer.[1]

The situation is no better when scholars assemble historical data on voter turnout and attempt to tease out the effects of campaign tactics by "holding constant" various background factors. Suppose that voter turnout rates were unusually high in areas canvassed by labor unions. Does this pattern mean that canvassing increased turnout or that labor unions deployed their canvassers in areas with unusually high turnout?

The scientific study of voter mobilization requires something more than correlations. It requires a method for making valid comparisons between instances where a campaign tactic was or was not used. It requires a method for establishing that the people who were canvassed, phoned, or mailed were similar to those who were left alone. Only one procedure ensures a fair comparison, and that is random assignment. Flip a coin to decide whether each person will be exposed to some form of "treatment" or instead assigned to a control group. Since random chance determines who receives the treatment, there will be no systematic tendency for the treatment group to contain a disproportionate number of frequent voters. As the number of people in the study increases, chance differences in the composition of the treatment and control groups will tend to disappear. When thousands of people are randomly assigned to treatment and control groups, experiments enable researchers to form a precise assessment of a treatment's impact.

What sets this book apart is that its conclusions about which campaign tactics work are based on evidence from randomized experiments. The remainder of this chapter provides an overview of how and where these experiments were conducted. If you are eager to hear about the conclusions of these studies, you may wish to skip this chapter and move on to chapter 3, but we encourage you to acquire at least some passing familiarity with experimental research. The more you understand about these studies, the easier it will be for you to recognize the strengths and limitations of the results when applying them to your own situation. Who knows? You may even be inspired to launch your own experiment.

Randomized Experiments

Randomized experimentation is the tool often used in medical research to gauge the effectiveness of new drugs. The reason is simple: in medical research, the stakes are enormous. Lives hang in the balance, and so do billions of dollars in pharmaceutical sales. In order to prevent profit-driven companies from exaggerating the benefits of their products, the

U.S. Food and Drug Administration maintains a high standard of scientific rigor when evaluating new treatments.

Compared with the world of pharmaceuticals, the world of elections is free-wheeling and unregulated. No government agency demands that consultants furnish proof to back up their claims about the effectiveness of campaign tactics.

Recognizing the importance of obtaining reliable evidence about how to increase voter turnout, we have made extensive use of randomized experimentation since 1998, and our work has inspired others to conduct experiments of their own. Hundreds of experiments have been conducted at various points in the electoral calendar: presidential elections, federal midterm elections, state off-year elections, municipal elections, runoff elections, and party primaries. Some of these studies have taken place in states with traditional voting systems (such as Virginia), while others have occurred in early-voting states (Texas) or in vote-by-mail-only states (Oregon). These get-out-the-vote campaigns have taken place in areas as different as Detroit, Eugene, Houston, and the rural outskirts of Fresno—not to mention France, Pakistan, and Uganda. Many of these experiments have involved nonpartisan efforts to get people to the polls; some, however, have studied attempts by partisan campaigns to both mobilize and persuade voters.

Despite these differences, the randomized studies of voter turnout discussed in this volume have a common structure, which consists of six components.

✓ A population of observations is defined. This population includes all the people or geographically defined groups whose actions will be measured (whether they are exposed to a GOTV intervention or not). Most studies draw their experimental subjects from lists of registered voters, although a few studies draw from lists of streets or precincts or media markets.

✓ The observations are randomly divided into a treatment group and a control group. Random assignment has a very specific meaning in this context. It does not refer to haphazard or arbitrary assignment. Random assignment refers to a procedure by which subjects are assigned to the treatment group with a known probability. In its most basic form, random assignment can be accomplished by flipping a coin for each individual and assigning all those who receive "heads" to the treatment group. In practice, random assignment is usually performed using a computerized random number generator.

✓ An intervention is applied to persons in the treatment group. For example, members of the treatment group may be sent mail encouraging them to vote.

✓ The outcome variable is measured for those in each group. In the studies we discuss, voting is measured by examining public records, not by asking people whether they voted. The percentage of people in the treatment group who voted is then compared to the percentage in the control group who voted.

✓ The difference between the treatment group's voting rate and the control group's voting rate is subjected to statistical analysis. The aim is to determine how much uncertainty remains about the true effect of the intervention. The larger the study (that is, the greater the number of observations assigned to treatment and control groups), the less uncertainty will remain after the experiment is analyzed. Statistical analysis also takes into account one of the annoying facts about both campaigning and experimenting: sometimes it is not possible to reach the people being targeted. If researchers know the rate at which people were contacted, they can calculate how much influence the experimental intervention had on those who are reachable. Both facts are needed to gauge how effective an intervention is likely to be when used in the future.[2]

✓ The experiment is replicated in other times and places. A single experiment can establish that a GOTV tactic works in a particular setting; a series of experiments is necessary to show that the experimental hypothesis holds when the political conditions are different. Replicating experiments also enables researchers to figure out whether variations in the way a treatment is administered affect the results and whether some voters are more responsive than others.

Conducting studies of this kind requires campaign management skills—in two senses. First, many of the experiments were the product of campaigns that the researchers themselves developed or helped to coordinate. The original 1998 studies in New Haven and West Haven, Connecticut, involved door-to-door canvassing, direct mail, and professional phone banks. Our research team plotted out canvassing routes, oversaw dozens of precinct walkers, worked with direct mail vendors to create and distribute nine different mailers, devised phone scripts, and monitored the calls from the phone bank. (The fact that we, as novices, were able to pull this off with only a few glitches should hearten those of you about to embark on your first campaign.)

The second sense in which we use the term "campaign management" refers to the fact that many of the experiments we report have grown out of collaborations with actual campaigns. We never turn down an opportunity to study campaigns experimentally and are proud to have worked with candidates and groups across the ideological spectrum: Republican gubernatorial and congressional campaigns; Tea Party campaigns on behalf of conservative state representatives; Democratic campaigns for state assembly and mayor; labor union efforts to mobilize supporters of statewide Democratic candidates; interest group campaigns designed to mobilize African Americans, women, and environmentalists; and nonpartisan campaigns designed to mobilize Latinos, Asians, and voters between the ages of eighteen and twenty-five. For these groups, mobilizing votes is understandably a higher priority than conducting research. Nevertheless, amid the time pressures of an impending election, these campaigns allocated a random portion of their target lists to a control group. Collaboration with actual campaigns has greatly enhanced our understanding of how various mobilization tactics work under a range of real-world conditions.

Many things can go awry in the course of these experiments. If canvassers are allowed to choose which houses to visit, they may inadvertently administer the treatment to people in the control group. We therefore take pains to make sure that these experiments are carried out according to the randomized experimental protocols that we have devised. We have orchestrated dozens of successful experiments but also several fiascos that had to be discarded because the experimental plan was not followed.

One final point bears emphasis. We believe in open science. When we evaluate voter mobilization campaigns, we present our results in public venues after the election has passed. When asked to maintain the anonymity of names and places, we have done so, but all of the experiments we conduct are arranged with the clear understanding that the results will be made public in a form that permits the accumulation of knowledge.

Some Illustrative Studies Described in This Book

This book reports the results of hundreds of experiments conducted from 1998 through 2018. Because the list of studies is too lengthy to describe one by one, we provide thumbnail sketches of just a few studies that give a flavor of how experiments have been used to assess the effectiveness of campaign tactics.

Federal Midterm Elections, 1998

Our first foray into the world of randomized field experiments was conducted in New Haven.[3] Under the auspices of the League of Women Voters, we launched a citywide nonpartisan campaign. We designed and managed a door-to-door canvassing effort that spoke with more than 1,600 people. One, two, or three pieces of direct mail were sent to more than 11,000 households. Thousands more were called by a commercial phone bank. Some registered voters received combinations of face-to-face canvassing, mail, and phone calls. All of the messages were strictly nonpartisan, but some urged people to vote as a matter of civic duty, while others emphasized that one vote could be decisive in a close election or that voting makes elected officials pay attention to your neighborhood. The study's principal findings have stood the test of time: canvassing raises turnout substantially (provided that canvassers are able to catch people at home), nonpartisan mailings boost turnout slightly, commercial phone banks produce disappointing results, minor variations in message make little difference, and there appears to be no special gain in turnout when canvassing, mail, or phone calls are used in tandem with one another.

Partisan Primary Election, 2006

Many of the experiments in this book assess the effectiveness of tactics designed to elect a particular candidate or pass a ballot measure. One example of this line of research comes from a campaign to reelect a Texas Supreme Court justice, who faced stiff competition in a Republican primary. The Republican governor, Rick Perry, who had initially appointed the candidate to the court, recorded a "robocall" encouraging Republicans to vote in support of his nominee, whom he praised as a true conservative. A team of researchers assessed the effectiveness of these calls in two ways.[4] First, in order to gauge turnout effects, the campaign divided approximately 130,000 target households into treatment and control groups. Official turnout records revealed that treatment households voted at a rate that was 0.2 of a percentage point higher than the control group. Second, more than 1,100 precincts were randomly assigned to treatment and control groups so that the net effects on vote share could be estimated. The results indicated that blanketing a precinct with robocalls on average raised the endorsed candidate's vote margin by just 1.7 votes.

Municipal and Primary Elections, 2009–2010

It is often speculated that voter turnout in low-salience elections would increase if voters were reminded that Election Day is coming up. Working with election officials in San Mateo, California, Neil Malhotra, Melissa Michelson, and Ali Valenzuela conducted a series of experiments to assess the effects of e-mail reminders sent a day or two before Election Day.[5] The researchers studied the effects of two parallel e-mail campaigns. One batch of e-mails was sent by the town's registrar of voters; the other by a nonpartisan group called People for the Advancement of Voter Education (PAVE). Both deployed the same messages to randomly assigned voters for whom the registrar had valid e-mail addresses. The messages addressed recipients by name and stressed the importance of the upcoming election. PAVE's 55,000 e-mails generated a meager 28 votes. The registrar's 55,000 e-mails, however, raised turnout by 0.56 of a percentage point, or approximately 308 votes. Although the registrar's e-mails were not terribly effective, they increased turnout by more than would be expected by chance alone.

Presidential Election, 2016

Elections during the nineteenth century were raucous affairs in which the all-male electorate often voted in saloons or locations where whiskey flowed freely. The Progressive reforms of the 1880s, which eliminated electioneering inside polling locations, are often blamed for the sharp decline in turnout that occurred between the 1890s and 1920s. One hypothesis about how to revive voter turnout is to reintroduce the festive environment surrounding elections (minus the whiskey). The nonpartisan group Civic Nation orchestrated Election Day festivals across the country, in collaboration with local volunteers who publicized the community event during the weeks leading up to the election. In each community, polling locations suitable for a festival were randomly assigned to either a festival or an untreated control, for a total of nine treatment sites and nine control sites. Voter turnout in treatment sites proved to be 3.8 percentage points higher than their control counterparts, a statistically significant increase despite the small size of the experiment.[6] This experiment inspired larger follow-up studies in 2017 and 2018, which are described in chapter 8.

GOTV Shoppers' Guide

These studies illustrate how experiments may be designed to assess the effects of various tactics, messages, and messengers on voter turnout and vote choice.

As you make your way through this book, consider the applicability of these studies to your particular circumstances and goals. Think about whether the tactics that have proven to be successful are feasible for you. For example, you may not have access to large numbers of canvassers or to the money needed to send out six pieces of direct mail. You may also want to think about whether you can tweak a strategy we discuss to fit your circumstances. If you cannot mount a door-to-door campaign, perhaps you can make face-to-face contact with voters in retirement homes, shopping centers, night schools, or religious centers. We have not studied these tactics directly, so there is more uncertainty about whether they work. Use your judgment when making the leap from our research findings to analogous situations that your campaign may encounter.

In order to help you to keep track of the uncertainty surrounding each of the lessons learned from the experimental studies, we have created a simple rating system.

★★★ A three-star rating indicates that the finding is based on experiments involving large numbers of voters and that the GOTV tactic has been tested by different groups in a variety of sites.

★★ A two-star rating indicates that the finding is based on just one or two experiments. We have a reasonable level of confidence in the results but harbor some reservations because they have not been replicated across a wide array of demographic groups or political conditions.

★ A one-star rating indicates that the finding is suggested by experimental evidence but subject to a great deal of uncertainty. The conclusion may rest on a single study, or the evidence across studies may be contradictory.

For example, we have a rather clear impression of how well commercial phone banks mobilize voters when callers remind people to vote in an upcoming election. Several truly massive experiments have estimated this effect with a great deal of precision based on studies of both partisan and nonpartisan campaigns. The results warrant three stars. Experiments gauging the effectiveness of Election Day festivals, by comparison, are fewer in number, and taken as a whole they provide less precise estimates than the typical phone bank experiment. Conclusions drawn from these studies therefore warrant two stars. Conclusions about the mobilizing effects of radio advertising warrant one star because the results to date are suggestive but remain statistically inconclusive.

Keep in mind that experimental evaluation of campaign tactics is a rapidly accelerating scientific enterprise. As this book goes to press, more studies are getting under way. The growing collaboration between scholars and practitioners promises to refine our current stock of knowledge and to broaden the range of campaign techniques that we have subjected to rigorous inquiry. Our research—like all research—is provisional and incomplete. Nevertheless, the findings reported here can help you to form realistic expectations about your GOTV campaign. How many votes would you realistically expect to generate as a result of 256,000 robocalls? How about 38,000 nonpartisan mailers? Or 2,500 conversations at voters' doorsteps? By the time you finish this book, you will understand why the answer is approximately 200.

CHAPTER THREE

Door-to-Door Canvassing

Visiting voters at their homes was once the bread and butter of party mobilization, particularly in urban areas. Ward leaders made special efforts to canvass their neighborhoods, occasionally calling in favors or offering small financial incentives to ensure that their constituents delivered their votes on Election Day. Petty corruption was rife, but turnout rates were high, even in relatively poor neighborhoods.

With the decline of patronage politics and the rise of technologies that sharply reduced the cost of phone calls and mass mailings, shoe leather politics gradually faded away. The shift away from door-to-door canvassing occurred not because this type of mobilization was discovered to be ineffective, but rather because the economic and political incentives facing parties, candidates, and campaign professionals changed over time.

Although local party organizations still tend to favor face-to-face mobilization, national party leaders typically prefer campaign tactics that afford them centralized control over the deployment of campaign resources. The decentralized network of local ward heelers was replaced by phone banks and direct mail firms, whose messages could be standardized and whose operations could be started with very short lead time and deployed virtually anywhere on an enormous scale. National parties and their allied organizations have invested more resources in "ground operations" in recent years, but these activities still account for a relatively small share of total campaign outlays.[1]

Candidates, too, gradually drifted away from door-to-door canvassing, lured by the short lead times and minimal start-up costs of impersonal campaigning. Furthermore, the ability to translate campaign funds directly into voter mobilization activities through private vendors selling direct mail, text messaging, or phone bank services meant that candidates were less beholden to local party activists. Candidates with money, but without much affection for or experience with their party, could run credible campaigns without many supporters.

Finally, a class of professional campaign consultants emerged to take advantage of the profits that could be made brokering direct mail, e-mail, phone banks, text messaging, and mass media. Less money was to be made from door-to-door canvassing, and campaign professionals had little incentive to invest in the on-the-ground infrastructure of local volunteers because there was no guarantee that they would be hired back to work in the same area.

You should therefore expect to get conflicting advice about the value of door-to-door canvassing. Campaign professionals, for example, sometimes belittle this type of campaign, because it is associated with candidates who must watch their budget and therefore make unattractive customers. Local party officials often swear by it, but because they are in a tug-of-war with their national party for resources, local activists have an incentive to tout these activities. Even the rhetoric surrounding door knocking is hard to decipher. Campaigns sometimes exaggerate the size of their ground game to create the impression that they have the enthusiastic support of local activists.

In this chapter, we discuss the practical challenges of organizing a door-to-door campaign and review the results from dozens of experimental studies. The evidence leaves little doubt that door-to-door canvassing by campaign workers can increase turnout substantially, but the studies also show that mounting a canvassing campaign has its challenges. Successful campaigns require planning, motivated canvassers, and access to large numbers of residences. As you review the evidence, think about whether your campaign or organization has the ingredients for a successful and cost-efficient door-to-door campaign.

Organizing and Conducting a Door-to-Door Canvassing Campaign

Door-to-door canvassing encompasses a variety of activities that involve making direct contact with citizens. In partisan campaigns, for example, canvassing may be performed by candidates themselves, their campaign workers, or allied groups. Canvassers may both talk with voters and distribute literature, absentee ballot applications, lawn signs, or other campaign paraphernalia. On Election Day, canvassers may coordinate rides to the polls. Last, canvassing should be thought of not only as a means of getting out votes, but also as a vehicle for recruiting campaign volunteers and improving the public visibility of a campaign.

Canvassing on a scale sufficient to reach thousands of voters over the span of three or four weeks requires a great deal of planning and organization. But even a small-scale canvassing effort requires a fair amount of preparation. When planning, it is often helpful to break the canvassing operation into a set of discrete tasks: targeting, recruiting, scheduling, training, and supervising.

Targeting

As with any get-out-the-vote effort, canvassing begins with a target population, that is, a set of potential voters whom you think it worthwhile to mobilize. For instance, your target voters might be all registered Republicans who voted in the last general election or all Latinos under the age of thirty. It is important to think about what you need to do to locate and visit your target group. Can you just canvass certain neighborhoods, or do you need to identify the specific individuals or households that fit your target?

If the latter, you will need to begin by creating or purchasing an accurate list of potential voters (see boxes 3-1 and 3-2 on obtaining, updating, and refining lists). Ideally, your list should be accurate in two ways. It should accurately reflect the pool of individuals you want to contact, and it should provide accurate contact information for those individuals. Maintaining an updated voter list is invaluable. You should download the list to your computer and adjust it as information comes in. Suppose your candidate is running as a Democrat. Some people listed as Democrats may no longer consider themselves Democrats. Some people, when canvassed, may indicate that they do not support your candidate. Take the time to drop them from your target list so that you do not inadvertently try to mobilize them later.

The task of meeting people at their doorstep poses a variety of challenges. How accessible are the people on your target list? There is no sense wasting time cursing locked security apartments. When are the residents likely to be home? If most registered voters in the neighborhood work, your canvassers will have to wait until evenings or weekends to make efficient use of their time.

Box 3-1. How to Get Lists

In most jurisdictions, lists of registered voters are accessible to the public and generally are available from local registrars, county clerks, and secretaries of state. The costs of these lists vary wildly across jurisdictions. You may pay $5 or $500. Depending on your needs and resources, you may also want to hire a private list vendor that consolidates voter files across counties or states. Lists of registered voters always contain addresses and sometimes other information that could be useful to a canvassing effort, such as an individual's party registration, sex, birth date, and turnout in previous elections. Private list vendors, for a fee, will provide phone numbers and e-mail addresses for some of the names that appear on the voter file.

Box 3-2. Refining the List

There are three ways to pare down a list to include only the subgroup you would like to canvass. Information on a particular ethnic or socioeconomic sector of the voting population is available from the U.S. Census Bureau at its website (www.census.gov). Although you cannot get information about individual households, you can get information about census blocks, the smallest geographic area delineated by the census. This will allow you to determine, for instance, which neighborhoods in a particular district have a high concentration of, say, homeowners or Asians or people living below the poverty line. You can then pull the names of registrants from those neighborhoods for your canvassing effort or just canvass those neighborhoods in their entirety, if you have reason to believe that doing so would be efficient.

List vendors can also help with ethnic targeting, for a price. A firm may be able to provide a list of registered voters in a given district whose last names are typically Latino or Chinese, for example. If you are handy with the software package R, you can find free open-source code to conduct ethnic surname matching yourself by googling "R code for ethnic surname matching."

Although the voter file does not say how a person voted, it often contains information about each person's party registration and record of voting in previous elections. Voting in closed primaries usually provides good clues about a person's partisan leanings. These clues can be useful when developing a targeted GOTV campaign.

If you plan to canvass in the evenings, consider the safety of your canvassers. By late October it may be getting dark before 7:00 p.m., and residents may react poorly to an evening visit from a stranger. You do not want to frighten or offend the potential voter you are trying to engage.

Recruiting Activists and Paid Volunteers

Unlike professional phone banks and direct mail, canvassing is almost entirely dependent on labor that, one way or another, you will have to produce. High schools and colleges are good sources of labor, particularly when students know the neighborhoods in which they will be working. Other sources of labor include churches, civic groups, unions, and interest groups, such as the Sierra Club or National Rifle Association.

There are, of course, advantages and disadvantages to forging an alliance with a social or political group that supports your candidate or shares a common political goal with your campaign. Any organization that becomes an ally has its own agenda. By collaborating on a GOTV partnership, you may be tacitly endorsing your ally's politics, and the canvassers it supplies may have difficulty staying on message for you. Beware of the fact that canvassers tend to be more ideologically extreme than the average voter.[2] In addition, if the partnership is seen as a personal favor, then a favor may be expected in return. The decision to collaborate may hinge on whether your ally will supply enough canvassing labor to make an alliance worthwhile.

Scheduling

The number of canvassers your campaign needs depends on how many contacts they will make per hour. An experienced canvasser working in an area with accessible apartments or other densely packed housing may be able to speak with members of eight households per hour. This rate may drop by a factor of two when it is difficult, dangerous, or time-consuming to reach voters' doors. Splitting the difference, we assume, for purposes of making some rough calculations, that canvassers on average speak with voters at six households each hour.[3]

With your best guess about your canvassers and the conditions they are likely to face, use the rate of contact to calculate how many hours of labor you will need for the campaign. Simply divide the number of contacts desired by the average number of contacts per hour. The resulting quotient is the number of volunteer hours required. Then divide the number of total canvassing hours into the number of weeks over which the canvassing will take place to obtain an average number of canvassing hours per week. The number of available canvassing hours in a week varies from region to region, but most campaigns conduct their canvassing efforts from 5:00 p.m. to 7:00 p.m. on weeknights and from 10:00 a.m. to 5:00 p.m. on Saturdays. Sunday canvassing depends entirely on the region and population but seldom takes place outside the hours of 12:00 p.m. to 5:00 p.m.

Safety

Unlike more impersonal GOTV tactics, door-to-door canvassing can place volunteers at some personal risk. However, you can minimize risk and increase the effectiveness of the campaign in several ways. First, you can send canvassers out in pairs. Each canvasser should go to separate doors, but they can do this while remaining near enough to each other (by working opposite sides of the street or visiting alternating addresses) that they can see or hear if the other encounters a problem. Sending workers out in pairs has the added benefit of providing some assurance that the canvassers are actually doing what they are supposed to, especially if you pair trusted canvassers with newcomers.

Second, you should provide canvassers with maps of their assigned areas so they do not get lost. The advent of smartphones and tablet computers has made it possible to provide canvassers with digitized maps and walk lists. Moreover, the geo-location signals sent by these devices allow field managers to keep track of the location and progress of each canvasser, which furthers the objectives of safety and quality control. Third, you should provide canvassers with an emergency number so that they can call you in the event they encounter a problem. Fourth, whenever possible, you should assign canvassers to neighborhoods with which they are familiar. Not only are canvassers less likely to face a problem in a familiar neighborhood, but familiarity also should strengthen their personal connection to the voters—something that may prove beneficial in getting those who are contacted to vote. Fifth, you should give canvassers something to identify them as canvassers and not marauders. For example, it is helpful for canvassers to wear a campaign T-shirt or campaign button. They also can put a campaign bumper sticker on the back of their clipboard, so that residents see it when they peek out their door. Finally, you should require all canvassers to reconvene at a predetermined time and location so that you can count heads and verify each canvasser's work.

Weather sometimes presents safety and efficiency concerns of its own. Getting stuck in a downpour or an unexpected snow squall can leave canvassers demoralized, not to mention wet and cold. It is useful to discuss ahead of time the contingency plans that will go into effect in case of bad weather. In principle, poor weather presents a good opportunity for canvassing, since more people can be found at home.

Training

Door-to-door canvassing is a simple technique that anyone willing to knock on a stranger's door can be taught to do. The specifics of training depend on the type of canvassing you plan to do. The easiest form of canvassing is nonpartisan encouragement to vote. Voters are typically receptive (and sometimes even grateful) when you simply encourage them to make their voices heard. The second form of canvassing involves mobilizing putative supporters of a cause or candidate. So long as the list of targeted voters in fact includes supporters, your job is still fairly easy: encourage like-minded people to vote. The hardest form of canvassing is outreach to people who are undecided or opposed. Here the objective is to make them see your candidate or cause in a positive light, with those who seem receptive receiving an encouragement to vote. More difficult canvassing missions will require more training and supervision, but for starters a half-hour session should include the following:

✓ An explanation of the purpose of the canvass;

✓ Instructions on what to say and do at each door;

✓ Division of volunteers into pairs and the assignment of a canvassing area to each pair;

✓ An opportunity for canvassers to practice the script with their partner, preferably under the supervision of someone who coaches them not to recite the script in a canned fashion;

✓ Distribution of all necessary materials, such as clipboards, walk lists, maps, and pens; if canvassers are equipped with tablet computers, they should receive instruction about how to access walk lists and, if necessary, how to show voters video clips related to the campaign;

✓ Explanation of what information canvassers should record after visiting an address;

✓ Expectations about how canvassers are supposed to dress and act while on duty (for example, no talking on cell phones or wearing earbuds);

✓ At least one phone number to call in the event of an emergency; and

✓ Designation of a time and location at which all canvassers will meet up at the end of the shift.

The message given in door-to-door canvassing should be consistent with the message of the overall campaign. The written pitch provided to volunteers should be treated more as a rough guideline than as a script to be read verbatim (see box 3-3). As we show in the chapter on phone banks, an informal style of communicating with potential voters works best. Scripts are necessary to provide guidance and confidence for inexperienced personnel, but the goal is not to create an army of automatons mindlessly parroting the same words. Encourage canvassers to make their presentations in words that are compatible with their own informal speaking style. Friendly enthusiasm will help them to convey their message in a manner that increases the listener's motivation to vote (see box 3-4).

Box 3-3. Script of a Nonpartisan Message Directed toward Latino Voters

A door-to-door campaign in Fresno, California, included some talking points directed specifically toward Latino voters:

Hi. My name is [your name], and I'm a student at Fresno State. I want to talk to you a few minutes about the elections this coming Tuesday. Here are some good reasons to vote in the upcoming election:

✓ Voting gives the Latino community a voice.

✓ Your vote helps your family and neighbors by increasing Latino political power.

✓ Voting tells politicians to pay attention to the Latino community.

Can I count on you to vote this Tuesday? Do you know where you vote and when the polls are open? If not, I can help you look up that information.

When done properly, canvassing opens a conversation with voters. Prepare your canvassers to field some basic questions that voters might throw at them. The more comfortable canvassers feel conversing with voters, the better. In the context of a campaign in support of a candidate or an issue, canvassers may be asked to explain a candidate or interest group's position. Unless you have an unusually savvy group of canvassers, it is probably best to instruct them to give voters an information sheet. To the extent that canvassers answer questions, they should focus on why they personally support the campaign.[4]

Supervising

Once the canvassers take to the streets, problems may range from bashfulness to drunkenness. Campaign managers have developed a number of tactics for monitoring the progress of canvassers, particularly those who are working for hourly wages. First, have them fill out the names of the people they meet at each door they visit. Since this report conceivably could be faked (claims to have contacted an unusually large number of people should raise a red flag), another useful tactic is to send canvassers out with lawn signs or placards advertising the campaign. The goal is to convince residents to plant the sign in their yard or put the poster in their window; seeing who can plant the most signs can be a useful source of friendly competition among canvassers. This visible indicator of success makes it easy for a supervisor to see where canvassers have been and to gauge how they are doing.

As mentioned above, monitoring the location and progress of canvassers has become easier thanks to smartphone apps that track canvassers and automatically update information they collect at the doors. These apps are part of a shift in the direction of digitized maps and walk lists, which have become standard among large-scale door-to-door campaigns. Googling "create walk lists for canvassing" will reveal a cottage industry of firms and organizations that provide software and training. Of course, even the smartest smartphone apps are useless if canvassers don't know how to use them, so expect an extra layer of training and supervision. One reason that campaigns have increasingly turned to for-hire canvassing firms is that they have streamlined the process of training an app-equipped team of canvassers.

If you are running your own canvassing operation with paid door-knockers, payment for services is best done on a weekly basis rather than on the spot. First, weekly payment schedules encourage canvassers to

Box 3-4. Script of an Advocacy Message and Mobilization of Supporters

A door-to-door campaign in North Carolina sought to identify and mobilize supporters of Hillary Clinton and to persuade those who were undecided or opposed.

Hi, my name is _____ with Working America. We're out today talking with folks in the neighborhood about the future of North Carolina. Are you [name]? Great! First—a quick survey. When you think about the upcoming election on November 8th, what is the most urgent issue to you and your family? [Record response: jobs, economy, public safety, etc.] Thank you. This fall, voters will be voting to elect our next President. If you were voting today, would you vote for Republican Donald Trump or Democrat Hillary Clinton? [Record response: Trump, Undecided, Clinton, Other]

Working America is an independent organization that represents over 40,000 North Carolinians who want an economy that works for working people. We are not part of any political party or campaign.

[IF Respondent supports CLINTON]: Earlier you said that you were supporting Hillary Clinton in the race for President. We are also supporting Clinton for President because of her strong track record on supporting working people. Thanks for your support! [Hand over literature.]

[IF Respondent is UNDECIDED]: You said earlier that [Issue Priority] was the most important issue to you. I understand. How you

think of this activity as an ongoing commitment. Second, it gives you a chance to discuss their performance with them after a day on the job, while they are still thinking about the payment that they expect to receive in the future.

Finally, you must take responsibility for dealing with unexpected events. Besides weather-related headaches, you should expect to field an occasional follow-up call from a resident, building manager, or local politician wondering what your campaign is up to. Think of canvassing as a big walk through town, a meet-and-greet with thousands of strangers. The outcomes are generally positive, but anything can happen.

vote is a personal decision. Working America has done the research on the economic issues and the records of the candidates. [Explain relevant issue background and candidate record.] Now that you have heard more about the candidates, who do you think you will be supporting in the Presidential Election, Donald Trump or Hillary Clinton?

[IF TRUMP]: You said earlier that [Issue Priority] was the most important issue to you. I understand. How you vote is a personal decision. Working America has done the research on the economic issues and the records of the candidates and we believe Hillary Clinton is the best candidate for our community. [Hand over lit and end conversation.]

[IF CLINTON]: When are you planning to vote? [Ask probing questions to help the voter visualize their voting day. The goal here is to have a conversation about their day to help the voter make a plan. If the voter is voting early, share county-specific early voting information.] What time of day do you normally vote? What do you do before you vote? Will you take time off work to vote? Do you know where your polling location is? How will you get there? Will you go vote with anyone else? Thank you. Have a good night.

Source: Kalla and Broockman (2018), supplemental information, pp. 63–67.

Experimental Research on Door-to-Door Canvassing

Dozens of door-to-door canvassing experiments have been conducted since 1998. Although the nature and scope of these campaigns varied from place to place, they shared many common elements. Registered voters in targeted neighborhoods were placed randomly into treatment and control groups. Canvassers, who usually were paid volunteers working under the supervision of campaign staff, were put through roughly an hour of training, given a list of target names and addresses, and instructed to speak only to voters on their target list. The particular GOTV pitches used by the canvassers varied from experiment to experiment (we discuss these variations momentarily), but the communication was designed to be informal and personal. In some cases, canvassers also distributed campaign material, voter guides, or information about polling locations.

The canvassing experiments can be grouped into four broad categories. The first encompasses nonpartisan canvassing efforts that were orchestrated by college professors. Such studies occurred in Dos Palos (a farm community in central California),[5] Fresno,[6] New Haven,[7] South Bend,[8] Brownsville (a largely Latino city on the Texas and Mexico border),[9] and River Heights, a small town in northern Utah.[10] The second category includes door-to-door campaigns that were organized and conducted by nonpartisan groups, such as Youth Vote,[11] and issue advocacy groups, such as ACORN (Association of Community Organizations for Reform Now),[12] SCOPE (Strategic Concepts in Organizing and Policy Education),[13] and PIRG (Public Interest Research Group).[14] Researchers helped to randomize the walk lists used by these canvassers but otherwise played a minor role. This type of canvassing occurred in Boulder, Bridgeport, Columbus, Detroit,[15] Eugene,[16] Minneapolis, Phoenix,[17] Raleigh, and St. Paul, as well as in several California sites.[18] In 2014, a conservative group in Texas canvassed on behalf of ideologically aligned legislative candidates in Texas primary elections and runoffs. In the final days of the 2016 presidential campaign, Working America canvassed on behalf of Hillary Clinton and other Democratic candidates[19] in North Carolina and Missouri. Another group, One Arizona, canvassed tens of thousands of young people, unmarried women, and nonwhites.[20] In 2017, Plus3, an organization that collaborates with other liberal grassroots organizations, orchestrated a GOTV drive in Virginia, urging its unpaid volunteers to mobilize a small number of their neighbors by any means they preferred, including face-to-face canvassing.[21] The third category includes precinct walking conducted by partisan campaigns. Here we have four studies: a 2002 GOTV effort funded by the Michigan Democratic Party,[22] which targeted young voters in approximately a dozen assembly districts; a 2004 Election Day mobilization effort targeting several inner cities within battleground states;[23] a 2005 GOTV campaign coordinated by the Young Democrats of America[24] targeting voters under thirty-six years of age; and a Republican candidate for local office in Kentucky.[25] In 2014, the Republican National Committee funded a study on the effects of intensive canvassing by "precinct captains" in three states with closely contested U.S. Senate elections.[26] The final category includes two instances in which candidates, rather than volunteers, canvassed voters. In the lead-up to a 2004 New Mexico primary election, Kevin Arceneaux randomly assigned precincts to three experimental groups: one to be walked by the candidate, one to be walked by campaign volunteers, and a control group.[27] In 2010, Jared Barton, Marco Castillo, and Ragan Petrie collaborated with a candidate for county legislature to assess whether canvassing and leafleting by a candidate affects turnout and vote choice.[28]

As this list of sites makes apparent, these experiments were conducted in a wide array of political and demographic settings. The precincts canvassed in Detroit were largely African American, whereas canvassers in Columbus and Eugene rarely encountered nonwhites. Bridgeport, Brownsville, and Fresno contained large Latino populations, and the areas canvassed in Los Angeles, Minneapolis, and St. Paul were multiethnic. The suburban areas of Raleigh and the rural precincts of Dos Palos stood in marked contrast to the urban environments of Detroit or St. Paul. The political climate also varied across sites. Bridgeport, Columbus, and Dos Palos were canvassed amid uncompetitive municipal elections. Somewhat more competitive were elections in Minneapolis and New Haven, where at least some of the races featured credible challengers. South Bend and Virginia were canvassed amid hotly contested general election campaigns, which saw both parties engaging in door-to-door campaigning. The U.S. Senate elections experiments in 2014 and the presidential election studies in 2004 and 2016 took place in contested states.

Lessons Learned

The lessons emerging from these studies are rated according to the system detailed in chapter 2: three stars are for findings that have received solid confirmation from several experiments, two stars are for more equivocal findings based on one or two experiments, and one star is for findings that are suggestive but not conclusive.

★ ★ ★ *Contacting eligible voters can be challenging.* Multiple attempts are often necessary to achieve contact rates of over 30 percent. For example, the Republican "precinct captains" who were deployed in Arkansas, Colorado, and Iowa in 2014 contacted 29.8 percent of their targeted voters on the first attempt, another 7.8 percent on the second attempt, and just 1 percent on the third attempt. Typically, higher-propensity voters (elderly voters, for example) have stable addresses and are easier to find at home, but don't expect to contact more than half of your targets. The Dos Palos study gives a sense of the maximum rate of contact that a GOTV campaign can expect to achieve. After combing the town for two weeks, making multiple attempts to contact each name on the target list, this campaign met up with three out of four voters it sought to target.

★ ★ ★ *When canvassers are able to reach voters, canvassing generates votes.* In forty-nine of fifty-six experiments, canvassing was found to increase turnout. (The odds of obtaining such a lopsided distribution of experimental results purely by chance are less than one in one million.)

★ ★ ★ *The effectiveness of canvassing varies depending on the type of election and type of voter.* When targeting voters whose "baseline" probability of voting—that is, the rate at which they would vote if they were left alone by your campaign—is between 30 percent and 50 percent, it takes about sixteen contacts to generate one vote. The number of contacts required to mobilize voters with less than a 30 percent baseline rate of voting rises to twenty-one. This figure is even higher when targeted voters have a baseline rate of voting in excess of 50 percent, which is typical of presidential elections.

Notice what this means for cost-efficient targeting of canvassing efforts. In a low-salience election, canvassing has the biggest impact on high-propensity voters, whereas in high-salience elections, canvassing has the biggest effect on low-propensity voters.[29] A few words of caution are in order, however. If you are walking a precinct in a low-salience election, it may not pay to bypass a door simply because infrequent voters live there. You have already paid the setup cost of the canvassing operation; the extra costs of contacting infrequent voters might still pay off, particularly if you think your campaign is especially effective in reaching out to the infrequent voter. Remember, too, that cost-efficiency is not everything. If your group or campaign is dedicated to mobilizing infrequent voters, your task is challenging but certainly not impossible.

★ ★ ★ *Canvassing is effective even in uncompetitive electoral settings.* Experimenters have found big canvassing effects in landslide elections where little was at stake and many candidates ran unopposed. It appears that canvassers can successfully motivate citizens to participate in the voting process even when the election seems to have few policy repercussions. The fact that canvassing attracts voters to the polls regardless of the stakes provides an important insight into how and why canvassing works. Canvassing evidently makes voters feel that their civic participation is valued.

★ *A GOTV canvassing effort may be less effective if conducted in areas that are being canvassed by other campaigns.* One caveat to the principle that canvassing can increase voter turnout in competitive races is that some races are so hot that your canvassing campaign duplicates the efforts of others. This explanation may explain the apparent failure of an Election Day canvassing effort in several inner cities during the 2004 election. The target sites in this experiment were all located in battleground states and therefore were saturated by months of canvassing by pro-Democratic campaigns. As a result, the treatment group may have received about as much canvassing as the control group.[30] Another challenge of staging canvassing campaigns in competitive electoral environments is that it may be difficult to hold on to capable canvassers. Several nonpartisan groups canvassing in battleground states during the 2012 presidential elections saw their canvassers melt away, lured by the higher wages paid by the presidential campaigns. Nevertheless, a well-executed door-to-door campaign can generate votes even in a presidential election, as illustrated by two successful canvassing efforts in North Carolina and Arizona in 2016.

★ *Canvass close to Election Day.* Three experimental studies randomized the timing and frequency of canvassing attempts. The two largest studies found canvassing during the last week of the campaign to be more effective than canvassing earlier. The smallest of the three studies found no added value of an additional contact during the weekend before Election Day. These studies took place in states that did not allow early voting; where early voting is available, it makes sense to put canvassers on the streets earlier, as they can urge people to vote immediately.

★ *The messenger matters.* It remains unclear whether canvassers who "match" the ethnic profile of the neighborhood tend to have more success than those who do not. In Dos Palos, a team of Latino Democratic canvassers were randomly assigned to canvass Anglo or Latino registered voters. The effects of canvassing were greater when these canvassers talked to Latino Democrats than to Latino non-Democrats or to non-Latinos. In contrast, the Fresno experiment in 2002, which involved both Latino and non-Latino canvassers and a target population of voters eighteen to twenty-five years of age, showed no consistent pattern. Obviously, it makes little sense to canvass in areas where language barriers disrupt communication, but the role of ethnicity per se remains unclear.

Putting ethnicity aside, there seems to be some evidence that local canvassers are more effective than canvassers from outside the turf they are canvassing. Researchers studying a large-scale canvassing effort in Los Angeles found that canvassers working in the same zip code in which they live are significantly more effective in mobilizing voters than those canvassing outside their home turf.[31] This finding may help to make sense of some of the variation in canvassing results across experiments. Groups who canvass close to their home base seem to be more effective, and when they spread out to other areas, their effectiveness diminishes. This hypothesis needs further testing, but the evidence as it stands suggests that, holding training and supervision constant, local canvassers may be especially effective at generating votes.

★ ★ *The message does not seem to matter much.* Experimenters have tried many variations of the door-to-door canvassing theme. Canvassers have distributed voter guides, polling place information, and pens bearing a candidate's name. Canvassing scripts have emphasized neighborhood solidarity, ethnic solidarity, civic duty, and the closeness of the election. Sometimes the scripts have focused on the candidates, sometimes on issues.[32] Although we cannot rule out the possibility that these variations in message and presentation make some difference, the effects seem to be so small that none of the studies were able to detect them reliably. And when we look across the dozens of canvassing experiments, the campaigns that were strictly nonpartisan were slightly but not significantly more effective on average than the campaigns that organized around an issue or a candidate. The only thing that seems to be required of a GOTV appeal is that the canvasser must urge voters to turn out. Experiments conducted by advocacy groups have repeatedly found that canvassing door-to-door has no effect on turnout when the discussion is solely about issues, candidates, or voters' concerns.[33]

Although we have concluded that the message does not matter very much, the data do suggest that some tactics might bump up turnout by an additional percentage point. One tactic is to ask citizens whether they can be counted on to vote. Another is to provide citizens with the location of their polling place. These effects are small, and researchers cannot claim to have isolated them with any precision, but they seem worth incorporating into most canvassing campaigns.[34] Canvassers seem to feel more comfortable conversing with people if they have information to convey and campaign paraphernalia to distribute, so nuances like providing polling information and asking for a commitment to vote may increase the effectiveness of canvassing simply by changing the tenor and length of the conversation on the doorstep.

★ ★ *Door-to-door canvassing allows a campaign to influence people incidentally and indirectly.* One attractive feature of knocking on doors is that it provides an opportunity to converse with multiple voters living at the same address. The canvasser first talks to the person who answers the door and then asks to speak to the targeted voter. Everyone is told the purpose of the visit: the importance of the upcoming election.

In part, elevated turnout rates among nontargeted people reflect the fact that canvassers give their GOTV message to everyone who comes to the door, but that is not the only thing that is going on. Using a clever experiment, David Nickerson demonstrated that voters living at the same address also mobilize one another.[35] Nickerson led a canvassing effort that knocked on doors and gave a message only to the person who answered the door. Half of the messages were get-out-the-vote appeals; the other half, reminders to recycle. No messages were delivered to others in the household, yet other registered voters in households receiving the GOTV appeal voted at higher rates. Evidently, those who received the GOTV message communicated something about the upcoming election to others in their household. In light of this experiment,[36] the one-for-sixteen rule understates the effectiveness of door-to-door canvassing because about 60 percent of the direct impact of canvassing appears to be transmitted to voters' housemates.

All in all, we see strong evidence that canvassing generates votes. Canvassing seems particularly effective when aimed at reliable voters who otherwise might skip a low-turnout election. Extras, such as providing polling place information or inviting people to make a verbal commitment to vote, may enhance slightly the effectiveness of door-to-door campaigns, although this conclusion remains tentative. Finally, well-crafted canvassing campaigns seem to encourage people to talk about the upcoming election with their housemates, thereby extending the influence of a canvassing campaign beyond those who are contacted directly.

Cost-Effectiveness

When you are evaluating the costs and benefits of canvassing, here are a few things to keep in mind. First, canvassing involves start-up costs.

If you intend to target specific individuals (as opposed to conducting a blanket GOTV campaign of all the residents living on certain streets), you need to obtain a voter registration list. It takes time to assemble walking routes, even with the help of mapping software. You may want to hire a supervisor to recruit and coordinate canvassers. You may wish to send out your team of canvassers wearing the campaign's T-shirts and armed with maps, clipboards, printed material, buttons, or refrigerator magnets, all of which require some up-front investment. High-tech walking campaigns use small handheld computers to record and transmit data about every canvassing target.

Second, what counts as a "benefit" depends on your goals. The accounting we perform in this section considers only one goal: getting out votes. Using canvassers to persuade voters to vote in a certain way may generate extra payoff. Indeed, canvassing potentially provides all sorts of collateral benefits: canvassers receive useful feedback from voters about issues and candidates; the lawn signs and campaign buttons that canvassers distribute may help to publicize the campaign and communicate its message; canvassers can help to clean up an outdated target list of voters, weeding out the names of people who have moved; as canvassers go door-to-door, they can register new voters; and, by conversing with people about the campaign, canvassers can help to create databases of residents who are sympathetic to a given candidate and therefore warrant special GOTV efforts on Election Day. We have not attempted to quantify these extra returns to canvassing. The cost-benefit analysis that follows is admittedly narrow in focus.

The number of votes produced per dollar is a function of labor costs, the number of people contacted per hour, and the effectiveness with which a canvasser mobilizes the people contacted. According to Susan Burnside, a consultant who specializes in canvassing campaigns, the wage rate for canvassers typically varies from $12 to $17.[37] In order to err on the side of caution, let's assume $16. If your canvasser speaks with voters at six households per hour, and each household contains an average of 1.5 voters, you are in effect getting six direct contacts and three indirect contacts per hour. Applying the one-for-sixteen rule for the direct contacts and Nickerson's one-for-twenty-seven rule for the indirect contacts implies that it takes $33 worth of labor to produce one additional vote. You may cut labor costs dramatically by convincing a team of canvassers to work all afternoon in exchange for a dinner of pizza and beer. Similarly, an unusually energetic and persuasive group of canvassers may increase the number of voters per dollar, just as a hard-to-canvass neighborhood may decrease it. Training and supervision drive costs up, so if you are hiring staff to manage your canvassing campaign, you might encounter substantially higher costs per vote.

If you are canvassing by yourself or are using unpaid volunteers, you may find it helpful to look at the efficiency problem in terms of the number of hours required to produce one vote. Contacting six households per hour produces one additional vote every two hours. Generating a serious number of votes requires a serious investment of canvassing hours.

Assessment and Conclusions

When we first began our experimental studies of voter turnout in 1998, we were eager to assess the effects of door-to-door canvassing. This campaign tactic has an almost mythic reputation. Talk to any veteran of local politics and you will hear a story about an overmatched challenger who used door-to-door canvassing to upset a complacent incumbent. Even campaign professionals who recognize the difficulty of mounting a canvassing campaign nonetheless advise, "If your program is well targeted, going door-to-door is the surest way to win votes."[38] We were at the time skeptical that a three-minute conversation with a stranger would be sufficient to increase turnout. Our first experiment showed canvassing to have a surprisingly powerful effect. Now that dozens of experiments have weighed in on the effects of canvassing, there no longer is any doubt that face-to-face contact with voters raises turnout.

Although canvassing has received a great deal of experimental attention, much remains to be learned. Just two studies, both small, have attempted to measure the effects of candidates themselves going door-to-door. The effects were mixed, and neither speaks decisively to the crucial question of whether candidates are more effective at the door than their volunteers. Given the many demands on a candidate's time and the inherent constraints on how many households can be visited, it seems strange that the payoff from a candidate's door-knocking efforts has so seldom been the subject of experimental inquiry. Also uncertain are the benefits of multiple visits with voters and the optimal timing of those visits. These questions, which are of enormous practical importance to campaigns, can be answered only by means of a very large-scale experiment. Finally, there remains the unsettled question of whether certain kinds of canvassers are more effective than others. A large-scale study is needed to gauge the relative effectiveness of canvassers drawn from inside and outside the targeted area. A key requirement of such an experiment is that canvassers must be randomly assigned their walk lists, which is often difficult to pull off in practice because canvassers often prefer to work in neighborhoods close to where they live.

Eventually, experiments will provide a more comprehensive and detailed account of which kinds of canvassing tactics do the best job of mobilizing voters. But even when best practices become clear, contacting voters at their doorstep will still present practical challenges. Precinct walking can be difficult and even dangerous. Anyone who has butted heads with managers of security apartments knows that some neighborhoods are inaccessible to political campaigns, notwithstanding court decisions that distinguish canvassing from commercial solicitation. Rural areas are often more hospitable, but the distance between houses undercuts the campaign's cost-efficiency.

Perhaps the biggest challenge is bringing a door-to-door campaign "to scale." It is one thing to canvass 3,600 voters; quite another to canvass 36,000 or 360,000. It is rare for a campaign to inspire (or hire) a workforce sufficient to canvass a significant portion of a U.S. congressional district. A million dollars is not a particularly large sum by the standards of federal elections; media campaigns gobble up this amount in the production and distribution of a single ad that airs for only a few days. But a million dollars will hire an army of canvassers for GOTV work during the final weeks of a campaign. Even if your campaign wins only your canvassers' affections and no one else's, the number of votes produced would be considerable.

The demonstrated effects of door-to-door canvassing suggest that other face-to-face tactics may stimulate voter turnout: shaking hands at a local supermarket, meeting voters at house parties, conversing with congregants at a church bingo night. We do not have direct evidence about the effectiveness of these time-honored campaign tactics, but they share much in common with conversations on a voter's doorstep. Face-to-face interaction makes politics come to life and helps voters to establish a personal connection with the electoral process. The canvasser's willingness to devote time and energy signals the importance of participation in the electoral process. Many nonvoters need just a nudge to motivate them to vote. A personal invitation sometimes makes all the difference.

CHAPTER FOUR

Leaflets and Signage

Leafleting is a get-out-the-vote tactic that shares much in common with door-to-door canvassing. Teams of canvassers comb neighborhoods, dropping literature at the doorstep (or inside the screen door) of targeted households. Like door-to-door canvassing, leafleting requires you to recruit and manage a pool of canvassers and to deal with the vagaries of bad weather, confusing street maps, and menacing dogs. But leafleting is easier, faster, and considerably less demanding than door-to-door canvassing. Just about anyone can do it, even those too shy to knock on doors. Leaflets can be distributed at just about any time of day, which vastly increases the number of hours that can be devoted to this activity during the final stages of a campaign.

Like leaflets, roadside signs require a delivery team. Campaign workers scout out prominent thoroughfares and plant signs where passersby are likely to notice them. A close cousin of the roadside sign is the yard sign, which is planted on private property, presumably with the owner's permission. As noted in the previous chapter, encouraging owners to display signs is a form of canvassing activity. The aim in distributing yard signs is not only to raise the visibility of the campaign, but also to signal the support it enjoys from local residents. Most down-ballot campaigns make extensive use of both types of signage in an effort to build candidates' name recognition and credibility. Bolstering voter turnout is seldom a candidate's main motivation for distributing signs; nevertheless, turnout may rise because a proliferation of signs raises voters' aware-ness of the upcoming election. Sometimes, however, signage is designed specifically to encourage turnout, whether in the form of billboards an-nouncing an upcoming election or handheld signs reminding voters that today is Election Day.

The aim of this chapter is to assess the cost-effectiveness of these tac-tics. On the one hand, leaflets and signage have the potential to commu-nicate a message inexpensively to a large number of voters; on the other hand, messages delivered in this way may do little to affect voter behav-ior. We describe some of the logistical issues with these tactics and then turn to the research literature to evaluate their effects on voter turnout.

Organizing a Leaflet Campaign

Although leafleting campaigns require less preparation than door-to-door canvassing efforts, planning is still an essential ingredient for suc-cess. Designing an effective leaflet, organizing walk lists, and assembling a corps of leafleteers require time and energy. If you wait until the last moment, the quality and distribution of your literature will suffer. Here are some things to consider as you craft your leafleting campaign.

Leaflet Design

When crafting a leaflet:

✓ Use a visually engaging layout to encourage recipients to glance at the leaflet before throwing it away.

✓ Use clear language and large print so that the gist of your message is apparent at a glance.

✓ Give the message credibility by including more detailed information for interested readers, perhaps directing them to a phone number or website.

A conventional leaflet is not much more than a printed sheet of paper, something that in principle could be produced by a desktop publisher. Bear in mind, however, that leaflets found lying on the ground in front of the doormat are less likely to attract attention than so-called door hang-ers. Door hangers, as the name suggests, have a perforated hole in the top that allows them to be hung on a doorknob (see box 4-1). Printing

Box 4-1. Sample Door Hanger

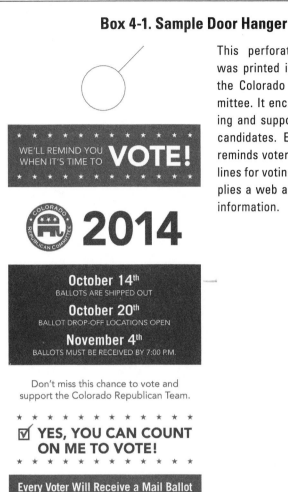

This perforated door hanger was printed in three colors by the Colorado Republican Committee. It encourages both voting and support for Republican candidates. Each door hanger reminds voters about the deadlines for voting by mail and supplies a web address for further information.

door hangers on this kind of card stock may require some professional assistance.

The lead time required to develop a leaflet depends on its sophistication. The easiest approach is to produce a generic leaflet for distribution to everyone. On the other end of the spectrum are leaflets customized for the recipients, perhaps listing their polling place or making a voting appeal tailored to their demographic profile. Somewhere in the middle are leaflets tailored to voting precincts; these might provide polling place information but not a message aimed at an individual recipient. This last approach is easy for even a low-tech campaign to pull off; just use adhesive labels to put polling place information on each leaflet.[1]

Voter Lists

Not all leafleting campaigns require target lists. Some campaigns are content to drop their literature at every household, regardless of whether it contains registered voters. Sometimes these "blind canvassing" efforts are used because they serve other purposes, such as encouraging voter registration or publicizing an event or organization. Sometimes they are used by necessity, because canvassers are too young or unreliable to follow a walk list. Blind canvassing speeds up the process of visiting addresses because canvassers need only check which street they are on. For neighborhoods with high registration rates, blind canvassing is often an efficient way to go. In areas with low registration rates, such as urban apartment complexes, blind canvassing may waste quite a bit of time and paper.

More sophisticated leafleting campaigns that target particular households require database management. Printing customized leaflets, for example, requires a current voter registration list (see chapter 3 on how to obtain and prepare such lists). Even if you plan to use a generic leaflet for everyone in your target population, you need to obtain a registration list and sort it by street or carrier route. Assign each canvasser a set of contiguous carrier routes. As leafleteers return from each day's work, you should update these computer records to indicate where canvassers have visited.

The decision whether to canvass by street or by individual address in part depends on the purpose of the leafleting campaign. Some partisan leaflets are designed to mobilize loyal voters, in which case it makes little sense to leave them at the doorstep of people registered in the opposing party. Other leaflets are intended to build a candidate's name recognition and communicate positive information about him or her. Unless you fear that these messages will produce a backlash among voters registered in the opposing party, you may distribute these leaflets blindly. If you are unsure about the likely effect of your partisan leaflets, it is probably safer to focus on people who either are registered in your party or are undeclared. That means targeting specific addresses.

Leafleteers

Distributing leaflets is a low-skill activity and one that is often assigned to teenagers. You do not need to train workers to deliver a script, but you should provide instructions about what to say if they encounter someone as they proceed from address to address. A bit of guidance should be given about where and how to position the leaflet on someone's property. It is a bad idea to place leaflets in mailboxes, which legally are the special domain of the postal service. In general, leaflets should be placed in ways that prevent them from blowing around and becoming litter. (Leaflets teeter on the edge of litter even under optimal conditions.) The great virtue of door hangers is that they stay put right where the voter is likely to see them.

Many of the same safety principles discussed in the previous chapter apply here. One further issue warrants mention. Leafleteers occasionally have the opportunity to sabotage other leafleting campaigns. On the day before the election, a leafleteer might encounter a stack of competing leaflets on a resident's doorstep. To prevent unpleasant confrontations with other campaigns, you ought to discourage your canvassers from discarding or destroying these competing messages, urging them instead to place your message on the top of the stack.

Conducting a Signage Campaign

The design and deployment of roadside signs is aided by specialized firms that print signs and ship them to campaign headquarters with accompanying wire frames that allow for easy planting along highways. The cost of printing and shipping is approximately $2 per sign for orders of at least 1,000. To guide your calculation of how many signs you might need, we note that the campaigns described below sought to place forty signs in each precinct they targeted. As with leafleting, labor and distribution comprise a large share of the overall cost. When distributing signs across an area the size of a congressional district, a rule of thumb is that each precinct requires one hour of labor and one gallon of gas.

No scientific studies have evaluated what kinds of signs work best. Campaign advisers recommend that signs feature simple lettering, large type, contrasting colors, and a message that consists of little more than a candidate's name and desired office. The challenge is getting signs into the ground and keeping them there. Many areas have ordinances prohibiting roadside signs, and so before planting your signs, figure out where they are likely to be removed by local authorities, sometimes with threats of fines. (Two of the roadside signs campaigns described below experienced this problem.) The presence or absence of signs from other campaigns is a good clue. Yard signs eliminate this concern, but obtaining the permission of residents requires canvassing labor. One shortcut is to obtain permission from likely supporters ahead of time (perhaps at fundraisers or over the phone) so that your team need only deliver the signs to supporters' addresses. Although the effectiveness of signage has seldom been studied rigorously, a measure of their perceived effectiveness is the frequency with which they are uprooted by competing campaigns and their supporters. Sign rustling occurred in one of the experimental studies presented below and seems to be a common occurrence, judging from the sheer number of scandals that Google returns when one searches the phrase "caught stealing yard signs." Instruct your team not to succumb to this temptation.

Assessing the Effectiveness of Leaflets

Eleven experimental leafleting campaigns—one by a partisan campaign that urged support for candidates, two by interest groups seeking to mobilize supporters of a presidential candidate, and eight by strictly non-partisan campaigns—have assessed whether leaflets boost voter turnout.

During the final days of the 1998 campaign, we conducted a nonpartisan experiment in the suburban town of Hamden, Connecticut.[2] Streets in the town were randomly assigned to treatment and control groups, and leafleteers distributed 8.5" × 11" postcards to every house on a treatment group street. Since this procedure was tantamount to a blind canvass, efficiency was compromised a bit, but in these neighborhoods a very high percentage of households contained registered voters. The leaflets featured a large picture of a patriotic symbol, such as the Constitution or American soldiers hoisting the flag, described voting as a civic duty, gave the date of the upcoming election, and encouraged voters to participate. Leaflets did not list the polling location. This experiment involved 2,021 registered voters, which makes it much smaller than some of the studies we discuss below. A year later, in the context of an uncompetitive mayoral election in New Haven, we replicated this leafleting experiment, again distributing large postcards to randomly assigned streets. This study, too, was small, encompassing 3,011 voters living on seventy-six streets.

In 2002, a much larger partisan leafleting study was crafted by David Nickerson, Ryan Friedrichs, and David King.[3] In this campaign, the Michigan Democratic Party targeted young voters in thirteen Michigan assembly districts during the weeks leading up to the general elections. This study involved a very large number of registered voters, roughly 2,500 in each assembly district. Because Michigan's registration system discontinued registration by party, the canvassing campaign targeted voters eighteen to thirty-five, focused on predominantly Democratic neighborhoods, and excluded voters who had registered as Republicans under the previous registration system. The Michigan experiment used a door hanger that conveyed a partisan message, encouraged voter turnout, and listed the polling place for residents of a given ward. Thus, the leaflet was customized for each precinct, but not each individual. Canvassers were instructed to deposit their door hangers only at specified addresses.

Two studies described by Julia Azari and Ebonya Washington examined the effects of leafleting in a battleground state.[4] During the closing days of the 2004 presidential election, an interest group supporting Democratic candidates conducted two leafleting experiments in Florida, one in Dade County and the other in Duval County. In both cases, the targeted precincts were predominantly African American. The leaflets conveyed an "election protection" message, encouraging voters to go to the polls and to report any problems they might encounter to a hotline designed to provide assistance. This theme was prominent among Democratic supporters in 2004, still chafing over what they perceived to be voter intimidation tactics in the 2000 election.

During 2006, several groups embarked on nonpartisan leafleting experiments. Valerie Frey and Santiago Suárez coordinated a leafleting experiment in Philadelphia.[5] The setting for the experiment was a special election to fill a vacancy in the state legislature. In order to test alternative messages, the researchers divided the target population of 15,550 voters by street into three groups: a control group, a group receiving a standard GOTV leaflet, and a group receiving a leaflet that encouraged voting and pointed out that bilingual ballots would be available at the polls. In California's June primary elections, two groups affiliated with church-based civic outreach campaigns leafleted neighborhoods in Orange County and Long Beach. The Orange County leaflets listed polling place locations, while the Long Beach leaflets provided voters with a voter guide that reported how candidates vying for local office responded to questions about various issues confronting the city. In the days leading up to the November elections, church-based groups again conducted leafleting in Fresno and Long Beach, this time without providing voter guides or polling places. Each of the five California studies reported by Melissa Michelson, Lisa García Bedolla, and Donald Green was relatively small in scope; combined, the five sites encompassed 7,655 registered voters.[6]

Assessing the Effectiveness of Signs

Six experiments have gauged the effects of signage: four involving roadside signs, one involving yard signs, and one involving handheld signs on Election Day. The first roadside experiment was conducted in collaboration with a New York Democratic congressional campaign during the November 2012 election. Because New York was not a battleground state, the overall level of campaign activity was fairly low. Conventional signs with the candidate's name were randomly assigned to a subset of the ninety-seven election districts (the term used for precincts in New York). To minimize spillovers from treated to untreated areas, the researchers stipulated that no election district could receive signs if a neighboring district had previously been selected to receive signs. This randomization scheme effectively divided the election districts into three groups: those treated with forty signs, the adjacent-to-treated, and the untreated. Outcomes were measured by the number of congressional votes cast in each election district.[7]

A second experiment was conducted in collaboration with Freedom Works, which opposed Terry McAuliffe, a Democratic candidate in the 2013 Virginia gubernatorial contest. The sign was critical of McAuliffe, mimicking a "For Sale" sign with his name on it. A subset of the 131 precincts in Northern Virginia was assigned to receive forty signs apiece, again subject to the constraint that no precinct could receive signs if its adjacent neighbors had. Precinct-level votes cast for governor were the measure of voter turnout.[8] A third experiment looked at a Republican primary election for county commissioner in Cumberland County, Pennsylvania. A random subset of the 88 precincts was assigned signs for the incumbent, who faced three opponents. In this study, the campaign placed only ten signs in each of the targeted precincts. A fourth study of signs planted along roadways was conducted by MoveOn in 296 Colorado precincts during the final weeks of the 2018 general elections. The signage read "I'm [blank] and I vote. So should you!" Those planting the signs were encouraged to fill in the blank with any phrase they liked, such as "a parent" or "for change."[9]

The sole yard sign experiment was conducted in the context of a mayoral primary election held in the fall of 2013. Signs were developed and distributed by the campaign team for one of the Democratic candidates. Electoral districts were once again assigned to treatment subject to the nonadjacency restriction, but this time signs intended for election districts were distributed directly to the candidate's known supporters for display in their yards. Turnout was measured by the number of votes cast for mayor in the seventy-one election districts.[10]

All but one of the aforementioned signage campaigns focused on candidates; only the MoveOn campaign explicitly promoted voter turnout. Another turnout-focused signage test assessed the effectiveness of handheld signs prior to the 2005 New York City municipal election.[11] Outside polling locations in fourteen randomly selected treatment sites, people working on behalf of the GOTV campaign held signs that read "VOTE TOMORROW" from 7 a.m. to 6 p.m. on the day before the election. Turnout rates for the treatment locations were compared with turnout rates in fourteen control sites.

Lessons Learned

The lessons emerging from these studies are rated according to the system detailed in chapter 2: three stars are for findings that have received solid confirmation from several experiments, two stars are for more equivocal findings, and one star is for findings that are suggestive but not conclusive.

★ ★ ★ *Leaflets and door hangers typically have weak effects on voter turnout.* A weighted average of all eleven studies suggests that for every 189 registered voters whose doors receive hangers, one additional vote is produced. Although based on more than 65,000 registered voters, the results fall short of statistical significance, because there is about an 11 percent chance that we would observe an estimated effect this large even if leaflets were ineffective. The statistical evidence, however, is strong enough to rule out the idea that leafleting on average produces big effects. The upper bound for the effectiveness of an average leafleting campaign appears to be one vote per seventy-two people who receive leaflets.

★ *Partisan door hangers appear to have a slight edge in effectiveness over nonpartisan leaflets, but the difference is not statistically reliable.* In the

Michigan experiment, for every seventy-eight registered voters whose doors received hangers, one additional vote was produced. However, the Florida leafleting campaigns, which had a less overt partisan message and did not include polling place information, failed to increase turnout. Combining Michigan's and Florida's results suggests that one vote is produced for every 127 people who receive leaflets. The corresponding number for the strictly nonpartisan leaflets is more than 500 recipients. In the absence of an experiment that pits partisan and nonpartisan messages head-to-head, we remain skeptical that the partisan content of the leaflet affects its ability to mobilize voters, particularly in light of the findings from the chapter on direct mail, which show few messaging effects and no superiority of partisan mailings.

Nonpartisan leaflets seem to be equally (in)effective for different segments of the electorate. After the initial 1998 nonpartisan experiment, it was thought that leaflets might have different effects depending on the recipients' party affiliation. Because undeclared voters receive less communication from campaigns, it seemed possible that leaflets might have greater salience for them. Consistent with this hypothesis, which was hinted at in the nonpartisan study, the Michigan experiment found fairly strong effects among young voters, who are usually ignored by campaigns. However, subsequent leafleting experiments failed to support this hypothesis. It now appears that recipients are about equally responsive to leaflets, regardless of party or past rates of voter participation.

★ *Door hangers that provide information about polling locations and local candidates may be more effective than standard leaflets.* Although the statistical results remain tentative, the most successful campaigns to date were the partisan effort in Michigan, which provided polling locations, and the nonpartisan effort in Long Beach, which provided local voter guides.[12]

★ ★ *Signage on private property or along roadsides has weak positive effects on turnout.* The two roadside experiments with candidate signs generated two small estimated effects, one positive and the other negative. The yard sign experiment generated a weakly positive estimated effect. The MoveOn signs, which were designed to promote voter turnout, were found to have a small positive effect on the number of votes cast in treated precincts as well as a small positive effect on adjacent precincts. None of the estimates are statistically distinguishable from zero. When the studies are pooled together, the evidence suggests that precincts that receive signs attract six additional voters to the polls. However, even this estimate is statistically equivocal, and the true effect could well be zero.

★ *Handheld signs advertising an upcoming election appear to boost turnout.* The sole study found surprisingly large positive effects on the order of 3 percentage points. The small size of this study, however, means that one cannot conclusively rule out the possibility that the apparent results are due to chance.

Cost-Effectiveness

Once a campaign has secured a target list, leafleting involves two principal costs: the up-front cost of printing and the hourly cost of distribution. Assume that you are producing a partisan door hanger that tells each resident where to vote. The printing costs depend on the print volume, card size, paper stock, and number of colors. Suppose that you are planning to spend $0.12 on each leaflet (which is what the Michigan Democrats paid to print 100,000 door hangers, converted to 2018 dollars).

Leafleteers are generally cheaper per hour than canvassers. Suppose you pay them $12 per hour with the expectation that they will drop leaflets at forty-five addresses per hour. Assuming that addresses contain an average of 1.5 voters, your leaflets reach 67.5 voters every hour. For every 189 voters contacted, one additional vote is generated. The labor costs of leafleting, therefore, come to approximately $34 per vote. Printing costs bring the total cost to approximately $49 per vote. The cost goes up still further if you print a voter guide instead of or in addition to a door hanger.

Leafleting thus appears to be less cost-effective than canvassing in terms of dollars per vote. However, the efficiency advantages of face-to-face canvassing may be offset by the greater supervisory costs associated with training and recruiting canvassers. One other consideration worth noting is that leafleting campaigns are easier to manage than face-to-face campaigns. Door-to-door canvassing requires the right type of people and a modicum of training; almost anyone can leaflet, so dealing with an unexpected shortfall of labor is less problematic for a leafleting campaign. There is an upper limit to what a leafleting campaign can accomplish, but it makes fewer organizational demands.

As for signage in yards and along roadsides, the research literature cannot say convincingly whether the turnout effect is greater than zero. But taken at face value, the evidence to date implies that six votes are generated per targeted precinct. If each precinct receives forty signs, and signs cost $2 apiece plus an additional $15 in labor (a higher wage rate than leafleting because a car is required) and $4 in gas, the cost per vote is an attractive $17. This figure looks even more impressive if we also consider the positive spillover effects to adjacent precincts; however, further experimentation is needed before we can say with confidence whether signs boost turnout.

Assessment and Conclusions

Leafleting operates on the principle that votes can be produced efficiently if political communication has even a small impact on a large number of people. If your target population is large, leafleting could be a cost-effective means of increasing turnout. However, if your jurisdiction is small enough to allow you to canvass the entire target population face-to-face, you should do so, because that will generate the most votes. Leafleting becomes an attractive option when vast numbers of voters otherwise would receive no contact from a face-to-face canvassing campaign.

Although leafleting experiments are relatively easy to conduct, they rarely have been conducted on a scale sufficient to produce informative results. The form and content of the leaflet have only begun to receive experimental attention. Do door hangers increase turnout regardless of whether they instruct people about their polling location, endorse candidates, or provide sample ballot information? Are door hangers better than other forms of leaflets?

More generally, does it matter how people receive GOTV literature? Are leaflets different from direct mail in terms of their effects on voters? Do recipients take notice of the manner in which they receive a given piece of printed material? Or are leaflets just direct mail delivered by volunteers? As experimental evidence about the effects of leaflets and direct mail has accumulated, their apparent effects have converged, but the definitive experiments on leafleting have yet to be conducted.

Signage experiments are even rarer, and the first experiments offer only tentative evidence about signs' effects on turnout. The lack of experimentation in this area is ironic given the ubiquitous use of signage in American elections. From a theoretical standpoint, one might expect signage to raise turnout by increasing voters' awareness of an upcoming election and familiarity with the candidates. However, as the next two chapters show, efforts to raise awareness of elections and candidates via mail and phone calls have only limited effects on turnout. An alternative possibility is that the public nature of signage conveys a social norm that one's fellow voters are engaged in the upcoming election, a theme to which we will return in chapter 11.

CHAPTER FIVE

Direct Mail

ust as commercial direct mail enables vendors of all sizes to distribute advertising to large numbers of households, political direct mail permits a campaign of any size to contact large numbers of registered voters with a small investment of time and staff. Direct mail requires no recruiting of volunteers and no battles with inclement weather. With direct mail, much of the work can be done well in advance of the election, and a few paid professionals can be employed to design, print, and distribute the mailings.

Although the administrative burdens of direct mail are minimal, the cost of preparation, printing, and postage can be considerable. At the high end of the market are direct mailings that are personalized for each voter. For example, in states that permit it, political campaigns send forms to voters enabling them to request an absentee ballot.[1] These forms have all of the necessary personal information already filled in; the addressee only needs to sign and mail the form. Another variation on this theme are mailings that remind the recipient of his or her polling location, perhaps even personalizing the campaign appeal based on the individual's demographic profile and place of residence. At the low end of the market are black-and-white postcards printed on relatively inexpensive paper stock. Regardless of the cost of preparing the mailer, postage must be paid for each piece of mail; for large mailings postage represents about half of the final cost. A typical direct mail campaign will cost somewhere between $0.50 and $0.75 per piece. If you were to mail 25,000 households three pieces of mail apiece, the final cost would be somewhere between $37,500 and $56,250. Cost per mailer drops when mailings are printed on a much larger scale or on small cardstock. And bear in mind that certain kinds of nonprofit organizations receive a special discount on postage.

Is direct mail worth the cost? Most campaign managers seem to think so. Direct mail enables a campaign to tell its side of the story, in print and often with vivid images. Enthusiasm for direct mail has, if anything, grown over time as campaigns use so-called microtargeting databases that enable them to tailor mailings to match the ostensible political viewpoints of different segments of the electorate.[2] Microtargeting might direct one set of mailings to voters who feel strongly about abortion and a different set of mailings to those who feel strongly about immigration. Another line of argument on behalf of direct mail is that it reinforces the effectiveness of other campaign tactics, such as the use of phone banks.

Skeptics question whether direct mail works (a view sometimes volunteered by consultants selling other kinds of campaign services). They argue that voters are inundated with junk mail and that at best they glance at campaign mail momentarily before putting it in the trash. The fact that these glances cost around $0.50 apiece is cause for concern.

After summarizing the practical aspects of how a direct mail campaign is put together, this chapter attempts to determine whether direct mail raises voter turnout rates. Two broad types of direct mail are considered: strictly nonpartisan mail that seeks only to mobilize voters and advocacy mail that urges recipients to support a particular candidate or ballot measure. Previewing some of the messaging techniques discussed in chapter 11, we briefly describe several tactics that have been shown to amplify direct mail's effect on turnout.

The bottom line is that conventional nonpartisan mail has, on average, a small positive effect on voter turnout, whereas advocacy mail appears to have no effect on whether people cast ballots. Over the past ten years, dozens of studies comprising more than a million voters have measured the effects of mail. Apart from special forms of messaging that exert social pressure, express gratitude for past participation, offer financial inducements, or provide official reassurances about ballot secrecy, the experimental literature as a whole indicates that direct mail is usually more costly than other methods of raising turnout. Mail may be the best option available to campaigns that seek to mobilize a large and geographically dispersed audience whose phone numbers are unlisted or unreliable, but unless one of these special types of messages is deployed, mail's effects on turnout are typically small. For that reason, this chapter should be read in conjunction with chapter 11 on messaging.

Organizing and Conducting a Direct Mail Campaign

When designing and implementing a GOTV direct mail program, plan ahead, line up your vendors, get an accurate list of voters, design the layout and content of your mailings, and learn the mechanics of sending mail.

Plan Ahead

Take a hard look at the calendar and set a production schedule. Almost invariably you will encounter a holdup somewhere along the line—a delay at the printer, a direct mail company that is behind schedule, or a post office that sits on your mail. Several extra days or, better, a week should be built into the schedule to account for the unexpected.

Get an Accurate List of Voters

As discussed in previous chapters, you can obtain voter lists from a number of sources (see also box 5-1), but it pays to obtain the most up-to-date list possible so that you don't waste money mailing to voters who no longer live at the listed address. Ask your list vendor to group voters by household rather than listing each voter individually. Addressing each mailer to all of the voters who are registered at a given address will save you the cost of sending multiple pieces of mail to one home. Any list that you assemble should also include your own address, so that you can verify whether and when the mail was sent.

Make Your GOTV Mail Readable and Memorable

Some examples of successful nonpartisan mail use evocative language and images to emphasize the importance of voting. Mail should try to communicate in words and images one or two simple take-home messages. Resist the temptation to put a lot of prose on your mailer. Bear in mind that most recipients will glance at the piece only momentarily en route to the trash can. If your mail looks like a wall of words, voters may

---

Box 5-1. Obtaining Mailing Lists

Registrars of voters, especially those in states that conduct elections by mail, keep fairly accurate records of current mailing addresses. If you get the most current list available prior to the election, expect less than 5 percent of mail sent to registered voters to be returned as undeliverable. If your target list comes from an interest group, such as a membership list, find out how recently the addresses were updated. One way to freshen a list is to pay a list vendor to check it against the national change of address registry. Some campaigns send a postcard to everyone on the mailing list in order to determine which addresses are no longer valid. Others restrict their target list to voters who have recently shown some sign of life, either by voting or by registering.

---

not even attempt to read it. This point should be emphasized in light of the messaging ideas discussed in chapter 11. You may want to use some of the messaging ideas, but resist the temptation to use all of them in the same mailer.

As for graphics and print quality, there are two schools of thought. One is that eye-grabbing graphics will catch voters' attention and encourage them to read the mailer before discarding it. Perhaps this is true, but the experiments presented below include many instances of stylish but ineffective direct mail. The other school of thought holds that homely mail gets more attention because it looks like something from a local organization or neighborhood group. One of the most effective pieces of mail tested was nothing more than plain text on a folded sheet of light blue paper.

Although experiments suggest that a variety of reasonable direct mail appeals can be effective in mobilizing voters, those results apply to mailings that achieve a minimum threshold of professional competence. As noted above, mail can be extremely simple, but if it appears sloppy or inaccurate, anything can happen, so take pains to ensure that your mailings do not become an embarrassment. This means checking for spelling and punctuation errors, out-of-focus photos, and factual mistakes. If you use photos or images, make sure they are in the public domain. In some jurisdictions, you are required to disclose the name of the campaign that funded the mail.[3] To avoid incurring unexpected costs, check with the post office to make sure that the piece envisioned is the proper size, weight, and format.[4]

Line up Your Vendors

If possible, check out references on both the printer and the direct mail firm that you plan to hire. Be sure that they have the capability to handle a job of the size envisioned and that they enjoy a reputation for producing quality work and delivering it on schedule. The printer needs to understand the scope of the print job, including piece specifications, number of copies of each piece, type of paper stock, number of colors, and turn-around time. The direct mail firm also needs to receive a detailed outline of the artwork specifications, the number of pieces to be mailed, and mail or drop dates. Discuss the logistics of how you will give them the list of addresses on your target list. Be sure to get written price quotes from any firm with which you do business.

Learn the Mechanics of Sending Mail in Large Quantities

A direct mail firm will handle the details of delivering your pieces to the appropriate mail facility. If you do not have a direct mail firm, you will have to do this yourself. Start by visiting USPS.com and reviewing their "checklist," which explains how to purchase permits and sort mail so that it conforms to the U.S. Postal Service requirements.

Once the mail is in the hands of the USPS, the length of the delivery process will vary. Some mail will move through the postal facility and the post offices in one day and arrive at voters' homes two to three days later. Some post offices, however, move more slowly than others. And some post offices and mail facilities get jammed with political mail during the days leading up to an election. Be prepared to track your mail by establishing a relationship with a supervisor in the bulk mail facility and pushing to get the mail out in a timely manner. If your schedule is tight, visit the mail facility in person when the mail arrives there. Following through can ensure that the mail is processed and distributed as quickly as possible.

For additional advice on designing and carrying out your mail campaign, you might look at Catherine Shaw's *The Campaign Manager*[5] or Judge Lawrence Grey's *How to Win a Local Election*.[6] Grey discusses a twist on conventional campaign mail. He proposes personalizing mail, explaining, "For the large campaign, bulk mail may be the only route, but for a small campaign without a lot of money, nothing is as effective as the personal letter. By a personal letter I mean a real letter with a stamp on it, written by a real, live person using a pen. This kind of letter gets read!"[7]

Before sitting down to write a few hundred letters, however, be advised that experiments testing the effects of handwritten messages have suggested that they are the equivalent of three or four pieces of conventional GOTV mail.[8] Letter writing is a good use of time for volunteers who are too shy to engage face-to-face with voters.

Experimental Research on Direct Mail

Since 1998, more than one hundred experiments have assessed the effects of direct mail. Rather than describe each one, we provide a brief synopsis of some illustrative experiments that provide a sense of the range of questions that have been addressed by this line of research.

Varying the Quantity of Mail

Campaign managers often wonder how much mail to send. Too much, and money is wasted. Too little, and the message won't get through to voters. Is there a sweet spot in terms of getting voters to turn out? Over the years, several experiments have sent up to twelve mailings in an effort to find out, and a recent experiment in New Hampshire illustrates how this kind of study works. Donald Green and Adam Zelizer worked with a conservative group seeking to encourage women to vote in the 2014 general election, which featured some closely contested statewide races.[9] The campaign mailed approximately 100,000 Republican women varying quantities of mail (none, one, three, five, or ten) thanking them for their past participation and stressing the importance of making their voice heard on Election Day.

Varying Whether Mailings Are in English or Multiple Languages

In New Jersey and Virginia's 2015 state elections, Christopher Mann, Matt Davis, and Melissa Michelson set out to test whether mailings that encouraged turnout among voters with Latino surnames were more effective when written in English or in both English and Spanish. In New Jersey, 26,900 voters were sent English mailers, 26,898 were sent bilingual mailers, and the remaining 125,597 were assigned to an untreated control group. In Virginia, these numbers were 24,041, 23,999, and 23,978, respectively. The mailings showed recipients whether they voted in four recent elections and said: "We appreciate your commitment to voting.

We hope that you will continue your record of exercising your civic duty by voting in the important election on Tuesday, November 3rd."[10]

Varying the Tone of Advocacy Mail

In the fall of 2012, David Doherty and Scott Adler worked with a conservative advocacy organization to evaluate the effects of the mailings it sent to voters in August and October.[11] In August, independent voters in a battleground state were either assigned to a control group or sent a pair of mailings that focused on state legislative contests. Negative mailings attacked the Democratic candidate, while positive mailings extolled the virtues of the Republican candidate. In October, new sets of targeted voters (some of whom had been sent mail in August) received a single mailing that was either positive or negative in tone or that presented a contrast between the candidates. Voter turnout records allowed the authors to compare voting rates in the November election to determine how the various combinations of mailings affected turnout among the roughly 25,000 registered voters. In addition, the researchers conducted surveys after each round of mailings to determine the extent to which they shifted vote preferences.

Varying Combinations of Mail and Other GOTV Tactics

In collaboration with NALEO (National Association of Latino Elected Officials), Ricardo Ramírez conducted the first large-scale experiment testing the effects of direct mail on Latino voter turnout.[12] The multistate study used bilingual mailings with high production value, designed by professional mail firms drawing inspiration from their conversations with Latino focus groups. In the four states where the experiment occurred, between two and four mailings were sent during the two weeks preceding the November 2002 elections. The target population was low-propensity voters with putatively Latino surnames whose average rates of turnout varied from 3 percent to more than 40 percent across sites. This multisite experiment was very large: roughly 300,000 voters were sent mail, and another 60,000 were relegated to a control group. Importantly, the experiment also tested whether the mailings were especially effective when paired with live or prerecorded phone calls.

Lessons Learned

The lessons emerging from the burgeoning experimental literature are rated according to the system detailed in chapter 2.

★ ★ ★ *Direct mail that merely reminds voters of an upcoming election and urges them to vote has no effect on voter turnout.* Five experiments that have tested reminders yield an overall estimate that is essentially zero. (This type of mailer is sometimes used as a placebo by researchers who seek to create a control group that receives some kind of mailing, however ineffective.)

★ ★ ★ *GOTV mailers increase turnout, albeit modestly, when they encourage turnout with messages that emphasize civic duty or stress the importance of making one's voice heard in an important election.* A meta-analysis of fifty-one studies of nonpartisan GOTV mailers (including reminders but excluding those that exert social pressure by making reference to voters' past turnout or that offer cash or other incentives to those who vote) shows that a mailer of this type increases turnout on average by just under 0.4 of a percentage point. More confrontational messages that scold voters to do their civic duty have been shown to produce stronger effects of between 1 and 2 percentage points.

★ *The mobilizing effects of nonpartisan direct mail appear to taper off after five or six mailings per address.* A 1999 nonpartisan mailing campaign in New Haven found that turnout among those sent civic duty appeals was highest among those who received six mailings as opposed to none, two, four, or eight. The 2014 New Hampshire study mentioned above indicated that turnout was highest among those who received five mailings as opposed to none, one, three, or ten.

★ ★ *Nonpartisan GOTV mail has weak effects among voters whose propensity to vote is very low.* The 2002 NALEO three-piece mail campaign in Colorado, which targeted Latinos whose base rate of voting was just 3 percent, had negligible effects. The same was true for several direct mail campaigns in California that were directed at low-propensity minority voters[13] as well as a 2012 experiment targeting minority voters in Virginia whose base rate of voting was just 4 percent.[14] Even the often highly influential "social pressure" mailings described below have weak effects when directed at those with very low vote propensities.[15] It may be that hardcore nonvoters are unreceptive to these encouragements to vote, but another explanation is that they never actually receive the mail. Direct mail vendors often advise against mailing registered voters who did not vote in the last presidential election (or any subsequent elections) on the grounds that they may no longer reside at the address listed on the voter file.

★ ★ ★ *Mail sent by an official source, such as a registrar of voters, is roughly twice as effective as ordinary nonpartisan mail.* A letter from a public official assuring voters that their ballots are secret seems to work well—better than a reminder to vote from the same official and better than reassurances about ballot secrecy from someone outside government.[16] As discussed in chapter 10, letters from state officials encouraging voter registration also raise turnout.[17]

★ ★ ★ *Advocacy mailings typically have negligible effects on turnout.* When advocacy groups or political campaigns use mail to "motivate their base" about the issues at stake in the coming election, the results tend to be disappointing. Sixteen separate studies, some of them quite large, suggest that the average advocacy mailer raises turnout by less than one-tenth of a percentage point. Advocacy campaigns that have sent up to twelve mailings have failed to produce effects, with no apparent "sweet spot" between zero and twelve.[18] In those rare instances where advocacy mail appears to work as well as nonpartisan GOTV mail, the content of the mailers focused primarily on the importance of turning out to vote.[19]

★ ★ *Turnout is unaffected by whether advocacy mailings are positive or negative in tone.* Positive mailings say something good about your preferred candidate or cause; negative mailings denounce the opposing side. The 1999 study of a Connecticut mayoral race hinted that nine pieces of negative mail might have a weakly demobilizing effect. Those who received the mail were 1 percentage point less likely to vote, but this apparent effect was not statistically distinguishable from zero. Subsequent research has cast doubt on the hypothesis that negative messages demobilize voters. A much smaller study of a Florida mayor's race found negative mail to have a positive effect on turnout. Doherty and Adler's head-to-head test of positive and negative advocacy messages showed that neither affected turnout in the context of a presidential election. An even larger head-to-head comparison in the context of a 2006 midterm election found weak turnout effects that, if anything, were slightly larger among those who received mailings that were negative in tone.

★★ *Efforts to impress voters with effort or expense do not produce corresponding gains in turnout.* It is sometimes suggested that voters respond if campaigns send a costly signal of how much their vote matters. However, mounting evidence suggests that expensively produced GOTV mailings are not especially good at raising turnout. The same may be said for mailing voter guides, a tactic tested in a series of experiments conducted in California and, more recently, in Chicago.[20] Here, the mailings were expensive and, in some cases, reached out to foreign-born ethnic voters in their first language, yet the mailings raised turnout by less than one additional voter per 100 recipients. Handwritten notes from volunteers are potentially more promising insofar as they convey a personal touch, but thus far the evidence suggests that they generate roughly one additional vote per 75 mailings.

★★ *Bilingual mailings are not more effective than mailings written solely in English.* If anything, the experiments that have tested bilingual mailings against English-only mailings have found that mailings written solely in English have done a slightly better job of mobilizing Latino voters.[21]

★★★ *The mobilizing effects of mail are enhanced by certain kinds of unconventional messages.* To this point, we have confined our attention to advocacy mail and conventional encouragements to vote. Within these broad categories, subtle variations in messaging seem to make little difference. We earlier mentioned that negative messages seem to have about the same effects as advocacy mailings that strike a positive tone. Similarly, researchers do not find GOTV mailings to vary in effectiveness depending on whether they appeal to ethnic solidarity, hope in the future, or the closeness of the election.[22] Providing extra information explaining the voting system does little to enhance effectiveness.[23] Evidently, a wide array of conventional variations on the "please vote in the upcoming election" theme seem to work equally well, producing a small lift in turnout.

As we leave the realm of conventional "please vote" messages, mail sometimes becomes substantially more effective. For example, turnout increases when voters are sent mail that scolds them about the importance of doing their civic duty and presents them with their own voting record and that of their neighbors. An experiment conducted in a 2006 Michigan primary, which involved 180,000 households, uncovered unexpectedly powerful effects. Showing voters their own voting record produced a jump of 5 percentage points in turnout, or one additional vote for every twenty recipients. Showing recipients both their own voting record and that of their neighbors boosted the effect significantly to 8 percentage points.[24] These effects are much smaller when such mailings are deployed in high-turnout elections, such as the hotly contested Wisconsin recall election in 2012, but remain larger than the effects of conventional GOTV mail.[25] We leave for chapter 11 a more extensive discussion of unconventional messages and the many studies that have sought to harness social pressure while limiting the backlash that it generates. For the time being, we mention one other messaging strategy of note: express gratitude to voters for their past turnout or involvement in politics, sometimes documented by reference to some past action, such as voter turnout. In a series of experiments, Costas Panagopoulos has shown that this approach generates substantial effects while generating few complaints.[26] It should be noted that, when calculating the average effects of nonpartisan direct mail, we have excluded all shaming and gratitude mailers so as not to inflate the apparent effectiveness of conventional nonpartisan mailings.[27]

★★ *Another especially effective message is a mailing that reminds the recipient of his/her earlier pledge to vote.* Most people who are asked to pledge to vote will do so. Following up with them later via a reminder postcard seems to be an efficient way to increase turnout.[28]

★★★ *There is no evidence of synergy between mail and other GOTV tactics.* Several experiments have examined whether mail enhances the effects of phone calls or visits. Only Emily Cardy's study of mail and phones in the 2002 gubernatorial primary found any hint of synergy, and this result is offset by an overwhelming array of studies. The 1998 New Haven experiment provided no support for the hypothesis that mail works better among those who are called or visited on their doorstep. The same may be said for other large studies, including the 2002 NALEO study mentioned above and the 2006 California Votes Initiative. No evidence of synergy emerged from nonpartisan studies conducted in 2010 or several large advocacy studies conducted in 2006 and 2014.

Cost-Effectiveness

Our assessment of the research literature suggests that partisan and issue advocacy mailings have a poor track record of generating increases in turnout. To raise turnout, mailings must stress the importance of getting out to vote. One additional vote is generated for every 282 people who receive a conventional nonadvocacy GOTV mailer. The typical address on a voter registration file contains 1.5 voters on average, so if mail is addressed to all voters at a household, voter turnout increases by one vote for every 188 pieces of mail. At $0.75 per piece of mail, it takes $141 of mail to produce one additional vote. At $0.50 per piece of mail, this figure drops to $94 per vote. This estimate makes direct mail more expensive than other nonpartisan GOTV tactics, such as door-to-door canvassing or, as we show in the next chapter, certain types of phone banks. On the other hand, the effectiveness of mail can be enhanced by various messaging tactics, such as personalizing the letter or sending it from a government official. This disparate category of enhanced GOTV mail is often two to three times more cost-effective.

What about mail that confronts people with their voting record in past elections? Although this type of mail is known to be highly effective (see chapter 11), we would warn readers against using this tactic. Social pressure mail is like lightning in a bottle, an interesting but dangerous curio. It is interesting because it reminds us that mail is indeed capable of producing big effects and that, in some cases, the message does matter. But it is dangerous because many people who receive this mail become irritated at the prospect of a campaign snooping on them and scolding them in front of their neighbors. Survey research shows that the public takes a dim view of social pressure mail,[29] and one campaign found that roughly one in every 300 recipients lodges a complaint by e-mail or phone.[30] If you send out thousands of mailers, you will quickly be inundated with complaints, not to mention calls from journalists eager to investigate accusations of voter intimidation.

The question is whether this type of mail could be repackaged in a more palatable manner. That is the inspiration for the gratitude mailings developed by Costas Panagopoulos. Their effects are not as large as sharp-edged social pressure mailings, but they generate solid returns in terms of cost per vote and provoke very little backlash. The experiments that have used expressions of gratitude to entice voters to the polls in low- and medium-salience elections have found effects suggesting that one vote is produced for every 89 recipients, implying a cost per vote of $30 ($0.50 × 89/1.5). Note, however, that gratitude messages—and mail in general—tend to produce weaker turnout effects in presidential elections.

Assessment and Conclusions

Advocacy mail and conventional GOTV mail are expensive, and their capacity to mobilize voters is typically rather limited. Nevertheless, direct mail makes sense for certain types of campaigns. If the campaign lacks the people power needed to distribute door hangers or the capacity to manage on-the-ground efforts, direct mail is a sensible alternative. Direct mail has the further advantage of allowing centralized control of very large campaigns, which explains why national organizations turn to direct mail when targeting hundreds of thousands of voters. Our results indicate that direct mail does nudge voter turnout upward, but it is important to be realistic about what to expect from such a campaign. Appendix B provides a useful statistical summary of how advocacy and GOTV mail campaigns have fared. To amp up the mobilizing effects of mail may require one of the messaging ingredients discussed in chapter 11, perhaps the most palatable being thanking voters for their past involvement. One attractive feature of direct mail is that the form and content of mail are flexible and lend themselves to experimental testing and refinement. Experimental research programs have repeatedly demonstrated success in raising the productivity of GOTV mail through messaging and targeting. This is good news for organizations that strive to mobilize voters in election after election.

CHAPTER SIX

Commercial Phone Banks, Volunteer Phone Banks, and Robocalls

You know them, you hate them: unsolicited telephone calls, typically occurring while you are eating dinner or settling down to relax for the evening. Phone calls from survey takers, telemarketers, or even campaign volunteers are rarely welcome. Nevertheless, every election year vast quantities of time and money are devoted to get-out-the-vote phone calls, some by paid professional callers, some by volunteers and paid campaign staff, and some by phone banks conveying prerecorded messages. Opinions about the effectiveness of phone calls vary widely. Some campaign experts regard them as an indispensable ingredient of a successful campaign, while others contend that "telemarketers have killed off the usefulness of this technique."[1]

In this chapter, we discuss the various ways in which campaigns use the telephone in an attempt to mobilize voters. After laying out the steps required to orchestrate phone campaigns, we evaluate the experimental evidence about the effectiveness of volunteer phone banks, commercial phone banks, and prerecorded messages.

Our findings suggest that phone banks work to the extent that they establish an authentic personal connection with voters. Prerecorded messages are rarely effective. Commercial phone banks that plow through get-out-the-vote scripts without much conviction do little to increase turnout. Phone banks staffed by enthusiastic volunteers are typically effective in raising turnout, although the vagaries of organizing volunteers for a sustained period of time often limit the number of people who can be reached in this manner. When commercial phone banks are carefully coached—and paid a premium to slow their callers down—they can be as effective as the average volunteer phone bank. Managing a phone bank campaign, therefore, requires attention not only to the mechanics of making a lot of calls, but also to the quality of each call.

Types of Phone Campaigns

There are five basic requirements for a telephone canvassing campaign: staff to make calls, several phone lines, a central location where callers can be supervised, a target list of potential voters (preferably with an up-to-date list of phone numbers), and a script that callers read or paraphrase. How these ingredients are put together depends on whether the phone bank in question is making prerecorded or live calls and, if the latter, whether the calls are made by campaign activists, paid staff, or professionals hired by a commercial phone bank. Before evaluating the performance of each type of phone bank, we first describe some of the practical aspects of each type of operation.

Professional Phone Banks

With the advent of commercial telemarketing firms, the technology used to conduct large-scale calling campaigns has become commonplace. Equipped with automatic dialers and computer-assisted interviewing technology, national and regional firms are capable of phoning hundreds of thousands of households each day. Commercial phone banks, moreover, require relatively little lead time; with the script and target list in hand, a telemarketing firm typically requires only a matter of hours before phone calls get under way. The capacity to generate large numbers of calls with little lead time gives phone banks an edge over other GOTV tactics during the waning days of a campaign. That is why at the end of a campaign the remaining contents of the war chest are often dumped into a commercial phone bank.

Even if you plan to conduct your calls during the last weekend before Election Day, make time beforehand to shop around and develop a thoughtful and well-executed phone campaign. Phone banks offer a wide array of pricing options, reflecting at least in part the fact that their callers and training practices vary in quality. As we show in this chapter, the quality of the calls plays a crucial role in determining whether they actually generate votes.

The typical campaign has little use for the data collected by telemarketing firms, but you should request this information anyway for accounting purposes. Unless you are a regular customer, you will have to pay phone banks a deposit up front, usually based on a setup fee and an estimated cost per completion. Be sure that you have a clear understanding of what counts as a completion before signing the contract. For example, if the respondent hangs up immediately, is that billed as a contact? After the calls have been completed, examine the records of whether and how target names were contacted in order to ensure that the charges are fair.

Put your own name (and the names of relatives and campaign workers who agree to be guinea pigs) onto the target list, so that you can track what the phone bank is doing. You also should take advantage of one of the high-tech perks of using a commercial phone bank, namely, the ability to listen in on GOTV calls. Monitoring the calls, especially early in the calling campaign, can be critical to your quality-control efforts. It is not unusual to encounter a particular caller who is misreading the message, going too fast, or speaking with an accent that your target audience will find jarring. Listening to the initial wave of calls also reminds you of small details that you may have missed, such as deciding whether callers should leave voicemail messages when they fail to contact voters directly.

Robocalls

A second approach to telephone canvassing is to contact voters with a prerecorded message known as a robocall. The recorded message may be provided directly by the candidate, by a member of the candidate's family, or by a prominent local or national figure endorsing the candidate. A nonpartisan campaign might enlist the help of a government official such as the secretary of state or might find a celebrity who is willing to deliver its nonpartisan message. Depending on the amount of demographic information that is available for individual voters, you can design different messages for different groups—one for young people, another for women, still another for Latinos.

The advantages of robocalling are that the calls are consistent in quality, relatively inexpensive, and easy to produce on short notice. They are designed as much for answering machines as for live respondents. Those who tout their virtues frequently recount anecdotes of voters who come home from work only to discover a memorable message on their answering machine from a movie star or a former U.S. president.

However, due to their extraordinary capacity to annoy recipients, robocalls are the subject of special regulations. Regarding content, the Federal Communications Commission declares that

> All prerecorded voice messages, political and otherwise . . . must include certain information to identify the party responsible for the message. In particular, all artificial and prerecorded voice messages must state clearly at the beginning of the message the identity of the business, individual, or other entity that is responsible for initiating the call.[2]

In addition, robocalls, like automatically dialed phone calls more generally, cannot be directed at cell phones:

> Prerecorded voice messages and autodialed calls (including autodialed live calls, prerecorded or artificial voice messages, and text messages) to cell phones and other mobile services such as paging systems are prohibited, subject to only two exceptions: 1) calls made for emergency purposes, and 2) calls made with the prior express consent of the called party. This broad prohibition covers prerecorded voice and autodialed political calls, including those sent by nonprofit organizations.[3]

The latter requirement has led commercial phone banks to change the way they do business. Back in 2004, when the first edition of this book published, these provisions of the Telephone Consumer Protection Act of 1991 seemed relatively innocuous, as just 5 percent of all households had no phone service other than cell phones. By 2018, that number exceeded 55 percent and is climbing rapidly.[4] The vast majority of voters under thirty live in cell phone–only households. The net effect of these trends is to skew the targeting of robocalls toward a diminishing and older subset of the electorate. On top of these federal restrictions are state restrictions that, in some jurisdictions, effectively prohibit robocalls.

Assuming you have recorded an acceptable message and assembled a permissible target list, the good news is that robocalls tend to be very cheap. Robocalls are usually priced in the neighborhood of $0.05 apiece or less, which is roughly one-tenth the cost of live calls. (Again, be sure that you are being charged per completion, not per attempt.) For an additional fee, simulated voice technology may be used to "personalize" the messages, say, by opening the script with the voter's name. The key question is whether robocalls actually increase recipients' likelihood of going to the polls.

Volunteer Phone Banks

A third option is to organize a calling effort yourself. A homegrown phone bank may be staffed by activists supporting your campaign, by paid staff, or by a combination of the two. For the purposes of explaining how a phone bank operation is put together, we lump activists and paid volunteers together under the heading "volunteers," but bear in mind that these two types of workers are very different. Callers who genuinely believe in the cause that they are calling for tend to be much more effective than those who view this work as just another job.

One motivation for building your own phone bank is to reap the benefits of an enthusiastic pool of supporters or at the very least the availability of able paid volunteers. Another is that cell phones are off limits to commercial phone banks that use automated dialers; legally, these numbers can be dialed only "by hand." This restriction implies that to speak with a large share of the electorate, a campaign must run two phone banking operations: its commercial phone bank calls landlines while the volunteer phone bank dials cell phones by hand.

Recruitment

Your first task is to recruit callers. Intuition suggests, and our research confirms, that callers who establish rapport have the greatest success in turning out voters via the telephone. Indeed, the principal advantage of organizing a volunteer phone bank is that the callers will convey an authentic sense of enthusiasm and commitment. The ease with which such callers can be found will depend on the nature of your campaign and those active within it. An articulate and motivated group of callers can move mountains; their evil twins (the ones who fail to show up, show up late, or accomplish little once they arrive) can be an expensive and demoralizing headache. It is important to recruit more volunteers than you will actually need, because many who promise to make calls will let you down.

Location

In principle, you can coordinate a phone bank in a decentralized manner, with callers working from home. Although less expensive, this type of arrangement creates potentially serious supervisory problems. Even if the callers are doing their work, you cannot monitor whether they are staying "on message" and conveying the proper tone. For this reason, many campaigns prefer to have phone bank volunteers make their calls from a central location. In assessing alternative sites, factors that must be taken into consideration include acoustics, physical layout (caller privacy has advantages, but so does a layout in which callers can be seen by one another and by the organizers), and facilities such as parking, restrooms, and perhaps even a refrigerator or vending machine.

When centralized calling is infeasible, the fallback is to rely on technology to allocate and monitor calls. A cottage industry has grown up around the coordination of calls made by political activists, who visit websites in order to pick up a list of target phone numbers. (Google "distributed phone banks" for examples.) When callers place their calls through these web interfaces, their progress can be monitored by a supervisor.

Work Shifts

After identifying your labor pool and workplace, try to determine how many calls you can expect to complete in the days remaining in the campaign. With an up-to-date list of phone numbers and a chatty script, a competent caller will complete sixteen calls per hour with the intended targets.[5] You can use this figure to calculate the number of person-hours that will be required in order to meet your objectives. For example, if you seek to complete 16,000 calls, your labor pool will need to furnish 1,000 person-hours.

Beware of the Automatic Dialer

Earlier, we mentioned that cell phones must be dialed by hand. But suppose you want your volunteers to call landlines; you may be advised to use an automated or "predictive" dialing machine. This technology dials many numbers simultaneously and alerts callers when someone has picked up. While the caller is being summoned to the line, however, the person who has picked up hears the telltale silence of a telemarketing call about to commence. Unless the targets of your phone calls are especially lonely or curious, they will hang up moments before the conversation begins. Hand-dialed phones have completion rates in the 50 percent range, but an automated dialer can lower those rates to 15 percent or less.[6] In more than one study, we have seen tens of thousands of target phone numbers devoured in a single evening, not because the calling crew was particularly large, but rather because large numbers of target voters hung up at the start of the call. From the standpoint of a commercial phone bank, which is paid by the completed call, automated dialers make good business sense. When managing your own phone bank, your political incentives are to contact a large share of the voters on your list even if it means more time spent per completed call.

Training

Although volunteers should devote as much time as possible to the central task of contacting voters, it is important to begin your phone drive (and to welcome each new group of volunteers) with a brief training session on how to deal with a variety of contingencies. Should callers leave messages on answering machines or voicemail? How should they respond to voters who are hostile to the candidate or to the GOTV effort? How important is it for callers to stay on script? Should they speak only with the person or persons named on a calling sheet, or should they give their pitch to anyone who answers the phone? How should they respond to voters who request more information about the campaign or who ask to be called back at another time? And what information should callers record on the calling sheet as they place calls?

With regard to this last question, you may wish to have callers record not just the names they contact, but also those who are not at home, those for whom recorded messages were left, and invalid telephone numbers or numbers that did not correspond to the voter named on the list. This information will enable you to track the progress of the GOTV effort and to direct volunteers to make a second or third attempt if time permits. The training session should provide volunteers with answers to all of these questions. Provide all callers with a printed instruction sheet, a copy of the script, and answers to frequently asked questions. This sheet will be especially important for volunteers who arrive late and miss some of the training.

Preparing a Script

The final task of the planning process is to script the pitch that volunteers will deliver to the voters they contact. Whether your script should be formal or more casual will depend on the specific goals of the phone drive, the characteristics of targeted voters, and the enthusiasm of the volunteers. Callers should be instructed on whether to adopt a crisp professional tone or to engage in a more conversational and unstructured discussion. Using a standardized script has advantages. A reasonable degree of consistency among your callers is guaranteed, and less supervision is required. Volunteers, especially those without past experience with phone banks, will have the psychological comfort of clearly understanding what is expected of them. Nonetheless, research suggests that more conversational calls—perhaps because they are unhurried and responsive to the reactions of the recipient—have a greater impact on voters than tightly scripted calls.

Morale

Nothing is more demoralizing to a group of volunteer callers than dialing nonworking numbers (see box 6-1). Nonworking numbers are less of a problem when working with professional phone banks, because they charge you per completed call. But nonworking numbers represent a major nuisance for volunteer phone banks. Another threat to morale is advocacy calls made to people who are hostile to the campaign. If you are calling primarily to identify your likely supporters and opponents, bear in mind that volunteers tend to burn out quickly after encountering opponents, who may be rude or abusive.

Supervision and Assistance during the Phone Drive

Campaign staff or a volunteer coordinator should be available throughout the phone drive. Volunteers may raise questions, need encouragement, or drift off message. Supervision will ensure that volunteers stay on task and that the phone bank proceeds smoothly. Good training will minimize the amount of oversight required.[7]

Box 6-1. Building a Targeted Phone List

Public voter files and even commercially distributed voter lists are often loaded with outdated phone numbers. Regardless of how you develop your list, if you are conducting a phone bank and have the resources, you probably should hire a phone-matching firm to match names with updated phone numbers or conduct an initial round of robocalls (if permissible in your state) in order to weed out nonworking numbers. When shopping for a firm, find out how recently the phone numbers were updated for your target jurisdiction.

Experimental Research on Telephone Calling

Several dozen experiments have assessed whether phone calls mobilize voters. As we review the experimental literature, we first consider the mobilizing effects of robocalls, both partisan and nonpartisan. Next, we summarize a series of experiments on the mobilizing effects of commercial phone banks. Finally, we discuss the array of volunteer phone banks that have been subjected to experimental evaluation.

Robocalls

In a study conducted in Seattle in November 2001, a nonpartisan group hired a robocall vendor to place 10,000 calls with a recorded message from the local registrar of voters reminding citizens to vote in the next day's municipal elections.[8] The turnout rate among those who were called was no higher than that of the control group. This pattern held for those who voted in person as well as those who voted absentee. Like the mail experiments summarized in chapter 5, the Seattle experiment shows that reminders to vote do not in and of themselves raise turnout rates. The significance of this point should not be underestimated. "Forgetting" Election Day is not why registered voters fail to cast ballots. Low voter turnout reflects low motivation, not forgetfulness.

Celebrity callers seem no more effective at mobilizing voters. In 2002, the National Association of Latino Elected Officials made robocalls to mobilize Latino voters in five states.[9] Two calls were placed to each voter, one from a Spanish-language television anchorwoman and another from a local radio or television celebrity. Both messages were conveyed in Spanish (except in one region, where one of the calls was in English). Robocalls again appeared to have a minuscule effect on turnout. Despite the enormous size of this experiment, which involved more than 250,000 people in the treatment group and 100,000 in the control group, the mobilizing effects of robocalls were so weak that they could not be distinguished statistically from zero.

The same goes for an experiment using a pair of messages recorded by actress and recording star Vanessa Williams.[10] During the final weekend of the 2004 presidential election campaign, either a GOTV message or an "election protection" message targeted large samples of black and white voters in North Carolina and Missouri, both nonbattleground but somewhat competitive states. Neither message had any effect on either racial group in either state.

Perhaps the problem is that people don't turn to celebrities for political advice. Looking for a more authoritative voice, faith-based mobilization groups in an area with a large Catholic and Latino population encouraged local priests to record bilingual robocalls encouraging voter participation. These experiments were much smaller in scale than the massive experiments mentioned above, but the result was the same: no effect.[11]

Perhaps the problem is that for political advice to be credible, it must come from a party's top political leader. The opportunity to test this hypothesis on a grand scale presented itself in a 2006 Texas Republican primary. One of the candidates for reappointment as state supreme court justice was endorsed by the popular Republican governor, Rick Perry, who had initially appointed him to the seat. Governor Perry recorded a robocall encouraging Republicans to vote in the primary in support of his nominee, whom he praised as a true conservative. Here was a Republican governor speaking to his fellow Texas Republicans about why they should reelect his conservative appointee. A robocall experiment was conducted involving hundreds of thousands of Republicans who had been "microtargeted" as Perry supporters.[12] The results indicate that those in the treatment group, on average, voted at 0.4 of a percentage point higher than the control group. Another endorsement call was a bit more successful. In advance of the 2014 midterm elections, a political action committee called voters in six states, reminding them "to vote on November 4th for our Republican candidates. Help send a message to Washington that you want your leaders to focus on conservative solutions for jobs and the economy. Vote on Tuesday, November 4th, for the Republican ticket." The experimental evaluation examined the effects of up to six calls and found, overall, that six votes were generated for every 1,000 people who answered at least one call.[13] It appears that endorsement calls generate small effects that are detectable by very large experiments.

Another class of exceptional robocalls draws attention to the recipient's failure to vote. To foreshadow the discussion of "social pressure" messages in chapter 11, we note that a robocall conducted in a 2008 primary election raised turnout by more than 2 percentage points, a statistically significant increase.[14] The targets of the call were one- and two-voter households whose members had the same profile of past voting: they voted in the preceding two November elections but not the preceding primary election. The noncelebrity female voice announced that she was calling to remind you to vote in tomorrow's election. Primary elections are important, but many people forget to vote in them. According to public records, you did vote in both November 2004 and 2006, but you missed the 2006 August primary. Please remember to vote tomorrow, August 5th. Press <1> if you would like us to provide future reminders like this one. Or press <2> if you would like your phone number removed from our list.

The same tactic had a weakly positive effect in the November 2008 general election, in keeping with the usual pattern of weaker turnout effects in high-salience elections.

What happens when advocacy endorsements and social pressure messages are combined? During the relatively low-salience 2016 primary elections, the Texas Home School Coalition used a similar approach, noting "We see from public records that you haven't voted yet, and we strongly encourage you to do so. Many voters skip over primary elections and vote only in general elections. But voting in the primaries is just as important." The call then urged the recipient to support the endorsed candidate for state legislature. This campaign randomly varied the number of calls from zero to seven and, like the GOP robocall study in 2014, found that heavy doses of robocalls were worse than moderate doses. Overall, the treatment group voted at a higher rate than the control group by about 0.6 of a percentage point, but on a per call basis the result suggests that for every 1,000 attempted calls, one additional vote is generated.[15]

Robocalls might help you to stretch your resources in ways that allow you to contact the maximum number of people, but don't expect to move them very much, if at all.

Commercial Phone Banks

Although more influential than robocalls, live calls from commercial phone banks often have modest effects on turnout. In 1998, we conducted two nonpartisan campaigns using a single commercial phone bank.[16] The smaller of the two campaigns was conducted in New Haven; a much larger study was conducted in neighboring West Haven. In both cities, the elections were rather quiet affairs, with relatively little campaign activity. In both experiments, the group receiving phone calls voted at rates that were no greater than the rates of the control group receiving no calls. None of the three scripts—one stressing civic duty, another, neighborhood solidarity, and a third, the possibility of deciding a close election—had any appreciable impact.

Curious as to whether this result was due to the failings of a single phone bank, we replicated the 1998 experiments on a grand scale in 2002.[17] Congressional districts in Iowa and Michigan were divided into two categories, depending on whether they featured competitive or uncompetitive races. Within each category, 15,000 randomly selected individuals at distinct addresses were assigned to be called by one of two commercial phone banks, each delivering the same nonpartisan message. Thus, 60,000 people in all were called in the treatment group, and more than 1 million names were placed in the control group. The estimated treatment effects were weakly positive. Taken at face value, the results suggest that these phone banks mobilized one additional voter for every 280 people they spoke with, but the apparent effects were not statistically distinguishable from zero. Another massive study in Illinois, which called voters before the 2004 November election using a similar nonpartisan script, found somewhat larger effects.[18] This time one vote was generated per fifty-five completed calls. However, this study is counterbalanced by a pair of large nonpartisan experiments in North Carolina and Missouri, which found conventional calls to have meager effects—just one vote generated per 500 contacts.[19] In a few instances, commercial phone banks have produced impressive results, notably in 2002, when a commercial phone bank was paid top dollar to deliver its GOTV appeal to young voters in a chatty and unhurried manner.[20] Another success story occurred in a study of turnout in three states leading up to the 2014 primary election; this GOTV message, which was delivered by a survey firm, produced one additional vote for each 48 contacts.[21]

These findings suggest that the quality of the phone calling operation makes all the difference. If this hypothesis is correct, a given phone bank can produce large or small effects, depending on the manner in which it conducts its calls. To test this hypothesis, an experiment was conducted in 2004, calling voters in North Carolina and Missouri.[22] A large phone bank deployed three kinds of nonpartisan scripts: a standard script akin to the ones used above; a longer, chattier script in which people were asked whether they knew their polling location, which was provided on request; and a still longer script in which people were encouraged both to vote and to mobilize their friends and neighbors to vote. The results are suggestive, if a bit puzzling. As expected, the standard script had weak effects, raising turnout by one vote for every eighty-three contacts. Also as expected, the medium script had a fairly large effect, raising turnout by one vote for every thirty completed calls. The puzzling result is the fact that the chatty recruit-your-friends script had an unexpectedly weak effect of one vote per sixty-nine completed calls. Apparently, coming up with the right chatty script is still more art than science.

Fast-forward to 2010, when Christopher Mann and Casey Klofstad conducted a head-to-head competition among different phone banks of varying quality.[23] On the high side of the quality spectrum were phone banks that specialized in fundraising or political calls; on the low side were phone banks whose business consisted of a wide array of nonpolitical as well as political clients. Mann and Klofstad reason that firms on the low end of the quality spectrum are incentivized to push through a high volume of calls in a mechanical fashion, whereas the focus and reputation of the high-quality firms required them to recruit and retain callers with a knack for political persuasion. Each of the four phone banks called more than 100,000 voters across several states. All the phone banks used the same "chatty" script, which blends several of the ideas discussed in chapter 11: gratitude, implementation intentions, and positive descriptive norms. Consistent with the quality hypothesis, the two low-quality phone banks generated weak results, raising turnout by one vote per 500 contacts. By contrast, the two high-quality phone banks raised turnout by one vote per 111 contacts or 71 contacts, respectively. Although the high-quality phone banks proved far less effective than the average volunteer phone bank or the vaunted high-quality phone bank in the Nickerson study, they were significantly more effective than the low-quality phone banks. (Ironically, the lower-quality phone banks also reported a higher rate of contacts, which meant that they ended up being more expensive on a cost-per-vote basis.) Given the immense size of this experiment and the tight controls that the authors imposed on the scripts used by the different phone banks, this study offers the most convincing evidence to date about the importance of that intangible ingredient—quality.

All of the aforementioned studies examined calls in the last few days before the election. Perhaps one way to bolster the quality of the calls would be to initiate a "conversation" with voters that begins with an early call and culminates in a call right before Election Day. Would this two-call package from a commercial phone bank be especially effective, compared to a late call alone or an early call alone? Three large experiments have assessed the effects of early calls, late calls, and combinations of the two. The largest took place in Colorado in advance of its 2014 midterm elections and found no gains in turnout when early calls were paired with late calls. The early call had the usual effect on turnout, and the late call added nothing (except cost).[24]

Such findings from experimental tests of commercial phone banks have received a chilly reception from those in the phone bank industry. Janet Grenzke and Mark Watts denounced the use of nonpartisan scripts on the grounds that such tests "betray basic misunderstandings about why and how GOTV efforts are conducted and to whom they are directed." "Effective GOTV campaign messages," Grenzke and Watts argue, "are [written for] and aimed at partisan audiences."[25] Their claim is that real campaign calls—the ones that seek to persuade people to support a candidate or issue—mobilize voters. That's a testable proposition. Let's see what the evidence says.

John McNulty conducted an experiment examining the effects of advocacy calls made by a campaign seeking to defeat a municipal ballot measure in San Francisco.[26] Close to 30,000 calls (about half resulting in successful contact) were made by a commercial phone center located in the Midwest. The script was as follows:

> Hello [name]. I'm calling on behalf of the Coalition for San Francisco Neighborhoods, reminding you to oppose Proposition D. Proposition D is a risky scheme that allows the PUC [Public Utility Commission] to issue revenue bonds without voter approval. These bonds would be paid back through higher utility rates. Can we count on you to join us in opposing Proposition D next Tuesday?

Consistent with other findings concerning the delivery of brief scripts by commercial phone banks, one vote was produced for every 200 successful contacts. A much larger experiment conducted by Christopher Mann tells the same story. GOTV phone calls before the 2006 general elections had no effect, regardless of whether these calls were made using nonpartisan messages or messages advocating support for a minimum wage measure.[27]

Turning from ballot measures to candidates, the pattern of results remains unchanged. Emily Cardy examined the results of an experiment in which a commercial phone bank called to persuade voters identified as pro-choice to support the pro-choice candidate in a 2002 Democratic gubernatorial primary.[28] Again, the turnout effects were minimal, amounting to roughly one vote for every 250 contacts. Weaker findings emerge from a hotly contested 2004 congressional primary in which a pro-choice interest group sought to encourage voters to support a pro-choice challenger to an incumbent in a solidly Democratic district. This large experiment found no difference in turnout rates between the treatment and control groups. The one head-to-head competition between advocacy and nonpartisan scripts was conducted in an Albany, New York, mayoral contest.[29] Targeting registered Democrats or Republicans, callers from a commercial phone bank read either partisan or nonpartisan scripts. The partisan scripts were drafted by seasoned political consultants from each party and encouraged partisans to support the party's nominee. Neither script had an appreciable effect on turnout; if anything, the nonpartisan script worked slightly better.

Volunteer Phone Banks

The relaxed, authentic style of most volunteer phone banks provides the right ingredients for success. (See box 6-2 for an example script.) A wealth of experimental evidence, however, cautions that volunteer phone banks are often, but not always, effective. For example, in the weeks leading up to the November 2000 elections, the Youth Vote Coalition of nonpartisan organizations targeting young voters had mixed success in generating votes.[30] Of the four sites in the experiment, two showed large effects (Albany and Stony Brook), and two showed weak effects (Boulder and Eugene). Overall, one vote was generated for every twenty-two contacts. When Youth Vote repeated this experiment in 2001—this time targeting voters of all ages—the effects were weaker but still positive.

In 2002, volunteer phone banks were pitted against the commercial phone bank described above in an effort to determine which approach produced more youth votes.[31] This time, the volunteer phone banks were given a very ambitious goal—to contact thousands or even tens of thousands of voters. Many sites got a late start in organizing their campaign and were forced to turn to paid staff, in some cases from temporary employment agencies. Turnover among callers was high, and supervisory staff was stretched thin by responsibilities other than the phone bank. This meant that local sites frequently relied on callers with minimal training. The net result was disappointing: the local phone banks increased turnout at a rate of one voter for every fifty-nine calls.

The importance of enthusiasm and training is illustrated further by three successful efforts in 2002. A volunteer calling campaign funded by the Michigan Democratic Party attempted to contact 10,550 registered voters between the ages of eighteen and thirty-five and completed calls with 5,319 of them.[32] The net effect was to raise turnout significantly among those contacted: one additional vote was produced for every twenty-nine people contacted. NALEO's local phone bank campaign, which was directed toward Latino registered voters in Los Angeles and Orange counties, raised turnout significantly among those contacted, producing one vote for every twenty-two contacts.[33] In 2014, NALEO's phone banking effort in California had low contact rates but seemed to produce one vote for every twenty-seven contacts when targeting single-voter households. Another campaign directed at multi-voter households sought to convince the high propensity voters in the household to mobilize their lower propensity housemates. This approach seems to have worked well in mobilizing housemates and merits further testing.[34] These findings echo other volunteer phone banking campaigns directed at Latino primary voters in California in 2010 and Texas in 2012, which were followed by reminder postcards or robocalls.[35]

Another good example of what committed volunteers are capable of achieving is illustrated by an experiment conducted by Joel Middleton in coordination with MoveOn.org. In a 2006 special congressional election in California, MoveOn directed its decentralized web-based phone bank effort at mobilizing voters who were identified as potential supporters of the Democratic candidate. The net result was one additional vote for every twenty-six contacts.

The MoveOn experiment illustrates one further point about volunteer phone banks, which is that a follow-up call just before Election Day can boost the effect of an initial call. This finding corroborates an earlier experiment conducted by the Public Interest Research Group (PIRG) in New Jersey. Before the 2003 state legislative elections, PIRG conducted a phone bank campaign targeting young voters. The experiment involved randomly assigning those who received the first call to a second round of Election Day phone calls. Interestingly, the effects of the second round of calls were large, but only among those who in the first round of calls said that they intended to vote. Recontacting intended voters was a tactic used by the Southwest Voter Registration and Education Project in its large-scale November 2006 campaign in Los Angeles, and the results were impressive: one additional vote for every eleven contacts. This finding, in turn, inspired the Orange County Asian and Pacific Islander Community Alliance to conduct a similar two-round calling campaign in the June 2008 election. Its multilanguage phone bank targeted low-propensity voters in five Asian groups and generated impressive effects— one additional vote per nine contacts. At the same time, the Asian Pacific American Legal Center conducted a parallel experiment, randomizing

Box 6-2. A "Conversational" Youth Vote 2002 Script

Hi [first name]. My name is [your full name], and I'm calling on behalf of the Youth Vote Coalition [pronounce slowly and clearly as it is hard for many people to understand "Youth Vote" the first time they hear it]. This is not a sales call, and we are not affiliated with any particular political party or candidate. Youth Vote is a national nonprofit, nonpartisan organization composed of diverse groups all working together to increase voter turnout among eighteen- to thirty-year-olds.

The reason we are contacting you is to thank you for registering to vote. You have taken the first crucial step in giving yourself the power to make your voice heard in our democracy. However, even more important than that is the fact that you actually DO vote on Election Day. This year's Senate race in Colorado is especially important and could have national implications in determining the balance of power in Congress. It is expected that less than 500 votes may determine the outcome of this race. Your vote can make a difference. Thus we encourage you to take the time to vote in the upcoming election on TUESDAY, NOVEMBER 5th, between the hours of 7 a.m. and 7 p.m.

Have you received your voter registration card in the mail?

[If yes:] OK, that tells you where your polling location is. But just so you know, your polling location is at [name of place and address]. Again, you can vote between the hours of 7 a.m. and 7 p.m. and will need to show your voter registration card and/or a government-issued picture ID. Lastly, we would like to provide you with a toll-free phone number and websites for obtaining nonpartisan information on the candidates and issues in your area. The number is 1-888-Vote-Smart (1-888-868-3762), and the websites are www.vote-smart.org [make sure you say vote-dash-smart.org] and www.youthvote.org.

Well [person's first name], I'd like to thank you for your time. Again, remember to mark your calendar to vote on Tuesday, November 5th, and encourage your friends and family to vote, too. Have a good evening.

Source: David Nickerson, "Quality Is Job One: Professional and Volunteer Voter Mobilization Calls," *American Journal of Political Science*, vol. 51 (2007): 269–82.

low-propensity voters into three groups, those who were not called, those who were called once, and those who would be given a follow-up call if in round 1 they expressed an intention to vote. Both rounds of calls were effective, especially the follow-up call.[36] Notice that follow-up phone calls have proven effective for volunteer phone banks but not commercial phone banks, which may reflect the rapport that volunteers are able to achieve.

Overall, volunteer phone banks have a fairly good track record of mobilizing those whom they contact. The rule of thumb that emerges from our review of this literature is that one additional voter is produced for every thirty-six contacts. The real question for volunteer phone banks is not whether they work under optimal conditions, but rather whether they can achieve a sufficient volume of calls to make a difference. It is the rare volunteer phone bank that can complete the 36,000 calls needed to generate 1,000 votes without compromising quality.

Lessons Learned

The lessons emerging from these studies are rated according to the system detailed in chapter 2.

★ ★ ★ *Robocalls have a weak effect on voter turnout.* Our best guess, based on experiments involving more than 1 million voters, places the vote production rate somewhere in the neighborhood of one vote per 390 contacts, with several experiments showing no effect at all. If you are attempting to mobilize voters in a constituency with millions of people with landlines and willing to gamble that robocalls do work, this tactic may be a cost-effective option, given the very low cost per call. But do not expect to notice the effects of a robocall campaign, since it takes roughly 390,000 contacted landlines to produce 1,000 votes.

★ ★ ★ *Live calls conducted by professional phone banks typically produce modest effects.* A standard commercial phone script of approximately thirty seconds in length on average increases turnout by 0.9 of a percentage point among those contacted. This figure is based on a large number of experiments and includes phone banks of varying quality. Telemarketing firms charge a substantial premium for more conversational and interactive scripts, as longer scripts increase the costs of training and supervision, while cutting the number of completed calls per hour.

These high-quality phone bank efforts appear to be more influential per contact in head-to-head competitions targeting the same population of voters in a given election. But although high-quality commercial phone banks came out ahead, they only increased turnout by as much as 1.4 percentage points among those contacted, which translates into one vote per seventy-one contacts.[37]

★ ★ *The effectiveness of professional phone banks has little to do with the specific reasons for voting stressed in the scripts.* The three nonpartisan scripts used in the 1998 New Haven and West Haven experiments were equally ineffective, as were the three scripts used in the 2002 Youth Vote campaign. Experiments that directly compare advocacy and nonpartisan scripts—the 2005 Albany experiment conducted by Costas Panagopoulos and the 2006 Missouri experiment conducted by Christopher Mann—found no difference in effectiveness.[38] There is some evidence that asking people to review when and how they will vote boosts turnout a bit (see chapter 11), although this effect may stem from the interactive nature of this type of conversation.

★ ★ ★ *Volunteer phone banks are often effective, but their quality varies, and their capacity to contact large numbers of people is often limited or unpredictable.* The average volunteer phone bank generates one vote for every thirty-six completed calls, but the effectiveness of volunteer phone banks varies widely. Roughly one-third of the experimental studies of volunteer phone banks reveal effects of less than one vote per fifty contacts.

★ ★ *Volunteer phone bank scripts that consist only of a brief reminder seem to produce votes at the lower end of the volunteer phone bank spectrum.* Janelle Wong's study of brief volunteer phone calls produced a weaker-than-average effect, and so did the volunteer phone bank organized by Jason Barabas and his colleagues, which called to remind Florida voters that certain ballot measures would be presented in the 2006 election.

★ ★ *Recontacting people who earlier expressed an intention to vote boosts the effectiveness of a calling campaign.* Volunteer phone banks have had good success conducting a second round of calls close to Election Day targeting those who earlier said that they intended to vote. Either people who express an intention to vote are especially receptive to reminders or they feel obligated to honor their previous commitment when reminded of it. Unfortunately, commercial phone banks seem unable to recreate the magic of an ongoing conversation. Three large experiments have tested the effects of recontacting voters, and only one of them found the follow-up call to be useful. The largest and most exacting test found follow-up calls to be ineffective, even when an initial call asked respondents whether they would like to be contacted to receive a final reminder to vote.[39]

Cost-Effectiveness

Gauging the cost-effectiveness of alternative phone bank strategies is no simple matter, because the effectiveness of phone banks varies depending on how the callers are trained and supervised. A commercial phone bank might charge $0.50 per completed call when contracting for brief scripts that involve little conversation between caller and voter. In contrast, top-of-the-line commercial phone banks cost $1.50 per completed call to cover the extra training and supervision required to execute a natural-sounding scripted conversation. It is easy to burn a lot of money paying triple rates to a high-quality phone bank in the hopes of recouping the investment with an effect that is at least three times as large. The one head-to-head competition among phone banks suggests that investing in quality pays off, but beware that you must monitor the quality of the calls yourself in order to reap the benefits of a premium phone bank.

Suppose you hire a commercial phone bank that is somewhere in the middle of the quality spectrum. Several experiments, many of them quite large, suggest that one vote is generated for every 106 completed calls. At $1 per completed call, that comes to $106 per vote. At $0.50 per completed call, the price per vote falls to $53. Bear in mind that nowadays, commercial phone banks typically reach only one-eighth of the voters they call, so your target list will have to be large if your phone campaign is going to generate an appreciable number of votes. And asking commercial phone banks to call cell phones using some form of "hand dialing" will raise the price to $1.50 or $2 per completed call.

Volunteer phone banks staffed by activists produce votes at an average rate of approximately one per thirty-six contacts (contacts here exclude messages left with housemates). If volunteers are paid at a rate of $16 per hour and make sixteen such contacts per hour, then one additional vote costs $36. If you have the good fortune of working with talented volunteers who generate votes at a rate of one vote per twenty completed calls, this rate falls to $20 per vote. Obviously, more unpaid volunteers mean better cost-efficiency, but higher recruitment, supervision, and training costs work in the opposite direction.

So, as you reflect on your own circumstances, ask yourself the following questions: How much dependable and committed labor can I muster and at what hourly rate? Do I have easy access to the resources that make a volunteer phone bank run smoothly (for example, a web-based distributed platform, supervisory staff)? Does my target list contain a large share of cell phone–only voters, whose number can only be dialed by hand?

Assessment and Conclusions

Although telephone communication is more than a century old, it continues to evolve rapidly. Cell phones, once the province of science fiction, are now ubiquitous even in the poorest neighborhoods. The portion of the electorate that maintains a landline is diminishing rapidly. Cell phones are off limits to phone banks using automated dialers, eliminating more than half of the electorate. Official "do not call lists" designed to prevent telemarketers from making unsolicited calls do not apply to live political phone banks, but they may discourage vendors who distribute phone databases for both political and other purposes from gathering these numbers. Several states have passed legislation restricting the use of robocalls, even robocalls by political campaigns. No one knows how these legal and technological trends will play out in the future, but it is reasonable to suppose that campaigning by phone will become considerably more difficult.

As it stands, phone-based GOTV campaigns are a hit-or-miss affair. Robotic phone calls may produce wonderful anecdotes about people coming home from work to find a phone message from their favorite celebrity, but the minuscule effect of these calls on turnout often defies scientific detection. Live calls made by the typical telemarketing firm are somewhat more effective, but are also more costly. Commercial phone banks, when well coached and carefully supervised, can produce votes, but their cost-effectiveness depends on the premium charged to deliver a longer, more naturalistic appeal. In terms of cost per vote, high-quality volunteer efforts have an edge over other types of phone banks—when they take shape as planned. Too often, they fall flat and fail to attract sizable numbers of motivated callers. Falling back on temporary workers means incurring all the hassles of maintaining a phone bank operation with very little payoff in terms of votes.

The ability to tailor a phone bank to serve your purposes has much to do with the resources at your disposal. Can you recruit capable volunteers? Do you have the time and energy to devote to overseeing a volunteer phone bank? If you hire a commercial phone bank, will you be able to work out an arrangement whereby you help to coach and monitor the callers?

The scientific investigation of GOTV phone calls has slowed in recent years as attention has increasingly focused on other tactics, such as texting and social media. Yet phone campaigns remain ubiquitous, and many questions about phone banks remain unanswered. Can volunteer efforts be made more effective, perhaps by assigning people to be in charge of mobilizing their friends and neighbors? Do phone calls directed to specific individuals have indirect mobilizing effects on other voters living at the same address? Can the crowd-sourcing model of coordinating calls by enthusiastic activists provide an ample supply of callers, or do their numbers and effectiveness dwindle over time or across elections? Campaigns may yet discover the optimal mixture of technology and political enthusiasm.

CHAPTER SEVEN

Electronic Mail, Social Media, and Text Messaging

Every new form of communication technology opens new opportunities for mobilizing voters. The explosive growth of the internet has drawn an increasing number of Americans into the world of electronic mail. According to national surveys, 89 percent of the adult population used the internet in 2018, up from 61 percent in 2003.[1] E-mail usage has become more or less universal, and social networking sites such as Facebook or Instagram regularly attract three-quarters of the adult population.[2]

From the vantage point of campaigns, communicating with voters via e-mail, texting, or social media channels has three attractive properties, at least in principle. First, if a group or campaign has access to e-mail addresses, cell phone numbers, or an audience of social media users, it may reach large numbers of people instantly. Second, e-mail and social network messaging enable recipients to forward messages easily to their friends, which creates the possibility of extending the influence of a given mailing. Finally, the content of political communication becomes very flexible. It is easy to design messages that direct recipients to websites, which in turn instruct them how to register, where and when to vote, how to find out more about the candidates, and whom to contact in order to become more involved in a campaign.

Despite the ease with which mass communication occurs through these channels, a host of practical challenges complicates political messaging. The downside of e-mail is that recipients are overrun with unsolicited communication, known as spam. Most e-mail servers are equipped with filters that automatically reject or reroute spam. And even when spam wends its way past these filters, there is no guarantee that the recipient will read the message after examining the subject line (the title of the e-mail). The same goes for ads placed on social media sites, which users typically ignore or circumvent. And as mentioned in chapter 6, automated communication with cell phones is subject to various restrictions. For these reasons, half the battle is getting your message through to your audience, which is why there is such a premium on messaging to audiences with which you have some sort of connection. They might trust you enough to read what you have to say.

Suppose the recipient does read your GOTV message; there remains the further question of whether this medium actually generates votes. It is one thing to present recipients with options that they can choose from immediately from the comfort of their chair, such as visiting a website that tells them where to vote. More difficult is to motivate the recipient to get out of that chair on some future date in order to cast a ballot. The same goes for advertisements that appear on social media sites, sometimes insinuating themselves into the "news feed" that reports what's going on in a user's social circle. It is far from obvious that incidental exposure to such political messages affects whether someone casts a vote in an upcoming election.

In this chapter, we evaluate the effectiveness of get-out-the-vote appeals conveyed via e-mail, texting, or social media. After describing the nuts and bolts of assembling a target list, we review a series of large-scale experiments that assessed the effects of e-mail, texts, and social media communications on voter turnout. These studies have examined the effects of messages from a wide array of senders: nonpartisan organizations, party committees, advocacy groups, local election officials, and personal acquaintances. Some of the studies focus on the effects of advertising, while others focus on the effects of social interactions that are facilitated by social media.[3] The surge of recent experiments reflects the rapid growth in campaign resources devoted to this form of voter mobilization.

The Nuts and Bolts of an E-Mail Campaign

Regardless of whether you plan to distribute e-mail in-house or via a commercial firm, the basic requirements are the same. You need a mailing list and a message. The challenge is to find the right list and the right message.

Lists

Like phone and direct mail campaigns, e-mail campaigns require a target list. These lists come in three forms. The first is an "opt-in" list of e-mails—addresses supplied by individuals who wish to be contacted by your campaign. Lists of this kind are hard to come by because they require advance work on somebody's part. For example, when registering new voters, you can encourage them to provide their e-mail address so that you can remind them when and where to vote. Some commercial vendors sell opt-in lists that are obtained by asking vast numbers of e-mail addressees whether they are willing to receive political communications via e-mail. What counts as opting in varies from vendor to vendor. High-quality opt-in lists include only those people who actively consent to receive political e-mail. Low-quality lists contain names of people who did not object when offered the opportunity to receive political spam. This type of opt-in list might be called a "neglected to opt out" list, since many of the people on it simply failed to read the fine print when they clicked on a link or signed up for some internet group. Before buying a target list, ask for details about how the list was generated and what other information (for example, physical address) is included.

The second type of list is an administrative database maintained by a particular group or organization. For example, colleges typically maintain a directory of their students' e-mail addresses. Political organizations periodically e-mail loyalists, resulting in a fairly reliable collection of e-mail addresses and high (by internet standards) percentages of people who open the e-mail. Depending on your connections and the purposes of your campaign, you may be able to use or purchase these lists or collaborate with the organizations that manage them. The advantage of administrative lists is that they often are linked to mailing addresses, information that allows you to target voters in your jurisdiction.

On the low end of the quality spectrum are generic lists of e-mail addresses. How commercial vendors obtain these addresses is often a mystery. One common technique is to write a computer program that crawls through millions of web pages, harvesting all of the e-mail addresses it comes across. These lists tend to be dirt cheap, but it is anybody's guess as to whether they contain any registered voters in your jurisdiction. Unless you are especially interested in getting the word out to people in faraway places, you should avoid generic lists.

Messages

An e-mail message should be thought of as three distinct components. The first is the subject line. This line frequently determines whether your message makes it past spam filters designed to prevent mass mailings (such as yours). The more personal the message, the less likely it is to be stopped by spam filters. There are, of course, all sorts of sleazy tricks to get past these filters, such as using deceptive subject lines. Do not resort to these tactics. It is hard to imagine that voters who open an e-mail with a misleading subject line will be receptive to the GOTV message that awaits them. Take the high road and formulate a short phrase that might plausibly encourage recipients to vote in the upcoming election. For example, "Need help finding your polling place in today's election?" or "Lincoln County elections today: Polls open from 6 a.m. to 8 p.m." This approach has the added benefit of getting the message across even to those who do not open your e-mail. Experiments suggest that concise subject lines about voting work best.[4]

The second component of an e-mail is the text. How the text looks to readers will depend on the e-mail service they are using. Some may read the text as though it were printed by an old-fashioned typewriter; others may be able to appreciate your choice of font and type size. Before sending a message, do a trial run with a few types of mail browsers to see how it will come across. One style of e-mail is to present people with a few simple messages, with web links to follow if they seek additional information. Another is to hit people with a few paragraphs of prose, as though they were delving into a newspaper story. The former has the advantage of being accessible to most voters, although the latter seems popular among universities, where messages about all subjects, including voting, tend to be wordy.

The final aspect of e-mail is graphics. Primitive e-mail readers will not display them, and neither will newer ones that are designed to filter unsolicited and perhaps distasteful images. But most e-mail users see graphics when they open up an e-mail. One advantage of sending graphics is that they make the message more vivid and memorable.

Another advantage of sending e-mail to HTML-compatible browsers is that your e-mail server is alerted when the message is loaded, enabling you to count the number of messages that have been opened. In the experiments described below, this information was crucial: without it, researchers would not have been able to distinguish an e-mail campaign that failed because no one read the messages from an e-mail campaign that failed because the messages, when read, failed to motivate people to vote.

Experimental Evidence Concerning E-Mail

E-mail has long attracted interest as an inexpensive and scalable way to encourage turnout. Although usage of the internet has changed dramatically over time, experiments have told a consistent story about e-mail's (in)effectiveness.

The midterm elections of 2002 marked the first time e-mail was tested on a grand scale. A nonpartisan organization called Votes For Students (VFS) sought to encourage voter participation by college students. VFS collaborated with colleges across the country to assemble an enormous database of student e-mail addresses. VFS programmers created a computer platform capable of sending large quantities of e-mail and of monitoring the rate at which these messages were opened. In order to allow for the possibility that students might forward the VFS e-mail to friends, these experimental e-mails were sent out in varying "density" to each campus. Some campuses received a high density of e-mail—90 percent of the students received VFS messages. On other campuses only one-third of the students received VFS messages. If students in the treatment group were infecting students in the control group, the low-density schools should show bigger treatment effects than the high-density schools.

The content and frequency of the e-mail campaign varied considerably from school to school. Students attending the University of Minnesota were treated to a dose of school spirit, inasmuch as the six e-mails encouraging voter participation typically ended with the cheer "Go Gophers!" In most other cases, students received four e-mails because Votes For Students obtained the school's e-mail database later than expected. An early-October e-mail conveyed information about how to register to vote. A late-October message provided information about how to obtain an absentee ballot. A few days before the election, students were reminded of the importance of voting. A final reminder was sent on Election Day.

As expected, many of the VFS e-mails went unopened. Combining all of the sites, 20 percent of the recipients appeared to open at least one of the VFS e-mails. At a minimum, students were exposed to a series of e-mail subject lines that called attention to voter registration deadlines and the impending election.

The massive size of the experiment enabled David Nickerson to pinpoint the effect of e-mail with a high degree of precision.[5] After the election was over, certain colleges furnished both home addresses and campus addresses for the students in the treatment and control groups. He then matched these names and addresses to the voter rolls in order to see which students registered or voted. Undoubtedly, some of these addresses were out of date, but the capacity to match names accurately was identical for the treatment and control groups, and the results remained unchanged when he increased the stringency of the matching criteria.

In his analysis of the results, David Nickerson looked for evidence that students in the treatment group registered to vote and voted at higher rates than students in the control group. Neither proved to be the case. Although "click-through" data showed that Votes For Students directed thousands of people to a website that enabled them to register to vote online, the treatment group was no more likely to be registered to vote than the control group. Either the people directed to online registration failed to register, or they would have registered anyway, without the e-mail stimulus. By the same token, the turnout rates were no higher for the treatment group than for the control group. For example, the registration rate among the 3,312 Eastern Michigan University students in the treatment group was 48.4 percent. The registration rate among the 6,652 students in the control group was 49.7 percent. The voter turnout rate in the treatment group was 25.3 percent, compared with 26.4 percent in the control group. Weak registration and turnout effects were observed at every college site. On the basis of more than 50,000 experimental subjects in five sites, David Nickerson concluded that e-mail does not increase registration or turnout.

The next step in this line of research is to investigate whether e-mail is more effective when sent to people who allow their e-mail address to be part of an opt-in list.[6] Before a Houston municipal election in 2003, Youth Vote targeted an opt-in list containing the e-mail addresses of more than 12,000 registered young voters. The treatment group was sent a series of three e-mails encouraging them to become informed about the coming election and to visit the Youth Vote website, which between

5 and 8 percent did following each e-mail. Turnout, however, was not affected by this intervention. When David Nickerson tabulated the voter turnout rates for the treatment and control groups, he found that among the 6,386 people in the control group, turnout was 9.2 percent. Among the 6,386 people in the treatment group, turnout was 9.0 percent. In sum, it appears that young voters were unresponsive to both the Votes For Students e-mail and the Youth Vote e-mail.

What about sending e-mail to a more diverse age range? Or sending e-mail to people who specifically request to be on a mailing list that reminds individuals to register and vote? Before the 2004 presidential election, a progressive organization called Working Assets sent GOTV e-mails to individuals who had visited its website and requested information about registration and voting. In all, 161,633 people who supplied their name and address received subsequent GOTV e-mail reminders. These reminders took several forms, two of which were studied. One reminded people that their state's voter registration deadline was approaching and encouraged them to vote. Another message, sent to those in same-day registration states, informed potential voters that they could vote even if they had not yet registered. Both of the messages encouraged their readers, saying, "One vote can make a difference! Just ask the folks in Florida." Participants in the study came from seven states. David Nickerson found that in all seven states those assigned to the treatment group were slightly less likely to register than their control group counterparts. Turnout rates were not affected by the intervention.

The Nickerson studies, taken together, suggest that e-mail is a poor vehicle for boosting registration and turnout. But Nickerson's reports have one limitation: all of his experiments involved nonpartisan messages. The next question is whether messages from a political party to its e-mail list of core supporters would produce larger effects. To test this hypothesis, Alissa Stollwerk collaborated with the Democratic National Committee to assess the effects of three e-mails encouraging voter turnout in support of the Democratic mayoral candidate in the 2005 New York City general election.[7] These e-mails were sent in the late afternoon on election eve, on the morning of Election Day, and during the mid-afternoon of Election Day. The subject lines referred to voting, and the text of the e-mail itself implored Democrats to "vote to ensure that our representatives protect the values and beliefs that we all treasure." Of the 41,900 people in the treatment group, 13 percent opened at least one of the e-mails. The partisan reminders, however, had no effect on voter turnout. Among the 41,900 people in the treatment group, the turnout rate was

58.7 percent. Among the 10,513 in the control group, turnout was 59.7 percent. Like the Nickerson studies, the Stollwerk study has a very small margin of error.

Alissa Stollwerk replicated her e-mail experiment in the days leading up to the 2013 New York City elections. Again, the Democratic National Committee sent three e-mails to its distribution list, but the content of the e-mails varied. One message conveyed the standard partisan appeal, another thanked voters for being registered to vote, and still another combined the two. Turnout was unaffected by the suite of partisan e-mails or the e-mails that mixed partisan appeals with gratitude. The gratitude-only messages seemed to work best, producing an increase in turnout of 1.2 percentage points.[8] Whether this positive result reflects the power of expressing gratitude (see chapter 11) awaits further testing. A skeptic might say that when that many tests are conducted, some positive results are bound to pop up by chance.

It is sometimes proposed that political messaging is especially effective if it comes from a credible source and announces an imminent threat to a group's core values. To test this proposition, a study was conducted with an environmental 501(c)(4) organization prior to the 2006 November election.[9] This organization sent its e-mail distribution list three messages urging support for a county bond measure designed to "preserve our last remaining open space for our children and our grandchildren before it is lost to development." Each of the messages contained graphics and text underscoring the urgency of protecting rivers and streams as sources of clean drinking water. A brief postelection phone survey of 2,024 respondents evenly divided between treatment and control groups was conducted to assess the e-mail campaign's effectiveness. Among those assigned to receive the e-mails, 14.1 percent recalled receiving them.[10] Validated turnout for the entire sample ($N = 18,818$), including those without phone numbers, was 52.0 percent in the treatment group and 52.4 percent in the control group. On the other hand, a nonpartisan organization called Oakland Rising produced a 1.1 percentage point increase in turnout via a series of three e-mails that included links to voter guides, although this study's margin of error is large.[11] A more reliable result comes from a large study conducted by Vote.org and its partners in the 2016 presidential election. Vote.org sent a series of four GOTV e-mails to 254,992 people who registered on its site, with another 255,087 held out as a control group. Both groups had the same turnout—75.1 percent.[12]

By this point, you have probably concluded that e-mail seldom works.

Few recipients open the e-mails, and those who do seem unmoved by their encouragements to register and vote. One caveat to this otherwise dispiriting conclusion comes from a series of three experiments conducted in 2009 and 2010 by Neil Malhotra, Melissa Michelson, and Ali Valenzuela.[13] Working with election officials in San Mateo, California, the researchers studied the effects of two parallel e-mail campaigns. One batch of e-mails was sent by the town's registrar of voters, the other by a nonpartisan group called People for the Advancement of Voter Education (PAVE). Both deployed the same messages (see box 7-1) to randomly assigned voters for whom the registrar had valid e-mail addresses. The messages addressed recipients by name and were sent either the Sun-

---

Box 7-1. Text of E-Mail Messages
Sent to San Mateo Residents

Subject Line: "Shape the Future—Vote on Tuesday!"

Dear [Voter's Name]
   I am writing to remind you to vote in Tuesday's Gubernatorial General Election. The future of California is in your hands. You will help set the course when you vote for our next Governor and the leaders to represent us in Washington and Sacramento. There are important statewide propositions (from money to marijuana) and county-wide measures (funding & elections). This election will also decide the run-off contests for County Supervisor and Treasurer–Tax Collector and some contests for city councils and school boards. Your vote is very important.

The messages sent by the local registrar of voters gave his name and contact information. The top of the message included the registrar's official logo. The messages sent by People for the Advancement of Voter Education were headed by a banner graphic with the name of the organization and its motto, "Paving the Way for a Better California." Both senders' messages contained unsubscribe instructions and contact information that linked to a working e-mail address and a telephone number.

Source: Neil Malhotra, Melissa R. Michelson, and Ali Adam Valenzuela, "Emails from Official Sources Can Increase Turnout," *Quarterly Journal of Political Science,* vol. 7 (2012): 321–32.

day or Monday before Election Day. In keeping with prior experiments, PAVE's e-mails were ineffective. Its 55,000 e-mails generated a meager twenty-eight votes. The registrar's 55,000 e-mails, however, raised turnout by 0.56 of a percentage point, or approximately 308 votes. This effect is rather modest and just barely exceeds conventional levels of statistical significance; however, like the mailings from the Secretary of State discussed in chapter 5, the result suggests that communication from public officials may be especially effective at raising turnout.

Text Messaging

Text messaging is analogous to e-mail in the sense that digital messages are transmitted instantly. Many of the same issues arise with respect to obtaining a target list, but with extra regulatory constraints on how texts may be sent out in bulk. In contrast to e-mail, which in principle could be distributed via one's own computer, large-scale texting campaigns are almost always conducted via a commercial interface. Many firms now specialize in orchestrated texting campaigns for political causes. A growing niche market includes services that match an official voter file to the "contact lists" from the cell phones of activists supporting a campaign; once the merged database is assembled, a centralized operation can distribute personalized texts. Another wrinkle is the "one-to-one" text messaging campaign: volunteers text strangers via a centralized interface and carry on a conversation with those who reply. This kind of activity grew dramatically in scale in 2018, as political campaigns began to tap the vast pool of part-time activists who are willing to volunteer for tasks that they can do from home.

Two things set text messages apart from e-mails. First, text messages break through the din of life. Most people check their smartphones immediately if they chime with an incoming message. Granted, they may scowl if the incoming message is about voting, but incoming messages tend to receive much more attention than the average unsolicited e-mail. The second difference between texts and e-mails is content; texts tend to be very brief. This constrained format might actually play to the advantage of text messages insofar as the receiver reads the incoming message expecting to glean something clear and concise. Given these two differences, it would not be altogether surprising if texts were to prove more effective than e-mail. Of course, like any medium, text messaging gradually becomes overrun by unwanted intrusions, and so the question is whether this mode of communication will continue to generate votes as more bulk messengers get into the act.

Experimental Evidence Concerning Text Messaging

The GOTV potential of text messaging attracted early attention thanks to Allison Dale and Aaron Strauss, who conducted an experiment involving more than 8,500 telephone numbers of people who had registered to vote with one of three nonpartisan groups. Half of these new registrants received text messages from the groups urging them to vote the following day in the November 2006 election.[14] Their results showed a powerful turnout effect of 3.1 percentage points and, when read in conjunction with two prior experiments on text messaging, suggest that this type of communication raises turnout by approximately 2.6 percentage points.[15] (As usual, there was no evidence of significant variations in the effect depending on whether the GOTV communication conveyed a "civic duty" or a "close election" message, and providing the number of a polling location hotline did not increase the effect.) Interpreted in light of the e-mail studies showing no effect, this intriguing result suggests that the mode of text communication is crucial. But what is it about receiving a message on one's phone that makes it so powerful? This finding seems to defy the basic thesis that impersonal communication is ineffective. Or does it instead show that the reason personal communication works is that it, like text messages on one's phone, commands the voter's attention?

Clues to these puzzles come from several further experiments. The first two were conducted in conjunction with the registrar of voters in San Mateo, California, amid the low-turnout elections of November 2009 and June 2010.[16] Both studies found small but clearly positive effects of text message reminders. Personalizing the messages by referring to the recipient by name did not enhance the effect. The third study was a large experiment conducted by Rock the Vote during the final days of the 2012 presidential election. More than 180,000 people who had given Rock the Vote their mobile phone numbers when they registered to vote were randomly assigned to one of five experimental groups: (1) an untreated control group; (2) a group that was texted the day before Election Day with the message "Tomorrow is election day! Get info on where to go and what to bring here: http://rtvote.com/Se2M18"; (3) a group that received the preceding message but with additional instructions to "reply with your address to find your polling location & time"; (4) a group that in addition to receiving one of the preceding reminders was sent an Election Day message; and (5) a group that in addition to receiving either reminder 2 or 3 was sent the Election Day message "Drop what you're doing and GO VOTE NOW!" Messages 2 and 3 worked equally well, boosting turnout by 0.6 of a percentage point. Further messaging on Election Day failed to boost turnout, and in fact the group that received the initial message and then the "Drop what you're doing" message voted at a lower rate than the control group. Taken together, the groups that received any text message from Rock the Vote voted at a rate that was 0.5 of a percentage point higher than the control group.[17] Returning to the context of federal midterm elections with messages from local groups, Lisa García Bedolla, Marisa Abrajano, and Jane Junn assessed the effects of texts sent by four California grassroots organizations prior to the 2014 election. They found an average increase in turnout of 3.1 percentage points.

By 2016, text messaging had become a staple of large, statewide campaigns. One study by David Broockman and Donald Green assessed the texting campaign of One Arizona, which targeted 205,358 registered voters who were nonwhite, under 35, or unmarried women and successfully delivered messages to 98 percent of the target list. Using a platform that allowed messages to be sent with personal follow-up in case the recipient responded, One Arizona sent an early message and a last-minute reminder to vote prior to the presidential election. The early message was a twist on social pressure mail: "[VOTER NAME], I'm [VOLUNTEER NAME] w/ One AZ helping folks vote. How you vote is secret, but if you vote or not is public & I saw you missed a past election. I want to be able to thank you for voting this year. [Please plan to vote!/Do you plan to vote?"] Regardless of whether the message ended with an injunction or a question, turnout increased by approximately 0.5 of a percentage point among those contacted. Asking a question increased the rate of conversation but did not increase turnout.[18] Another study leading up to the 2016 presidential election involving 20,015 voters was also inspired by social pressure messaging, but this time without the pretext that the messages were coming from a particular individual or group. During the final eight days before the election, five texts were sent to voters in all 50 states with messages such as, "Do you know that whether you vote or not is public info? If you don't vote, YOUR FRIENDS will find out!" Turnout, however, was identical—80.6 percent in both the treatment and control groups.[19] Further evidence calling into question the value of social pressure messaging in this context is a head-to-head experiment conducted by Vote.org and its partners in twenty-seven states leading up to the presidential election. The target population, people who had registered to vote with Vote.org, was divided into three groups of approximately 108,000 apiece: a control group that received no messages; a treatment group that received a total of ten messages, the first of which called attention to the recipient's personal vote history; and a treatment group that also received ten messages but without any reference to personal vote history. Compared to the control group, turnout in the social pressure group was 0.35 of a percentage point higher, while the no social pressure group was 0.65 of a percentage point higher.[20]

Other messaging experiments in 2016 focused on the role of polling place information. One study targeted 188,486 Illinois voters under 40 who were targeted as probable Democrats. Messages read, "Hey Stephanie, I'm Justine, a volunteer working to get folks in Illinois out to vote. Election Day is Nov 8 and IL has early voting locations open now. You can find your polling location at http://nxtgn.us/vote—can we count on you to vote no matter what?" The results showed a turnout increase of 0.25 of a percentage point in the treatment group, or one vote per 400 people who were texted.[21] A larger and more direct test of polling place information comes from a study of more than 1.2 million nonwhite and single women voters that compared a control group (N = 301,920) to a plan-making message group (N = 301,751) and a group that received polling place location information (N = 603,645). The plan-making group was sent seven texts yet voted at a rate of 52.1 percent, compared to 52.2 percent in the control group. The polling location group received up to four texts and voted at a rate of 52.4 percent.[22] An almost identical experiment conducted in a low-salience election, the 2017 Virginia gubernatorial primary, targeted the same type of audience and produced a 0.62 percentage point increase in turnout. These effects were slightly larger when the text included polling place information.[23]

Making sense of these results requires a bit of guesswork because no single study systematically tests each of the constituent parts. It seems clear that effects are smaller in presidential contests. Within a given electoral context, it appears that effects are larger when a GOTV message comes from a public official or a grassroots organization. Social pressure messages have produced mixed results and, on the whole, seem not to be worth the trouble. Other nuances of message content appear to have negligible effects (for example, asking questions), but there is reason to believe that providing polling place information is helpful. Overall, text messaging is a more reliable way to increase turnout than e-mail.

Social Media

The sheer volume of human activity that takes place on platforms such as Facebook, Instagram, or Twitter is mind-boggling. Facebook users, for example, comprise 68 percent of the American adult population and spend on average fifty-eight minutes per day using the service.[24] The question for political campaigns is how to convey messages to this vast audience. One answer is to generate the kind of news, blog post, or video that quickly spreads through social media channels. Generating this so-called earned media coverage is the specialty of many publicists and political consultants.

Another approach is to buy ads on social media sites. Depending on the site, such ads may be sold by a price per "impression" (that is, each time an ad is displayed to a user) or a price per click-through (that is, each time users click on a link image that redirects them to another web page, such as the campaign's home page). Sometimes prices are flat fees; in other cases, they are purchased through auctions. Perhaps because advertisers remain skeptical about the returns from online ads, these ads tend to be relatively inexpensive. For example, a week's advertising budget designed to saturate Facebook users in a congressional district in 2012 cost only a few hundred dollars.[25] The unit cost of advertising rises, however, when ads are insinuated more subtly into the user's online experience. Advertisers pay a premium to place their messages into the "news feed" of social media sites so that viewers will come across them as they scroll through their friends' postings. The question, of course, is whether such ads pay off in terms of votes.

A third messaging approach is to use social media platforms as an opportunity for person-to-person communication about politics. Social media sites comprise a wide array of groups that are drawn together by common interests, be it sports, entertainment, or politics. Personal conversations within these social circles are potentially a way to increase their interest and involvement in an upcoming election.

Experimental Evidence Concerning Social Media

Although the experimental literature on social media and voter turnout is not large, the studies that have been conducted are quite instructive. Academic researchers and Facebook researchers teamed up to conduct a massive study of turnout among Facebook users in the 2010 general election.[26] Millions of Facebook users were randomly assigned to one of three conditions. The first was a control group that received no encouragement to vote. The second group received an information treatment that consisted of several elements: users were shown a banner at the top of their news feed announcing that "Today is Election Day," encouraged to indicate whether they voted by clicking an "I Voted" graphic, provided a link to locate their polling place, and presented with a counter tabulating the cumulative vote count among Facebook users. The third group received a social treatment: they received the same encouragement as the information group and were also shown profile photos of up to six friends who had voted along with a count of friends who had voted. Data gleaned from Facebook users' personal profiles allowed the research team to assess actual turnout for about one in ten subjects, which nevertheless left approximately 60,000 subjects in the control and information conditions and millions in the social condition. Two key findings emerged. The first is that the information treatment had precisely zero effect on turnout. This finding reaffirms results from other experiments suggesting that reminders to vote have little effect on turnout. The second is that the social treatment increased turnout by 0.39 of a percentage point. This effect is not large, but thanks to the enormous size of the experiment it cannot be attributed to chance. Turnout in the social group was significantly higher than in the control condition or the information condition. Evidently, the active ingredient in the social condition is the presentation of friends' turnout, a theme that we will revisit in chapter 11, when we discuss the influence of social norms on turnout. When the experiment was repeated prior to the 2012 presidential election, the results were similar. Among those who logged in to Facebook sometime during Election Day, turnout was 0.35 percent higher among those who were exposed to voting messages that showed the names of friends who ostensibly voted.[27]

The idea of putting an "I voted" widget on Facebook users' news feeds is a creative one, but this intervention is not something that those outside Facebook are at liberty to do, even for a fee. The fallback position is to buy ads on Facebook. Over time, Facebook has become more accommodating to advertisers. In 2012, the site allowed Rock the Vote to place ads on news feeds only when the targeted users "liked" Rock the Vote or had friends who had done so. By 2013, this policy was relaxed so that Rock the Vote could deliver news feed ads to all Facebook users they sought to target. In a pair of large-scale experiments, Kevin Collins, Lauren Keane, and Joshua Kalla tested whether Rock the Vote ads placed in Facebook's news feed in fact raised turnout.[28] In 2012, they assigned approximately 365,000 people to an untreated control group and another 365,000 to a treatment group that received encouragements to vote via sidebar ads and in their news feeds (the latter were actually delivered to 41 percent of the assigned treatment group, who "liked" Rock the Vote). These encouragements showed, for example, the number of days left before the election and a display of friends who "liked" this countdown. Because Rock the Vote had a positive image among the subjects who received its message, having helped many of them register to vote, it was a credible source of information and encouragement. However, voter turnout records later revealed that the treatment and control groups voted at identical rates: 56.5 percent. The following year, another experiment using the same design was conducted in fourteen states where November elections were being held. Roughly 46,500 voters were assigned to an untreated control and a like number to the treatment group exposed to Rock the Vote advertising. This time, a slightly higher proportion of the assigned treatment group, 54 percent, received ads embedded in their news feeds. Turnout, however, was 14.6 percent in the control group and 14.0 percent in the treatment group. In both elections, Facebook ads proved ineffective at increasing turnout. What went wrong? It is hard to say. The experiments themselves were meticulously executed, and even if half the subjects in the treatment groups went untreated, the groups were large enough to reveal an effect if news feed ads in fact boosted turnout to an appreciable extent among those who received them. Putting the two experiments together suggests that the average effect of news feed ads on those who were eligible to receive them was probably no greater than zero and at most 0.15 of a percentage point. Two GOTV campaigns conducted in California prior to the 2014 midterm fall exactly in this range. One conducted by Rock the Vote sent digital ads to 1,926,000 people, with 472,141 in an untreated control group. The other conducted by Mi Familia Vota sent ads to 1,859,837, with 464,504 in control. In both cases, turnout was 0.1 of a percentage point higher in the treatment group.[29] Studies of local elections generate similar conclusions. A cookie-targeting digital advertising campaign conducted by Katherine Haenschen and Jay Jennings in partnership with the Dallas Morning News sought to promote turnout in a municipal election among registered voters ages 23 to 35. More than 70,000 voters were randomly assigned to receive either reminder ads with links to polling locations and times, information ads with links to news stories about issues and candidates, both treatments, or nothing. Control group turnout was

5.83 percent, and the only treatment group with higher turnout was the group receiving both messages, which voted at 5.95 percent.[30]

The largest and most informative digital advertising experiment was conducted by Joshua Kalla during the 2016 presidential election.[31] The advertiser was a 501(c)(4) that targeted 1.2 million voters ages 18 to 35 in New Hampshire, Nevada, and Pennsylvania, all battleground states. The ads, two-thirds of which were deployed through Facebook, urged viewers to turnout and support Hillary Clinton. Turnout in the treatment group of 1,041,952 was 0.14 of a percentage point higher than that of the control group of 195,368. Despite the enormous size of this study, that effect is not statistically distinguishable from zero; it is, however, right in line with other tests of online advertising. This advertising campaign cost $691,005 and produced 1,459 votes at a cost of $474 per vote.

To this point we have considered only aspects of the social networking experience that are directed by impersonal forces—ads and news feed items from interest groups as opposed to personal acquaintances. What happens when Facebook users are exposed to updates that are generated by a person whom they "friended"? In an experiment conducted at a university, Holly Teresi encouraged students to friend her on Facebook. She randomly divided the roughly 600 who did so into a control group that periodically received nine updates on nonpolitical topics and a treatment group that received these updates as well as fourteen additional updates on matters related to the upcoming 2010 general election. Using information on the subjects' Facebook profiles to match records to the Georgia voter file, she found the treatment turnout rate to be 31.2 percent, compared to 23 percent in the control group. This large effect is statistically significant, despite the fact that only 344 participants could be matched to the voter file.[32] The direction and magnitude of this effect is broadly consistent with other experimental evidence suggesting that augmenting the political content of Facebook users' news feed increases their interest in politics and interest in voting.[33] Another powerful effect observed within Facebook social networks is Katherine Haenschen's study of social pressure. In the first study, she matched seven people's "friends" list to the Dallas County voter file and divided the 293 registered voters into experimental groups. During the early voting period prior to the 2014 midterm elections, some people were scolded for their failure to vote, others were praised for voting early, others were encouraged to do their civic duty, and others were part of an untreated control group. Turnout in the "shame" condition was 76 percent, as compared to 68 percent in the "pride" condition, 48 percent in the "civic duty" condition, and 52 percent in the control group. Interestingly, the effects were much more muted in a separate experiment in which the researcher's accomplices called out one another for their failure to vote but did not direct their ire at the experimental subjects; evidently, scolding only raises turnout when it is directed at the target voter.[34]

Lessons Learned

The lessons emerging from these studies are rated according to the system detailed in chapter 2.

★ ★ ★ *E-mail designed to encourage voter participation has negligible effects on voter registration.* Although thousands of recipients of these e-mails followed links to sites where they could register online, registration rates for the treatment and control groups were almost identical. Absent these e-mail campaigns, the people who registered online would have registered anyway.

★ ★ ★ *E-mail messages rarely increase voter turnout.* Studies of encouragements to vote by nonpartisan, partisan, and advocacy organizations found e-mail communication to have no positive effect on voter turnout. This finding holds across a range of target groups and message styles. One noteworthy exception is e-mail sent by a local registrar of voters, which produced small but statistically significant positive effects, suggesting that one vote is produced per 180 e-mails sent.

★ ★ ★ *Text messages from public officials or grassroots organizations increase voter turnout.* These effects tend to be smaller in presidential contests. Averaging across all studies, including several large studies conducted during the 2016 presidential election, the average effect of a text messaging campaign (sometimes consisting of multiple messages) is 0.29 of a percentage point, or one vote per 345 targeted phone numbers.

★ ★ *Social media information campaigns consisting of prominently displayed banner ads and "I voted" widgets have no effect on voter turnout; such campaigns raise turnout only when users are also presented with news showing which of their friends have voted.* The average effect of this social prime is small but positive, with one vote produced for every 256 users presented with this package of information. Although the average effect of the social prime is small, when administered to 60 million Facebook users, this intervention translates into more than 230,000 votes.

★ ★ *Advertisements on social media platforms such as Facebook produce little or no apparent increase in turnout.* This pattern holds regardless of whether the ads in question appear in the sidebar or the news feed.

★ *Friend-to-friend communication about an upcoming election can raise voter turnout.* The two studies to evaluate communication within a social network found large effects from encouraging friends to vote or monitoring their turnout on a daily basis during the period of early voting. Although provisional pending replication, these effects are on par with the effect of face-to-face canvassing.

Assessment and Conclusion

Given the current state of the evidence, the cost assessment of mass e-mail is rather dismal. Setting up a target database and hiring technical staff to design and distribute e-mail involve substantial start-up costs. The marginal cost of sending each e-mail is minimal, but, unfortunately, the effects on registration and turnout are minimal as well. The sole exception is messaging from the local registrar. One may be tempted to conclude that the registrar of voters is an especially credible source of information about the importance of an upcoming election. The puzzling thing is why stalwart Democrats were unmoved by blandishments from the Democratic National Committee. One would think that those who routinely receive DNC communications would follow its lead at election time. Evidently not. The same goes for social media users, many of whom registered to vote with help from Rock the Vote. One would think that Rock the Vote would be a credible source of "news" in one's news feed, yet its blandishments had no effect on turnout.

Could the way forward be to send more personalized e-mail or social media communication, perhaps propagated by friends encouraging each other to vote? A small experiment designed to test this proposition showed some promising initial results. Tiffany Davenport conducted a friends-to-friends e-mail experiment in which each sender's network of friends was randomly assigned to receive either a mass GOTV e-mail (presumed to have no effect) or a personal e-mail note encouraging voter turnout.[35] Her results suggest that personalized friend-to-friend contact substantially increases turnout vis-à-vis the mass e-mail control group. This line of research in conjunction with Holly Teresi's study of friend-to-friend communication via Facebook may pave the way for a new generation of mobilization campaigns. Using the vast number of social connections provided by Facebook and other online communities may be the key to effective—and relatively inexpensive—voter mobilization.

Text messaging from personal contacts, public officials, or grassroots organizations seems to benefit from their authenticity coupled with their ability to briefly command the attention of recipients. Texting campaigns, including those conducted in the final days of presidential elections, have tended to produce approximately three votes for every 1,000 targeted voters. For this mobilization tactic to generate a sizable increase in turnout, the scale of the texting campaign must be enormous. If you pay a list vendor $2 per 100 eligible cell phone numbers and pay a texting service $7 per one hundred messages sent, texting one million voters five times apiece costs $370,000, without accounting for the recruitment and supervision of volunteers to send texts. If you raise turnout by 3 voters per 1,000 targeted voters, the resulting 3,000 votes will cost $123 apiece. But if you can generate the kind of text messaging campaign that raises turnout by 10 voters per 1,000 targeted voters (that is, akin to the effects that are often observed in nonpresidential elections), a cost-per-vote calculation implies an attractive $37 per vote. Differences in effectiveness can have profound implications, which is why R&D in this area is currently so vigorous.

CHAPTER EIGHT

Using Events to Draw
Voters to the Polls

I t is the rare campaigner who looks forward to the prospect of calling and canvassing for weeks on end. Even people who genuinely love to talk with voters blanch at the prospect of contacting several hundred households. At the same time, most people who enjoy politics and political organizing relish the prospect of coordinating and attending campaign events.

Campaign events may take many forms. Events such as Election Day festivals attract potential voters by turning the polls into social gathering places. Forums and debates attract potential voters by bringing them into close contact with candidates, perhaps providing an opportunity for citizens to question candidates directly.

Over the years, we have found that many organizations that lack the capacity to conduct large-scale GOTV efforts are nonetheless quite good at organizing and publicizing events. This chapter aims to assess the effectiveness of these efforts. The evidence base suggests that events represent a valuable supplement to conventional voter mobilization campaigns.

Campaign Events in Historical Perspective

Since the late 1880s, state laws have gradually distanced the individual voter from the hoopla surrounding Election Day. Before the introduction of the secret ballot, voters cast their votes in front of their neighbors, bosses, and ward heelers. The political parties supplied printed ballots of varying colors. Voters could scratch out the party's suggested names and write other names instead, but these marks and the partisan complexion of the ballot were apparent to party onlookers. In Connecticut, for example, voters were required to place their filled-out ballot atop the ballot box; if no one challenged their right to cast a ballot at that point, their ballot was placed into the box. The reforms of the late nineteenth century replaced party-printed ballots with ballots distributed by the state, required party workers to remain seventy-five feet or farther from the polling place, and provided booths for voters to cast their ballots in secret. A century later, in an effort to make voting more convenient, several states instituted no-fault absentee voting, allowing people to vote from home, even further from the reach of electioneering activities.

The net effect of these reforms has been to change the character of Election Day. Before the reforms of the 1880s, voters often lingered for hours at the polls, consuming the free booze and entertainment that the candidates and parties provided. As historian Richard Bensel points out, polling places were sometimes located in saloons or other gathering places where a raucous, freewheeling atmosphere prevailed. Voting in federal elections was a men-only affair in those days, and brawls and catcalls frequently accompanied the act of voting. Bensel reports that the jurisprudence of that era set the bar rather high for charges of voter intimidation, requiring only that "a man of ordinary courage" must be able to cast his ballot.[1] Nonetheless, voting rates were much higher than anything seen in the twentieth century.

Once voting was moved out of sight of onlookers and party officials, Election Day whiskey ceased to flow, and crowds no longer congregated at the polls. Turnout abruptly declined.[2] A century later, reforms allowing people to vote by mail or in advance of Election Day further diminished interaction between voters and the social significance of Election Day itself.

The events leading up to Election Day have also changed. Consider, for example, the presidential election of 1884, in which 71 percent of eligible voters cast ballots. What did campaigning look like in the heyday of voting? Connecticut was a "battleground state" in this election, giving

Grover Cleveland a narrow 51.3 percent victory statewide. The city of Hartford saw a steady stream of campaign events—parades, speeches, and rallies—that drew large numbers of people in the evenings and on weekends. The *Hartford Courant* paints a picture of one procession:

> A grand parade of uniformed republican clubs took place in the Eighth ward last evening. . . . All along the line of the march there were fine illuminations of private residences, displays of flags, burning of colored fires, and large numbers of people in the streets to witness the procession. On Grand and Lawrence streets there were some particularly fine displays, and the whistle of the Billings & Spencer company's factory on the latter street blew a continuous salute while the procession was passing. . . . At one place on Park there was a pyramid of six or eight children in front of a house with fancy dresses, and waving flags, making a beautiful tableau, as illuminated with colored lights. . . . There were nearly 600 men in line, including the drum bands.[3]

These kinds of events are difficult to imagine today. Unless a presidential candidate makes a personal appearance, rallies are rare. Processions are even rarer.

The one enduring feature of old-fashioned elections is the candidate forum. At the state and national levels these debates are nowadays highly scripted events directed at a television audience, but they nonetheless offer an opportunity for interested viewers to get a sense of the candidates' issue positions and personal style. At the local level, they attract smaller audiences but often serve the purpose of encouraging candidates to address the concerns of specific segments of the electorate and allow voters to size up the styles and issue stances of the candidates.

Although it is not possible to measure the impact of nineteenth-century campaign events, one can test the effectiveness of contemporary events, some of which are designed to create the same feelings of interest and engagement. In this chapter, we discuss Election Day festivals, patterned after those of the late nineteenth century (minus the liquor). We also summarize the research literature on other events, such as candidate forums and town hall meetings that voters listen to by phone. The take-home message of this chapter is that the personal touch of face-to-face gatherings has the potential to increase turnout.

Modern Day Festivals

In 2005 and 2006, Elizabeth Addonizio, Donald Green, and James Glaser set out to explore the feasibility of creating a more festive and community-focused atmosphere at the polls.[4] This line of inquiry turns the usual approach to GOTV on its head. Researchers and policymakers tend to focus on the costs of voting and ways to reduce those costs. But rarely do they address the potential benefits of casting a ballot.[5] This line of research attempted to quantify the impact of imbuing polling places with the attractiveness of a local fair.

These poll parties, while inspired by those of the nineteenth century, departed from their historical models in significant ways. Elections and Election Day activity are highly regulated today, and most state and federal laws prohibit not only vote buying, but also any kind of quid pro quo inducement to vote. Researchers were therefore informed by local and state officials that the parties had to be advertised and carried out in such a way as not to link the casting of a ballot with the receipt of food and entertainment. Provided that these restrictions were respected, the festivals were well within the bounds of election law. And unlike the social activities surrounding elections in the nineteenth century, which catered to the tastes of male voters, these parties were meant for general audiences, including children. The empirical question the researchers thus addressed was whether these family-friendly, alcohol-free variants of the old-time poll party raise turnout.

Over the course of two years, Addonizio and her co-authors evaluated a series of sixteen experimental festivals. These festivals were held in a wide array of locations, ranging from middle-class, all-white suburbs to poor, largely minority inner cities. All of the festivals followed a common model, which was developed in New Hampshire, where the authors conducted a pilot study before municipal elections held in the spring of 2005. The authors began with two towns—Hooksett and Hanover—that had similar populations and voting rates. A coin was flipped, and the researchers organized a party in Hooksett, leaving Hanover as the control group.

The festival was preceded by a week of publicity and local organizing. Flyers were handed out at town meetings, and posters were displayed in local stores and meeting spots. On the Saturday before Election Day, the regional newspaper included a flyer advertising an "Election Day Poll Party," giving the location and time. The local paper also advertised the event. On the Sunday before Election Day, a story describing the party appeared in one of the papers. At the same time, three dozen lawn signs advertising the event were planted on busy streets in town. Finally, two prerecorded thirty-second phone calls were directed to 3,000 Hooksett households. Both extended an invitation to the party and gave details about its hours (3:00 p.m. to 7:00 p.m.) and location.

Election Day in Hooksett featured beautiful spring weather, perfect for an outdoor event. The festival took place immediately outside the polling place, on the front lawn of the local middle school. A large tent was set up, surrounded by signs encouraging people to enjoy free snacks, drinks, and raffles. A cotton candy machine, expertly staffed by political science professors, attracted a steady stream of children. People of all ages milled about the party tent, eating, drinking, and listening to music supplied by a local disk jockey. People at the party seemed aware of the event before coming to the polls to vote. They had read the flyer, received the calls, or heard about the various advertised activities from other residents.

Judging from the size of the crowd it attracted and partygoers' positive evaluation of the event, the party was deemed a success. Hooksett, despite having no contested candidates on the ballot, garnered a higher voter turnout rate than Hanover. After replicating the experiment in a local election in New Haven in 2005, the authors attracted the involvement of Working Assets in 2006, which coordinated local festivals in every region of the country during the primary and general election season. In each site, target precincts were identified, some of which were randomly assigned to a treatment group in which a festival was held. Turnout rates of the treatment and control precincts were compared; because these additional sites were not matched in terms of past voter turnout rates, a multivariate analysis was conducted to control for past turnout differences across precincts.

Across all thirty-eight precincts, the results indicated that festivals—or to be more precise, the festivals and the pre-election publicity surrounding them—increased turnout by approximately 2 percentage points. Because many of these precincts were small, the festivals together generated approximately 960 additional votes at a cost of $33,168 in 2018 dollars. These figures imply a cost per vote of $35, which puts festivals on the same general plane as other face-to-face tactics.

Despite the promising results from these early festivals, political campaigns and nonpartisan groups seldom used festivals to bolster turnout between 2005 and 2016. The breakthrough came when a nonpartisan group called Civic Nation took an interest in promoting festivals during the 2016 presidential election. These festivals, coordinated by Edna Ishayik in collaboration with local organizations, equaled or surpassed the earlier festivals in terms of the energy that went into local canvassing to spread the word to local businesses and nearby homes. All of the festivals featured free food, and local sites offered various forms of entertainment: live broadcasts from a local radio station, dance troupes, photo booths, arts and crafts, lawn games, and puppies. A total of nine festivals took place in an assortment of battleground (North Carolina, Ohio) and nonbattleground states (California, Tennessee, Texas). All of the sites enjoyed pleasant weather. The total cost of the festivals, including advertising, food and beverages, staff, venue, and entertainment—as well as the value of in-kind donations from local businesses—was approximately $28,000.

Donald Green and Oliver McClellan designed an evaluation patterned after the earlier studies. Each local organization that planned to throw a party was asked to nominate more than one feasible site. The researchers then randomly assigned some of the sites to a treatment group and others to a control group. Despite the fact that the study involved just eighteen voting sites (nine treatment and nine control), the statistical results were surprisingly decisive. Turnout was 3.8 percentage points higher in treated locations, and the chances of obtaining an estimate this large simply by chance was about one in forty-five. This boost in turnout implies a cost-per-vote of $34, which is quite good given the challenges of increasing turnout in a presidential election.[6]

Coincidentally, an advocacy organization also took an interest in festivals during the waning days of the 2016 presidential election. This 501(c)(4) organization sought to increase turnout among college students in the battleground state of Pennsylvania. Most of its festivals were not evaluated experimentally, but five were. Following the same experimental protocol as the Civic Nation study, this group picked two possible voting sites, and the researchers randomly selected one to receive treatment. In contrast to the Civic Nation festivals, which focused on getting the word out in advance to the local community, these festivals popped up suddenly in off-campus precincts where students vote and primarily consisted of free food and shuttles from campus. Turnout was higher in treatment sites in three of the five pairs, but the average effect was almost exactly zero.[7]

Civic Nation coordinated a larger festivals program in 2017, which featured an assortment of state and local elections. Civic Nation developed training materials to introduce local groups to the legal requirements of hosting a nonpartisan festival and to provide pointers for planning the festival and getting the word out. This decentralized model included small grants to local organizations to defray the costs of food and advertising. The character of the festivals varied. Some were relatively low-key affairs consisting of pizza, soft drinks, and a boom box; others reflected far greater community involvement, such as local entertainer performances and catering from well-known local eateries. Perhaps more important, advance work leading up to the festivals also varied. Some local groups publicized the event through door-to-door canvassing and posters in local shops, but most relied on flyers, robo-calls, or direct mail. This variation in pre–Election Day advertising was reflected in highly variable festival attendance. While the smallest parties received as few as fifteen or twenty attendees, larger parties received hundreds of party-goers. The weather was no help—rain afflicted 85 percent of the festival sites, which were outdoors. When the results were tallied, precinct-level voting rates were on average higher in treatment sites than in their control group counterparts, but only by 0.9 of a percentage point, implying a cost-per-vote that was four times higher than in 2016. However, the researchers took note of the fact that while the treatment has only a weakly positive effect on turnout in the sites that were hit by rain, the sites where no rain fell experienced a substantial increase in turnout on par with the results from 2016.[8]

By 2018, Election Day festivals had begun to attract attention among civic leaders and donors. The organization #VoteTogether, a spin-off of Civic Nation and under the leadership of Angie Jean-Marie, set out to orchestrate hundreds of parties in advance of the midterm elections. #VoteTogether coordinated grants to train local organizations, publicize the idea of hosting voting events, and defray the costs of throwing festivals. A total of 1,946 events received #VoteTogether's encouragement or assistance. The vast majority of these parties took place outside any experimental evaluation, but some groups were willing to do the extra legwork to pick more than one feasible site and let researchers randomly select which site would receive a festival. In all, a total of 56 sites were assigned to treatment and were each paired with a control site. Drawing on the lessons from 2017, #VoteTogether provided clear guidelines to local groups about the importance of community outreach in advance of a festival, but the weather was again uncooperative, with rainfall in 77 percent of the sites. Attendance was uneven, perhaps due to the lack of personalized outreach efforts in many sites. At the time of this writing, preliminary results suggest that the turnout boost was negligible, at more than $200 per vote.

The results from 2017 and 2018 serve as a reminder that the main challenge is drawing a crowd. In effect, the turnout problem shifts from getting people to vote to getting people to attend (and then vote). Building festival attendance is as yet more art than science, but the trick seems to be to maximize outreach, community involvement, and economies of scale. Future experiments will offer guidance on many untried tactics for building attendance. For example, a lineup of all-school musical performances serves the dual purpose of providing performers and an appreciative audience of family members. Jurisdictions that permit voting by mail allow festival planners to hold their parties after church or as part of a prelude to a weekend concert or sporting event. In places that have consolidated voting locations to accommodate early voting, one could hold a festival on a weekend and advertise to the entire city. House or office parties can bring friends together to congregate for drinks and snacks before walking en masse to a nearby polling place. Variations on the festival theme are almost limitless. The challenge of putting together a successful festival stems from the fact that contemporary Americans do not associate festivals with elections, and some election officials worry that even a nonpartisan festival might appear to serve some partisan purpose. It might take a series of festivals before locals see social gatherings as an expected and attractive aspect of coming to vote.

Candidate Debates

To what extent does watching a debate increase a person's probability of voting? Social scientists have often speculated that exposure to the candidates and the issues they discuss causes voters to become more interested in the campaign and therefore they are more likely to vote. However, experimental evidence is thin. Just two studies have randomly encouraged people to watch candidate debates. Adria Lawrence and Bethany Albertson report the results of an experiment conducted in 2000, which showed that people who are randomly encouraged to watch the presidential debates are significantly more likely subsequently to report an intention to vote.[9] The problem with this study is that it relied on self-reports in the context of a follow-up interview; it did not document whether people actually voted. A study by Sendhil Mullainathan, Ebonya Washington, and Julia Azari in the context of the 2005 mayoral election in New York City overcame this problem by randomly encouraging people to watch the mayoral debates a few days before the election and measuring their behavior using public records.[10] Again, a positive effect was found, although it falls short of statistical significance. Taken together, these studies hint that viewing debates may increase voter turnout.

What about attending a debate in person? Live debates are the kind of event that can be staged relatively easily among down-ballot candidates, and the question is whether these events have any effect on those who attend. David Nickerson studied a creative attempt to bring out the lighter side of a meet-the-candidates event.[11] The event, called "Candidates Gone Wild" (CGW), was hosted by the Oregon Bus Project and a local counterculture newspaper in the hopes of boosting young people's interest in local politics. The event took place in Portland two weeks before its 2006 primary election, and candidates for county and city offices were invited to participate. Candidates had an opportunity to make themselves known and to show their lighter side. CGW was held in a local theater, and several hundred potential voters attended the event. Tickets were sold in advance for $3.

The CGW study was small but cleverly designed. For the purposes of the experiment, fifty tickets to CGW were set aside. After the remaining 950 tickets were sold, Oregon Bus Project volunteers signed interested individuals up for a lottery to distribute the fifty remaining tickets. Those signing up became the subjects of the study. To register for the lottery, individuals had to fill out a card with their full name, address, phone number, and e-mail address. In the end, 100 people signed up for the lottery, and fifty names were randomly selected to receive tickets. A postelection survey confirmed that, for the most part, the lottery winners attended the show, and the control group did not.

Before describing the effects of the program on turnout, let's first consider how the event affected voters' opinions, based on a postelection interview that David Nickerson conducted with thirty-nine of the participants. Given the content of a program like Candidates Gone Wild, one might expect the audience to become more informed about the election and to feel more connected to the politicians and the political system in general, resulting in higher turnout rates. In fact, the findings are mixed. A significantly higher proportion of the treatment group could correctly identify whether the seven candidates who participated were challengers or incumbents, but the treatment group was no better than the control group at answering four factual questions about the candidates. (The particular questions were selected because the content was mentioned during the event itself.) All in all, voters who attended CGW seemed to be more familiar with the candidates but retained little substantive information two weeks after the event.

The picture is similarly mixed with regard to attitudes about politics. When asked to agree or disagree with a series of statements, members of the treatment group were no more likely to express interest in politics or to think that voting is particularly important. This finding echoes the study of the New York mayoral debates, which also found them to have little effect on interest in the election. Nevertheless, participants in the CGW treatment group were far more likely than their control group counterparts to think that local elections are important.

The most striking finding in this study is the turnout effect. Although the treatment and control groups expressed similar attitudes about voting, the average rate of turnout was substantially higher in the treatment group. Among the ninety-one people whose vote could be validated using public records, turnout in the control group was 17 percent, compared with 31 percent in the treatment group. The small size of this experiment means that its results must be interpreted with caution, but the results remain intriguing. The "random invitation" design is an underutilized experimental approach, and more experiments are needed to verify the results of these three promising studies.

One such study distributed random invitations to a "tele–town hall meeting" to discuss the issue of mass incarceration and to encourage voting on this issue in the 2014 midterm election.[12] A grassroots group called likely voters residing in South Los Angeles, inviting them to participate. Then, on the day of the telephone town hall, they received another call that patched them through to the 42-minute discussion of criminal justice reform. Of the 28,969 households that were invited, 3,960 actually participated, listening for an average of eight minutes. Given the limited take-up rate, it is perhaps not surprising that the researchers found no increase in turnout. This kind of study merits replication, perhaps with a focus on candidate debates.

Conclusions and Thoughts for Further Research

The findings of this chapter are summarized according to the rating system detailed in chapter 2.

★★ *Election Day festivals increase voter turnout.* The array of experiments conducted to date suggests that festivals draw voters to the polls—if the weather cooperates. When festivals are well advertised and conducted in coordination with local organizations and businesses, they may provide a cost-effective means of increasing turnout. Pooling all five studies of festivals, including those with bad weather or limited community outreach, suggests that festivals raise turnout by 1 percentage point. If the average precinct includes 2,700 voters and the average festival costs $1,900, the cost per vote comes to $72.

★ *Viewing candidate debates in person increases turnout.* Experimental findings remain ambiguous but suggest that viewers vote at higher rates even if they do not show higher overall levels of interest in politics.

The varied and sometimes offbeat interventions described in this chapter serve as reminders that scientific discoveries draw their inspiration from many sources. One important and underutilized source is our own history. We tend to view our politics as fundamentally different from the electoral battles that predated television sets and Progressive reforms. We tend to view ourselves as markedly different from our poorer and more insular predecessors. And yet, experiments continually turn up evidence that old-fashioned campaign tactics work. The simple fact that experiments show the efficacy of low-tech, personal mobilization techniques suggests that the distant past ought to be mined more frequently for ideas about how to mobilize voters.

The experiments reported in this chapter underscore, among other things, the importance of making civic engagement engaging. Festivals and candidate events are sources of fun. Although the Progressive reformers were bent on making elections sober affairs (literally) that turn on issues rather than petty bribes, their insistence on imbuing polling places with what Bensel calls a "morgue-like atmosphere" meant that elections ceased to attract interest as social events. How much of the precipitous drop in voter turnout rates between the 1880s and 1920s is due to this transformation remains unclear. What does seem clear is that the process is, at least to a limited extent, reversible.

CHAPTER NINE

Using Mass Media to Mobilize Voters

The three traditional forms of mass media—television, radio, newspapers—have long been staples of both campaign craft and social science inquiry. Presidential, senatorial, and gubernatorial campaigns spend enormous resources trying to reach voters through paid advertisements and so-called earned media, such as public appearances and announcements that attract news coverage. For decades, social scientists have studied the ways in which these campaigns are shaped by efforts to attract media attention and by the ways, in turn, that voters are influenced by what they see, hear, and read. During the 1930s, at the dawn of modern social science, teams of researchers set out to measure the effects of political propaganda on voters' opinions and behavior. Unfortunately, despite several decades of research by thousands of scholars, surprisingly little progress has been made.[1]

The basic problem is that social scientists have seldom gauged the media's influence using field experiments. Most research on the media's influence relies on surveys. Survey researchers ask respondents what they have been watching and perform a statistical analysis to assess the correlation between media consumption and political attitudes or behaviors. This research design suffers from two drawbacks. The first is that respondents are often asked to characterize their viewing patterns in vague terms (for example, How many days per week do you watch television?), which means that the "treatment" is measured with error. The second problem is that media consumption reflects personal tastes. It may be that those who watch Fox News are, on average, more sympathetic to Republican policies than nonviewers, but does exposure to Fox News cause viewers to become more sympathetic to Republican policies? Or does Fox News simply attract viewers who tend to have Republican sympathies? Survey data cannot distinguish between these two hypotheses. At most, survey data can narrow the comparison to those people who have similar background characteristics (they grew up in similar places, had similar experiences, and so forth). But narrowing the comparison is not the same thing as forming truly comparable groups of viewers and nonviewers. We are left to speculate about whether the Fox News effect is real or illusory.

In response to this conundrum, social scientists have turned to laboratory experiments in order to assess whether mass media influence political attitudes and behaviors. Laboratory studies expose subjects randomly to different media, and random assignment means that we can trust the treatment and control groups to be comparable. However, laboratory studies have at least three limitations. First, they typically expose subjects to the media in a contrived way. Subjects might be invited into the lab and asked to watch a news program during which randomly assigned ads are aired. Or subjects may be asked to read newspaper articles as part of a copyediting exercise. The manner in which these subjects are exposed to the media is potentially quite different from how they would receive these messages under ordinary conditions. Second, laboratory researchers tend to measure outcomes in ways that make it difficult to interpret an experiment's practical consequences. Rarely do laboratory experiments measure actual voter turnout; instead, as part of a post-treatment interview, they measure whether subjects say that they are likely to vote. Third, college students make up an overwhelming preponderance of subjects in media experiments. One is left to wonder whether the experimental results that college students generate apply to the broader population of voting-age adults.

The bottom line is that, although university library shelves sag with books and articles purporting to measure the effects of the mass media, rarely have these effects been measured using field experiments. And when we further restrict our attention to the effects of the mass media on voter turnout, we are left with only a handful of studies. Ordinarily, we would exclude from our review any nonexperimental study, but in this chapter we discuss a small number of quasi-experiments, or studies in which the treatments vary in a haphazard but not strictly random fashion. In future editions of this book, we hope that these studies will be superseded by randomized experiments.

This chapter provides a summary of research findings for readers who are thinking about conducting a media campaign to encourage voter turnout. Because media campaigns tend not to be do-it-yourself affairs (those with sufficient resources to conduct this type of campaign generally rely on consultants to produce and distribute advertisements or public service announcements), we focus our attention primarily on the research findings rather than on the how-to aspects of conducting a media campaign. For further reading on how to implement mass media campaigns, see box 9-1.

Do Persuasive Campaign Ads Mobilize?

One of the most intriguing theories about the media's influence holds that television hoopla signals to voters the importance of an upcoming election. The idea is that the content of political ads is secondary; what

---

Box 9-1. Practical Guidance for Designing and Implementing Media Campaigns

The following reference books offer how-to advice for those who seek to craft and implement a mass media campaign.

Michael McNamara, *The Political Campaign Desk Reference* (Parker, Colo.: Outskirts Press, 2012). A brief how-to guide that covers everything from campaign logos to messaging. The appendix presents sample TV and radio scripts.

Catherine Shaw, *The Campaign Manager: Running and Winning Local Elections*, 5th ed. (Boulder, Colo.: Westview Press, 2014). This canonical how-to guide for local candidates devotes a chapter to the development and implementation of media campaigns.

Judith S. Trent, Robert V. Friedenberg, and Robert E. Denton, *Political Campaign Communication: Principles and Practices*, 7th ed. (Lanham, Md.: Rowman & Littlefield, 2011). A broad introduction to political advertising that describes the history and evolution of modern campaign tactics.

matters is the fact that the airwaves and newspapers are filled with ads and political banter. When voters see or hear a lot of political ads, they infer that an important election is coming up. Elections that are perceived to be important attract higher rates of turnout. What makes this theory interesting is the notion that campaign ads—even those that make no mention of voting or Election Day—produce higher turnout.

Although this theory has intuitive appeal, it has been challenged by quasi-experiments in which exposure to ads varies haphazardly. Consider, for example, the way in which accidents of geography cause some people to be inundated with television ads, while others nearby receive none at all. These accidents are especially common where presidential ads are concerned. People living within the same state are sometimes subjected to widely varying numbers of presidential ads, depending on their proximity to media markets that serve battleground states. For example, voters in western Maryland receive Pittsburgh television broadcasts. In the last few presidential elections, Pennsylvania was a pivotal battleground state, and both presidential contestants aired thousands of ads on Pittsburgh television stations during the final weeks of the campaign. These ads were directed at those in Pennsylvania, but they were just as pertinent to Maryland voters, who voted in the same presidential election but whose Electoral College votes were sure to go to the Democrats. Unlike their counterparts in western Maryland, voters in central Maryland saw almost no ads because their television signals did not emanate from Pennsylvania. The same intrastate contrasts may be found in places such as Indiana and Georgia, which border battleground states. Within states, the idiosyncrasies of geography cause some counties to be blanketed with ads while others remain untouched.

Because this type of study is not a randomized experiment, its findings must be read with caution, as the treatment and control groups may differ in ways that affect turnout rates. Nonexperimental studies that seem to be sound might nevertheless contain hidden biases, and their conclusions must be interpreted as provisional, pending experimental confirmation.

With this warning in mind, we note the weak correlation between advertising volume and turnout. Examining 128 geographic zones in which people living in the same state were subject to different amounts of televised presidential campaign advertising, Jonathan Krasno and Donald Green found no evidence that exposure to ads during the final weeks of the campaign increased turnout in the 2000 election.[2] The largest volume of advertising exposure—enough advertising to expose each member of the television audience approximately 132 times—raised turnout by less than 1 percentage point. Scott Ashworth and Joshua Clinton came to a similar conclusion when comparing different regions of New Jersey, some of which received a torrent of presidential ads from Phila- delphia, while others received no ads, as they were in the New York City broadcast area.[3] Again, there was no evidence that those exposed to an avalanche of presidential ads voted at higher rates.[4]

Sometimes presidential ads are blamed for decreasing turnout. Attack ads are said to polarize the electorate and alienate moderates. But Krasno and Green found no support for this theory. Perhaps more important, neither did Joshua Clinton and John Lapinski, researchers who tested this hypothesis by randomly exposing large numbers of viewers to posi- tive and negative ads.[5] Their analysis of voting records found no effect on turnout. Apparently, attack ads do not demobilize voters, and more upbeat ads do not mobilize voters. Regardless of their tone, campaign ads have little effect on turnout.

For campaigns, the finding that thousands of gross ratings points (GRPs) fail to increase turnout in presidential elections can be read in two ways. First, the finding implies that one should not count on per- suasive ads to mobilize. Perhaps the lack of effect reflects the fact that televised campaign advertising, like partisan direct mail, tends to focus almost exclusively on candidates and issues. Rarely do they mention vot- ing or Election Day. Perhaps campaign ads could mobilize if voting were a more prominent theme, but the ads we see have little effect.

A second interpretation holds out the hope that campaign ads mobi- lize voters in nonpresidential elections. The hypothesis is that voters do not need any reminders about the significance of an upcoming presi- dential election. Presidential campaigns dominate the news every day for weeks leading up to the election. The situation may be quite different in state or local elections. Below, we revisit both issues, as we consider whether advertisements that encourage voting in presidential and other elections, in fact, increase turnout.

Conveying Social Norms

Another theory about why the media might influence voter turnout is that media messages express "social norms," ideas about what kinds of behaviors are appropriate. Just as radio, newspapers, and television tell us what fashions are in style, they also tell us how right-thinking people regard Election Day.

With this theory in mind, Lynn Vavreck and Donald Green sought to link voting to the strong feelings of patriotism that flourished after the September 11, 2001, terrorist attacks on the United States.[6] The idea was to employ evocative imagery to suggest that voting is a patriotic responsibility. Two ads were created by a team of UCLA film students. The first used a sequence of still images of inspiring American scenes (firemen hoisting a flag, the AIDS quilt, and children playing) as the percussive cadence in the background escalated in complexity and volume. The female narrator observed, "Even as the world changes, your role as a citizen remains the same." At the end, the images coalesced into the shape of the United States, under which the tagline read, "Shape your country, vote this Tuesday."

The tone of the second ad was much darker, this time addressing the fear of violent extremism. The ad flashed still images of swastikas, notorious dictators, and frightening moments from famous wars defending freedom. The voice-over challenged viewers with an ironic observation about the pictured dictators: "Not interested in politics? That's OK. Really, that's OK. Plenty of others are." The anti-democratic images increased in speed as the same percussive cadence increased in volume. At the end, the tagline read, "Stand up for democracy, vote this Tuesday." Unlike the first ad, which identified voting with national pride and solidarity, the second ad warned viewers to consider the negative consequences of neglecting their civic responsibilities.

In order to test the effects of these ads on voter turnout, an experiment was conducted in the context of four statewide elections during 2003. In Kentucky and Louisiana, statewide offices were contested, and Kentucky's gubernatorial election was relatively competitive. In New Jersey and Virginia, legislative elections were by and large low-salience affairs. Across all four states, a total of 156 cable television systems were randomly assigned to four groups: a control group receiving no ads, a group receiving the "shape your country" ad, a group receiving the "stand up for democracy" ad, and a group receiving a mixture of both ads.

The ads ran from October 30 through November 3, immediately before the general elections of 2003, on TNT, USA, and Lifetime networks in New Jersey, Virginia, and Kentucky. In Louisiana, the ads ran on the same networks from October 30 to November 14, the date of the Louisiana election. These cable networks were selected because of their broad appeal and high ratings during prime-time viewing hours at this time of year. Each ad ran twice on each channel every night before the election, for a total of thirty spots in each cable system in New Jersey, Virginia, and Kentucky and ninety-six spots in Louisiana. After the election, voter turnout data were obtained for zip codes that were encompassed by a single cable system.

The pattern of turnout suggests that the ads may have led to a small but statistically equivocal boost in turnout. A simple comparison of the control group to all of the treatment groups suggested an increase of approximately half a percentage point. When one controls for past voter turnout, the "shape your country" ad appears to be the most effective, although the results fall short of statistical significance. In an attempt to bring more statistical precision to this estimate, Vavreck and Green also conducted an automated telephone survey of more than 25,000 registered voters living in the experimental cable television markets. Respondents in both the treatment and control groups were asked whether they received cable television and whether they recently watched several specific shows, the idea being to identify comparable viewers in the treatment and control groups, some of whom randomly encountered the voter turnout ads. By refining the comparison in this way, the authors expected to observe larger treatment effects when examining official turnout records. Instead, this analysis again showed weak and statistically insignificant positive effects.

One pair of ads hardly exhausts the range of possible treatments that must be tested, but the lack of effectiveness of these ads tentatively suggests that television ads merely affirming the norm of participating in an election do not generate higher turnout rates in low- and medium-salience elections. The null result cannot be blamed on low rates of exposure to the ads because even when one compares likely ad viewers, the treatment effect remains small.

Emphasizing What's at Stake

Perhaps imploring people to vote is not enough. Perhaps media appeals must also include a persuasive reason why the issues at stake in an upcoming election merit viewers' participation. This hypothesis inspired an experimental test of television ads produced by the Rock the Vote organization, which was at the forefront of efforts to increase voter turnout among young people.[7] Rock the Vote has a long history of producing memorable and sometimes controversial public service announcements. Rock the Vote's 2004 ad campaign dealt with two themes, the prospect of a military draft and the high cost of secondary education.

In the "military draft" advertisement, a young couple dancing at a party discussed the man's new job. He was very excited to be working in promotions and hoped to start his own firm in six months. The woman interrupted him and said, "That's if you don't get drafted." The man was puzzled. She clarified, "Drafted, for the war?" He responded, "Would they do that?" The ad closed with everyone at the party looking into the camera and the words "It's up to you" on the screen. The voice-over said: "The draft. One of the issues that will be decided this November. Remember to vote on November 2nd." The closing image was of the Rock the Vote logo on a black screen.[8]

In the "education" ad, a young man arrived at work with news that he had been accepted to college. His colleagues congratulated him, but one of them asked, "Books, room, board, tuition . . . how can you pay for all of that?" The ad closed with everyone looking into the camera, as the words "It's up to you" filled the screen. The voice-over was similar to the one above, but with education substituted for the draft.

The experimental evaluation conducted by Lynn Vavreck and Donald Green focused on twelve nonbattleground states in order to gauge the effects of the treatment with less interference from presidential campaign ads. Random assignment placed forty-two cable systems into the treatment group and forty-three into the control group. In this experiment, both ads were shown with equal frequency as many times as budget constraints would allow. During the last eight days of the election campaign, the ads aired four times per night in prime time on each of the following channels: USA, Lifetime, TNT, and TBS. At the time, two-thirds of American households subscribed to cable television, and according to the National Cable Commission, these were among the most popular cable channels.

Given the ads' content, the focus of the experimental evaluation was the 23,869 eighteen- and nineteen-year-olds living in these cable markets. For them, 2004 marked their first opportunity to vote in a federal election. The authors reported an increase of 3 percentage points in turnout in this age bracket, which is both large in absolute terms and statistically significant. Interestingly, the effect was strong among those up to twenty-two years old (the end of the college years) and small for older people. This experiment provides the first clear evidence that televised ads can increase turnout within a targeted audience. Equally interesting is the fact that turnout among other age groups was only mildly affected. Although the ads were placed on programs watched by a wide age spectrum, only young viewers seem to have responded with higher levels of turnout. This finding again suggests that ads are effective only when they engage viewers with messages about the importance of the upcoming election.

Another test of the "what's at stake" message comes from a pair of radio experiments conducted in 2008 and 2010 by Eline de Rooij and Donald Green.[9] Working with dozens of stations that broadcast programming intended for Native Americans, the authors randomly assigned some to air public service announcements encouraging Native American participation in the upcoming election. Across both elections, turnout increased by approximately 2.3 percentage points among Native Americans living in the treated coverage areas at a cost per vote of $18. Although this pair of estimates falls shy of conventional levels of statistical significance, the results suggest that group-based appeals to "make your voice heard" may boost turnout.

What's at Stake and Who's on the Ballot

Persuading people of the importance of an upcoming presidential election is one thing; persuading them of the importance of an upcoming municipal election is quite another. Few local elections are closely contested; incumbent mayors tend to win more than 90 percent of their bids for reelection. Moreover, the issues at stake in local elections tend to be less lofty and engaging than the topics that usually take center stage in federal elections. As a result, it is not uncommon to see municipal elections attract less than one-third of all registered voters to the polls.

The question is whether turnout in municipal elections responds to a mass media campaign that calls attention to the significance of local elections, provides some basic information about the contestants, and tells voters when the election will take place. Costas Panagopoulos and Donald Green tested this proposition by conducting an experiment in seventy-eight mayoral elections occurring in November 2005 and 2006.[10] In the thirty-nine randomly selected treatment municipalities, radio ads were placed by a professional ad buyer on local radio stations that were thought to reach a broad cross section of the electorate. For each city assigned to the treatment group, between fifty and ninety GRPs were purchased. A gross ratings point is a metric used to gauge the size of the projected audience. Each GRP represents enough advertising to expose 1 percent of the media market to the ad once; fifty GRPs are enough to expose 50 percent of the media market once or 1 percent of the media market fifty times. The quantity of advertising is relatively small compared with what a political campaign might purchase in a hotly contested race, which leaves open the question of whether more intensive (and expensive) advertising campaigns might be more effective.

The script was customized for each location. For example, the following sample script was used for Syracuse, New York:

> Many people don't realize how important local government is. But think about it. Your local government is in charge of things that affect your life every day: police protection, transportation, garbage collection, tax assessment. From fire departments to libraries to safe drinking water—it's all part of local government.
>
> Here's where you come in: Voting. If you're a registered voter in SYRACUSE, you have an opportunity to shape the direction of your city by electing the mayor and other local officials. On Tuesday, November 8th, residents of SYRACUSE will vote to decide whether to RE-elect Democratic MAYOR MATTHEW DRISCOLL or to support his opponent, Republican JOANNIE MAHONEY.
>
> Take part in shaping your city's future. Be sure to vote on November 8th.
>
> Paid for by the Institution for Social and Policy Studies, a nonpartisan organization that encourages citizens to take an active role in their communities.

Note that this script was strictly nonpartisan. It neither endorsed a candidate nor hinted which one might be better at addressing local issues. And unlike the Rock the Vote ad, it neither tailored its message to specific subgroups nor used vignettes to dramatize the importance of the upcoming election.

The results of this experiment were positive but inconclusive. In twenty-three of the thirty-nine pairs of local elections, voter turnout was higher in the treatment group. The average rate of turnout in the treatment group was approximately 1 percentage point higher than in the control group. Although these results are encouraging, they fall short of statistical significance in the sense that there is a one-in-six chance of coming up with at least twenty-three heads if thirty-nine coins were flipped.

Murky results are not unusual in science, and the best way to clear the fog is to conduct more experiments. In 2006, Panagopoulos and Green conducted a follow-up experiment in which Spanish-language radio stations encouraged listeners to consider the significance of the imminent congressional elections.[11] As in the mayoral experiment, the script (in Spanish) described some of the important issue domains that are affected by federal elections, presented the names of candidates for the U.S. House of Representatives, and mentioned when the election would occur. Because Spanish-language radio is rarely heard by non-Latinos, the focus of the evaluation was voter turnout among those with putatively Latino surnames.

Results from 204 congressional districts indicate that the radio ads boosted turnout among voters with Hispanic surnames and, as predicted, had no effect on non-Hispanic turnout.[12] These experimental results are on the border of statistical significance, but it appears that radio ads stressing the stakes of the upcoming election nudge turnout upward.

Newspapers

Notwithstanding the fact that newspapers have played a central role in democratic politics for centuries, they have rarely been the subject of experimental inquiry. Those who study nonexperimental data have often speculated that newspapers supply political information and increase voter turnout. This argument has been bolstered recently by a clever analysis of a quasi-experiment associated with the rise of television during the 1950s. Matthew Gentzkow demonstrated that, as television stations acquired licenses across the country, newspaper readership fell, and so did voter turnout.[13] This thesis implies that a profound transformation in voter turnout could lie on the horizon. Newspaper readership has plummeted among young people, and the average daily reader grows older each year.

The question is what would happen to voter turnout if people were randomly induced to read a daily newspaper. A pathbreaking experiment conducted by Alan Gerber, Dean Karlan, and Daniel Bergan provided several hundred Virginia households living in the Washington area with free newspaper subscriptions in 2005.[14] One group of households was randomly assigned to receive the conservative *Washington Times,* while another group was randomly assigned to receive the more liberal *Washington Post.* A control group of households received no subscription. Subscriptions were distributed during the final weeks of the statewide election campaign in Virginia, enabling these researchers to test whether receiving a daily newspaper boosts turnout.

Among the 2,571 people whose names could be matched to voter turnout records, turnout was 56.3 percent in the control group, 57.4 percent among those assigned to the *Washington Post,* and 56.1 percent among those assigned to the *Washington Times*. Overall, the subscriptions generated a half percentage point gain in turnout, a small effect that persisted through the 2006 midterm elections a year later. Could it be that receiving a daily paper sets in motion lasting involvement in elections?

A related question is whether turnout rises when newspaper readers are presented with half-page advertisements encouraging them to vote in local elections. This experiment is a twist on the mayoral experiment involving radio, except that it targets newspaper readers, who tend to be high-propensity voters. Costas Panagopoulos conducted a small study involving four pairs of towns, all of which held municipal elections during 2005.[15] The towns were each paired according to past voter turnout, and one member of each pair was randomly assigned to receive a half-page ad in its local newspaper on the Sunday before the election. The ad stressed the importance of local issues and urged voters to cast ballots on Tuesday.

Due to the small size of this experiment, the results must be interpreted with caution. Turnout was higher in the treatment town in three of four pairs. Of course, this pattern could emerge merely by chance; flip four coins, and about one-third of the time you will get three or more heads. Nevertheless, this finding merits further investigation, because if newspaper ads really do boost turnout by 1.5 percentage points, as this pilot study suggests, the implied cost per vote would be very attractive. Fortunately, newspaper experiments are relatively easy to conduct across a broad array of settings. One could, for example, place ads in randomly assigned college newspapers and look at turnout in different campus precincts. Or one could pick locations such as Los Angeles or Queens and randomly assign some of the local ethnic newspapers to treatment and control groups, looking for interethnic variation in turnout. Given how straightforward it is to experiment with local newspapers (or their online equivalents), it is surprising that the academic study of newspapers has so rarely employed experimental designs.

Messages Embedded in Entertainment Programs

Advertisers of commercial products pay extraordinary sums of money for what are known as product placements, defined as "insertion of branded products or services into mass media content with the intent of influencing consumer attitude or behavior."[16] Examples of writing products into scripts range from shopping trips to Pottery Barn in the TV series *Friends* to James Bond quaffing Heineken beer rather than his usual martini in the movie *Skyfall*. The operative assumption is that viewers emulate the behaviors they see on screen. Much the same thinking has encouraged soap operas around the globe to model positive social behaviors, such as taking literacy classes or accepting people from other ethnic groups. Could this same approach encourage political participation?

A team of researchers led by Elizabeth Levy Paluck tested this hypothesis by working with writers of three Spanish-language soap operas that aired on a large U.S. television network.[17] The idea was to weave stories about voter registration into a soap opera plotline at a randomly chosen point in the calendar in order to assess whether it produced a surge of voter registrations among Latinos. The four episodes involving voter registration appeared in early May 2012. But daily registration figures show no corresponding surge in registrations among Latinos in the wake of these messages. At best, there was a modest increase in the visits to the Spanish-language version of the Rock the Vote website. Apparently, the civic analog to product placements does not generate much imitative behavior from the audience. As it turns out, these authors found little in the way of behavioral responses to any of the product placements they studied, such as the opening of bank accounts or the purchase of healthy foods. It may be that product placements are overrated.

Conclusion

Surprisingly, few field experiments have evaluated the mobilizing effects of the mass media. Using the rating system detailed in chapter 2, each of the conclusions is rated with one star, indicating that the findings are suggestive but not conclusive.

★ *The sheer volume of political ads is a poor predictor of voter turnout.* Mere exposure to a large number of campaign ads does not, in itself, raise voter turnout in presidential elections. The conclusion derived from quasi-experiments involving television ads fits well with the experimental finding, noted in chapter 5, that partisan direct mail tends to have little effect on turnout.

★ *Television ads that specifically urge voter turnout have the capacity to mobilize targeted viewers.* The Rock the Vote ads, which used vignettes to dramatize the significance of the upcoming election, produced statistically significant increases in turnout among eighteen- and nineteen-year-olds. The ads had minimal effects on voters older than twenty-two.

★ *Broad-based television ads that encourage voter turnout appear to have weak positive effects on voter turnout.* The two experiments testing the effects of ads that urged voters to "shape your country" or "stand up for democracy" increased turnout by less than a quarter percentage point.

★ *Radio campaigns that stress the importance of upcoming local elections appear to have some positive effect on voter turnout.*

★ *Daily exposure to newspapers raises turnout to a small extent, at least among those who do not ordinarily receive a daily paper.* Virginians given free subscriptions to Washington daily newspapers became slightly more likely to vote in subsequent state and federal elections.

★ *Newspaper ads urging voters to participate in upcoming local elections may increase turnout, but this finding is subject to a great deal of statistical uncertainty.*

★ *Product placements that dramatize voter registration on televised soap operas do not seem to induce viewers to register.*

How do the media results fit with our general pattern of results in this book? On the one hand, mass media appeals resemble direct mail or robotic phone calls in the sense that they are delivered in an impersonal and mechanical fashion. On the other hand, the Rock the Vote experiment suggests that vignettes that dramatize the meaning of an upcoming election can be influential (at least among their target audience), perhaps because they succeed in simulating a personal appeal. If this interpretation is correct, the success or failure of any mobilization campaign hinges on whether it increases the audience's motivation to participate. Evidently, some, but not all, ads or product placements succeed on this score, and the challenge for those who launch media campaigns in the hopes of raising voter turnout is to craft a message that truly motivates the audience.

What do our findings suggest about the cost-efficiency of using the mass media to raise voter turnout? Any calculation of dollars per vote must be regarded as tentative, but the following numbers provide a good starting point for discussion. The 2003 televised public service announcements had disappointing effects, apparently raising turnout by just 0.22

of a percentage point. However, the cable systems that were targeted included more than 2.3 million registered voters, so the ads generated just over 5,000 additional votes. The total cost of producing, distributing, and running the ads was $92,800 (in 2018 dollars), which puts the cost per vote at approximately $19. The Rock the Vote ads were shown on cable television systems comprising more than 350,000 voters and had an average treatment effect across the whole age spectrum of 0.56 of a percentage point (mostly concentrated among young voters). The total number of votes generated was approximately 2,000. We do not know the cost of producing the ads, but distributing and airing them in the experimental study cost $37,125 (in 2018 dollars), which again implies $19 per vote. These rosy cost-per-vote estimates must be interpreted with extreme caution, given that the estimated effects are subject to a great deal of statistical uncertainty, but they remind us that when television reaches vast audiences, even a small effect goes a long way.

As for radio, the results are again subject to some interesting, if tentative, back-of-the-envelope calculations. The mayoral election experiments cost a total of $143,195 (in 2018 dollars) in order to increase turnout by an average of 0.79 percentage point in the treatment towns. These thirty-nine towns contained an average of 50,000 registered voters, so the radio ads generated roughly 15,400 votes, which comes to $9 per vote. The cost calculations for the 2006 Spanish-language radio experiment are similar. An expenditure of $195,170 (in 2018 dollars) generated votes at a rate of $13 per vote. The cost per vote from the 2008 and 2010 Native American radio ads was $19.

The bottom line seems to be that certain types of mass media ads represent a potentially cost-effective means of raising turnout. The jury is still out on many types of advertising campaigns, such as product placements, and even the effects of conventional TV or radio ads have not been estimated with precision. Advertising effects seem to be subtle, and it is hard to detect them unless one conducts an experiment involving dozens of media markets or, using new technology, media platforms that serve "addressable" ads to specific households.

Next Steps in Media Research

The first and most obvious next step in this line of research is to replicate and extend existing experiments so that issues of cost-efficiency can be assessed more precisely. Thus far, media experiments have generated small but cost-effective voter mobilization effects, though these results are nowhere near as robust as the findings in well-established areas of GOTV research. Until more experimental results come in, we cannot rule out the possibility that the effects are zero, in which case cost-effectiveness goes out the window. Those in the advertising business like to joke that half of all money spent on television is wasted; the problem is that you don't know which half it is. Our view is more skeptical: How do they know that only half is wasted?

A further question is whether media campaigns amplify the effects of ground campaigns. Organizations that conduct both types of campaigns sometimes offer anecdotes suggesting that the media messaging makes it easier for canvassers to strike up a conversation with voters who have heard about the organization and perhaps endorse its electoral aims. This hypothesis does have an air of plausibility, but like many claims about synergy, it must be viewed with caution until supported with experimental evidence.

The array of unanswered questions about long-standing forms of mass communication is the great irony of media research. Given the amount of money at stake for political campaigns, one would think that the experimental literature would be extensive and nuanced. Instead, several decades after the development of television and radio, we know relatively little about their effects on voting behavior. As field experimental inquiry gains momentum, that is likely to change.

CHAPTER TEN

Voter Registration and Voter Turnout

One of the practical questions that confronts any campaign seeking to increase turnout is whether to devote resources to voter registration. For decades, scholars and campaign professionals have opined on this question, offering advice ranging from an emphatic yes to an emphatic no. Those offering an emphatic yes argue that 85 percent of those who are registered vote in a presidential election, whereas no unregistered people vote. They reason that registration is simply an impediment to voting. Eliminate the hurdle of registration, and the formerly unregistered will vote at the same high rates that registered voters do. Those offering an emphatic no caution that registered people vote at high rates because they have an intrinsic interest in politics and elections. That's why they bothered to register in the first place. Unregistered people will not vote if you register them because they are not interested. Somewhere between these two extremes is the view that some unregistered people will vote if they were to become registered, whether through a relaxation of registration requirements or through the help of a registration drive.[1]

As you can imagine, this debate tends to be tinged with political overtones. Those who take the emphatic yes position contend that registration requirements were a late nineteenth-century scheme by the affluent to discourage turnout among the working class. The unregistered were pushed out of the political process but are perfectly capable of voting if registration requirements were relaxed.[2] Those on the other side of the aisle tend to be skeptical of the claim that registration requirements are onerous and are even more skeptical of easing requirements in ways that open the door to voter fraud. For decades, political scientists have weighed in on this debate by staking out a middle position. The dominant argument has been that relaxing registration requirements by allowing people to register on the same day that they vote will increase turnout modestly without materially affecting election outcomes.[3]

All sides of this debate have relied on rather flimsy evidence. Those who argue that registration causes turnout have adduced survey data showing a correlation between registration and voting, aggregate data indicating that states with permissive registration rules tend to have high turnout, and trends showing that turnout falls immediately after the introduction of registration requirements. Those skeptical that a causal relationship exists between registration and turnout point out that the relaxation of registration requirements has not produced appreciable increases in turnout.[4] Only rarely have experiments been conducted to assess whether randomly targeted registration drives produce concomitant increases in turnout.[5] The first edition of this book said next to nothing about registration because the body of experimental evidence was so thin.

Such experiments have become increasingly common in recent years, although many remain outside the public domain because they were commissioned by partisan or advocacy groups and never posted on a public website or presented in a public forum. This "gray literature" poses a problem for scholars who seek to provide a comprehensive assessment of what is known about registration. Our policy is that we do not reveal the results of proprietary studies, but we also take care not to give undue weight to public studies if we know their results are contradicted by proprietary research. In other words, we are careful to neither disclose secret information nor adduce evidence that we know to be misleading. With those ground rules, we summarize the results of experiments that assess the effects of canvassing, classroom visits, mail, e-mail, and phone calls. Although each of these tactics sought to increase registration, our metric for evaluation remains the same as in previous chapters: the number of votes produced per dollar. We conclude by commenting on the implications of these experiments for long-standing debates about how registration affects turnout.

Registration Drives: Practical Considerations

The main logistical challenge in conducting a registration drive is finding ample numbers of eligible voters who are unregistered. According to census data and election tallies, 231 million Americans were eligible to vote in 2016, of whom 157.6 million were registered and 138.9 million actually voted. Because 68 percent of eligible voters are currently registered (including everyone in North Dakota, which does not require registration), voter registration drives must be selective. Among citizens of voting age, registration rates are lowest among those under twenty-five (55 percent), Asian Americans (56 percent), and Hispanics (57 percent).[6] Many registration drives and accompanying experiments target these groups as well as those who recently moved from one town to another.[7] It may be that movers are just less interested in voting, but moving clearly depresses turnout as well. Evidently, it takes time for new residents of a community to integrate themselves into the voting process. Experiments that have tracked people who were randomly encouraged to move out of public housing found a sharp drop in voter registration.[8] Another vein of unregistered people may be mined from large consumer databases. By crossing these lists with voter registration rolls, one may extract vast numbers of unregistered adults; however, many of them may be ineligible to vote or may no longer live at the listed address.

The key tactical question is how to go about registering the unregistered. (We realize that the phrase "registering the unregistered" seems pedantic, but we want to call attention to a common problem with voter registration drives: they often re-register the already registered.) There are four different approaches. The first is site-based registration. Picture a team of clipboard-toting people in front of a supermarket accosting shoppers and inviting them to register. Public places with a lot of foot traffic lend themselves to this sort of activity. Favorite sites include college campuses, concerts, sports arenas, community centers, and shopping areas. Second is blind canvassing—going door-to-door through a neighborhood in search of the unregistered. This approach has some of the same requirements and drawbacks as GOTV canvassing, and campaigns sometimes combine both GOTV and registration drives in states where the registration deadline is close to or on Election Day. When doing registration work months before an election, canvassers confront the challenge of locating the unregistered but nevertheless available-at-home eligible voter. In an ordinary residential neighborhood, it would not be uncommon for each canvasser to register just one such person per hour. That number goes up when canvassing college dorms or areas with a high density of unregistered eligible voters. A third approach is to target specific individuals, whether in person or by mail, phone, or e-mail. Again, this approach hinges on having an accurate list of target individuals. Given the hit-or-miss nature of canvassing this population, in-person visits are rarely attempted. Much more common are registration campaigns via mail, phone, or e-mail. The most common tactics are to use driver's license records to identify soon-to-be eighteen-year-olds and send them a registration form on their birthday, and to use change-of-address data to identify those who have recently moved and send them a registration form at their new address. Finally, mass media appeals may be used to target specific demographic groups (for example, young Latinos) to register. This approach is relatively rare on TV or radio but more common via social media advertising.

What are the special requirements of a registration campaign? At first glance, site-based or door-to-door registration looks similar to canvassing in terms of recruitment, training, and supervision. However, laws concerning the handling of filled-in registration forms make supervision more demanding (see box 10-1). It is illegal to fill in a registration form with a fake signature or false information. Some states also punish mishandling of completed forms. For example, those who collect registration forms must submit them to the registrar in a timely manner—registration drives sponsored by a political group must not "lose" the forms completed by voters seeking to register with the opposing party. One must be careful, therefore, when supervising people who are paid per registration or who display excessive partisan zeal.

Experimental Evidence Concerning Registration

The first place to look for unregistered adults is in schools. By the spring of their senior year, a large proportion of high school students have reached voting age, but only a small proportion are registered to vote. The First-Time Voter Program is a school-based outreach program developed by Elizabeth Addonizio to encourage high school seniors to vote.[9] The program consists of three elements. A young volunteer, rather than a high school teacher, leads the seminar. The seminar's format is informal and interactive. The seminar focuses on providing students with the experience of registering to vote and casting a ballot using the type of voting machine that is used in their jurisdiction.

Box 10-1. Meeting the Legal Requirements for Conducting a Registration Drive

Before launching a voter registration drive, learn about the legal requirements that apply in the state(s) in which you plan to operate. Some states (Kansas and Montana, for example) have no specific regulations on registration drives, while others (California and Texas) have an array of laws that campaigns must be careful to follow. Violating these laws can have serious consequences, including criminal sanctions, fines, and disqualifications.

Go to your state's official election administration website or contact election administrators directly to get up-to-date information about the following:

✓ Are those who conduct registration drives required to be officially certified?

✓ Are an organization's leaders and/or volunteers required to undergo training before launching a registration drive?

✓ Is an organization that conducts a registration drive required to provide detailed information about its staffing and structure?

✓ Is an organization required to report (or pre-report) when and where it conducts its registration drives?

✓ Are there deadlines by which completed registration forms must be turned in to election officials? Note that some states impose punishments when registration forms are not returned to election officials, even when forms are mishandled or lost for seemingly innocent reasons.

Source: Diana Kasdan, *State Restrictions on Voter Registration Drives*, report prepared for Brennan Center for Justice (New York University School of Law, November 30, 2012).

Although students are not required to register or to cast a practice vote, they are encouraged to do so. Generally, about 90 percent of the students cast a practice ballot. The First-Time Voter sessions tend to run about forty minutes, involving about twenty to thirty students per session. An effort is made to keep the sessions as small and as intimate as possible so that students can comfortably learn to register and cast a ballot.

In order to evaluate the effectiveness of this program, Elizabeth Addonizio conducted a series of experiments. Before fall and spring elections in 2003 and 2004, seniors in participating high schools in Connecticut, Indiana, Kentucky, Nebraska, New Hampshire, and New Jersey were randomly divided into two groups, one of which was assigned to participate in a First-Time Voter seminar. The total subject pool for the study consisted of the 840 students who were old enough to be eligible to vote at election time. Experiments were conducted in different states at different times to investigate variation in the salience of the election and the socioeconomic level of the population under study. The experiment was replicated in areas with competitive and noncompetitive local, statewide, and presidential elections and in high- and low-socioeconomic communities in order to determine whether the competitiveness of the election and the affluence of the community influence the effects of the mobilization effort.[10] Addonizio's results indicated that students attending the First-Time Voter Program had turnout rates that were approximately 10 percentage points higher than their control group counterparts. These effects held across different electoral and socioeconomic settings.

Analogous programs in colleges have also been found to be similarly effective. Elizabeth Bennion and David Nickerson conducted a vast experiment prior to the 2006 midterm election in which 1,026 classrooms in sixteen colleges were assigned to one of three conditions: an untreated control group, a treatment group in which registration forms were placed on every desk before class and an instructor urged students to register, and a second treatment group in which forms were distributed and the encouragement to register came from a fellow student.[11] Both encouragements worked to roughly the same extent, raising registration rates by 6 percentage points and raising turnout rates by 2.6 percentage points. Evidently, when a captive audience is presented with an opportunity to register under close supervision, registration rates climb, and roughly 40% of those who are induced to register in the classroom go on to vote.

Looking for potential registrants classroom by classroom is productive but slow work that requires coordination with campus administrators and instructors. An alternative approach that lends itself to inexpensive, large-scale outreach is to e-mail students, directing them to online sites where they can obtain registration forms. This type of outreach often appeals to campus administrators, because the 1998 amendments to the Higher Education Act require colleges and universities to distribute registration materials to their students, and online registration systems are an inexpensive option. In chapter 7, we discussed a slew of voter mobilization experiments showing that e-mail appeals to students fail to increase turnout. The same studies also showed no gains in registration rates in the wake of e-mail messaging, even when a reasonable proportion of recipients opened the e-mail or clicked on web pages that provide downloadable registration forms.[12]

Consider, for example, the multisite evaluation of e-mail appeals to register and vote conducted by Elizabeth Bennion and David Nickerson.[13] This enormous study comprised more than 250,000 students at twenty-six colleges and universities in the weeks leading up to the 2006 midterm elections. The crux of the e-mail was encouragement to use an online voter registration tool. Scripts varied across and sometimes within sites according to whether the sender was a university administrator or a student leader, whether the scripts were short or long, whether the text of the e-mail was personalized in some way, and whether students were sent one, two, or three e-mails. The many varieties of e-mail all led to the same dismal conclusion. In keeping with previous experiments on e-mail encouragements to students, the estimated effect proved to be slightly negative, with registration rates declining by 0.3 of a percentage point overall. Evidently, you can talk to students in person about registration and get them to fill out a form right then and there, but if you set them down the path of doing so online, they get lost in some sort of vortex due to confusion or procrastination.

If there is a bright spot in this story of oddly negative effects, it is that text message reminders boost registration rates among those who visit an online registration system and agree to receive text message "updates."[14] This select group may be characterized as those who sense that they may need a nudge. In a 2008 study, thousands of such visitors to Rock the Vote's online registration system were randomly assigned to receive text reminders. Reminders boosted registration rates by 4 percentage points. So if your e-mail sends recipients into an online registration vortex, text messages might extract those who are willing to accept a text reminder.

The bottom line appears to be that old-fashioned in-person appeals work best on college campuses. The personal touch also seems to perform well in site-based registration drives that target neighborhoods with low rates of registration. What we know about the effectiveness of this tactic comes primarily from a half-dozen experimental evaluations of nonpartisan registration drives conducted by David Nickerson from 2004 to 2007.[15] This collection of experiments encompasses six urban areas (Denver, Memphis, Louisville, Detroit, Tampa, and Kalamazoo) and spans presidential, gubernatorial, and mayoral elections. Several months before each election, targeted streets were randomly assigned to treatment or control conditions. On treatment streets, canvassers knocked on every door at least twice, contacting between one-third and one-half of the residents, providing registration forms, and collecting them when completed. The canvassing organization selected the targeted neighborhoods in three cities; in the other three cities the research protocol assigned canvassers to neighborhoods that varied markedly in affluence so that the relative efficiency of different targeting strategies could be assessed. One attractive feature of this study is that the researcher took steps to prevent the canvassing organization from recontacting the newly registered, so any turnout effects are likely due to the act of registration itself rather than subsequent mobilization activity. Four key results emerge from this remarkable collection of experiments. First, the registration drives produced, on average, ten new registrants per street (approximately one new registrant per sixteen households). Second, the addition of ten new registrants translated into 2.6 additional votes in the subsequent election. Both the gains in registration and accompanying gains in turnout are estimated with a good deal of precision, thanks to the scale of these experiments. Third, the number of new registrants per street proved to be about five times greater on low-income streets than on high-income streets. Finally, more votes were generated per new registrant in more affluent areas. In low-income areas, 20 percent of new registrants voted, as compared with 50 percent in high-income areas. Nevertheless, when one takes both registration rates and voting rates into account, registration drives produce twice as many votes on low-income streets as on high-income streets.

Not every campaign has the means or motivation to conduct door-to-door registration drives. An alternative approach is to use impersonal tactics, such as mail and robocalls. This strategy has proven to be ineffective when organizations have targeted broad swaths of unregistered people.[16] For example, in October 2005, a pro-Republican group in Texas conducted an experiment in which more than 300,000 unregistered adults were slated to receive a first-class mailing with a note from a little girl urging them to register; those with listed phone numbers also received a robocall from the same girl reiterating this message. The targeted individuals were selected based on microtargeting algorithms that declared them to be likely Republicans based on their income, magazine subscriptions, and precinct-level voting patterns. (A similar program had been used a year earlier and had achieved a kind of mythic status based on its reputed success, although no rigorous evaluation had been conducted.) Approximately 1,600 precincts were randomly assigned to treatment and 250 to control. The total expenditure on the mail and calls exceeded $392,000 (in 2018 dollars) but produced just 713 new registrants.

When impersonal tactics are used, a more promising approach is to craft messages that address specific types of unregistered people. Using motor vehicle records of teenagers who are about to turn eighteen, non-partisan organizations periodically mail them birthday envelopes that include registration materials. For example, an experiment in thirteen states prior to the 2008 election tested whether birthday mailings lift registration rates among young people whom commercial databases identified as likely belonging to ethnic- or racial-minority groups. Registration rates were 1.5 percentage points higher in the treatment group, and voting rates in the November election were 0.4 of a percentage point higher. Both effects are statistically distinguishable from zero and together imply that each additional registration generates 0.26 votes, a figure very similar to Nickerson's estimate from site-based registration drives. An even larger set of experiments conducted in 2008 and 2010 assessed the effectiveness of sending registration packets to minority voters who recently moved across county lines. Registration rates increased by 1.8 percentage points and turnout rates by 1.0 percentage point, implying that each new registrant generated 0.55 votes. Two smaller follow-up experiments in 2010 using the same demographic target found a 1.2 percentage point jump in registration with no corresponding increase in turnout and a 2.8 percentage point increase in registration accompanied by a 1.7 percentage point increase in turnout. All told, it seems that approximately 0.4 additional votes are generated for every newly registered minority mover, reminiscent of Nickerson's findings for door knocking in middle-income urban neighborhoods.

A variant of this approach is for state agencies to encourage voter registration. In a series of large-scale experiments conducted in collaboration with Oregon's Secretary of State and Delaware's Office of the State Election Commissioner, Christopher Mann and Lisa Bryant evaluated the effects of direct mail appeals designed to encourage voter registration.[17] Prior to the general elections of 2012 and 2014, these state agencies targeted large lists of people who were believed to be eligible to vote but were unregistered. Official letters sent a few weeks before the registration deadline explained to recipients that "Our records indicate you may be eligible to vote, but do not appear to be registered to vote" and stressed the urgency of registering in advance of the deadline (by mail in Delaware in 2012, online in Oregon in 2014). A variety of appeals were tested, including plan making (see chapter 11), but in the end all of them proved about equally effective. In 2012, Delaware's mailings raised the registration rate prior to the election from 6.8 percent in the control group to 9.0 percent across all treatment groups. Turnout in the 2012 election went from 6.8 percent in the control group to 8.8 percent, implying that almost everyone who became registered due to the treatment went on to vote in the presidential election. In 2014, Oregon's mailings raised registration rates from 4.6 percent to 6.8 percent, but this time the effect on voting was somewhat smaller. Turnout in the control group was 2.0 percent, as compared to 3.7 percent in the treatment groups, suggesting that about three-quarters of those who registered due to the state's encouragement went on to vote. Another large study was conducted in collaboration with the secretary of state of Pennsylvania in 2016. Lisa Bryant and Michael Hanmer designed an experiment in which official mailings were sent to more than 2.2 million eligible but unregistered people, generating a one percentage point increase in registration. Almost everyone who was induced to register went on to vote in 2016.[18] Taken together, the three experiments suggest that although relatively few unregistered people register when contacted by a secretary of state or state election commissioner, those who are induced to register in advance of a presidential election are highly likely to vote.

Can nongovernmental organizations produce similar effects? Vote.org texted a "public service announcement" to 512,083 unregistered nonwhites under age 40 and unmarried women, with another 341,400 held out as a control group.[19] Prior to the registration deadline, targeted people were sent a series of four messages, such as: "**Only days left to register to vote.** Use Vote·org now: Tap the link to register to vote: [link] This is a FREE and secure service message from Vote·org." The treatment group registered to vote at a rate that was 0.3 of a percentage point higher than the control group, and turnout was also 0.3 of a percentage point higher. The effect was smaller than mail communication from the secretary of state and state election commissioner, but it appears that everyone induced to register also went on to vote.

Lessons Learned

The findings of this chapter are summarized here using the ratings systems detailed in chapter 2.

★ ★ ★ *Mass e-mail is a poor method for generating new registrants.* An impressive body of experiments shows it to be ineffective. This conclusion holds regardless of the number of e-mails sent to each recipient, the e-mail's format, or the sender.

★ ★ ★ *Personal appeals that accompany the distribution and collection of forms increase registration rates.* The studies of registration drives in classrooms and neighborhoods indicate that face-to-face appeals work well.

★ ★ *Generic mailings, automated calls, and web advertisements have little effect on registration rates.*

★ ★ ★ *An important exception is mailings sent by state agencies, which raise registration rates significantly in both midterm and presidential election years, with the biggest turnout effects coming in presidential elections.*

★ ★ *Mailing registration materials and accompanying instructions to those turning eighteen or to recent movers increases registration rates.* The effect is on the order of one new registrant per sixty-six mailings.

★ ★ ★ *Registering the unregistered increases turnout.* Pooling several experiments, one new vote is produced for every three or four new registrants. The translation of registrations into votes, however, seems to vary markedly across elections and the socioeconomic status of those encouraged to register. Registration in advance of a presidential election yields the most votes.

Conclusion

Whether registration drives are cost-effective depends on one's access to the unregistered, how one encourages them to register, and the translation of registrations into votes. If one conducts a house-to-house search for the unregistered in low-income neighborhoods, one might expect to obtain one new registrant per hour. If an hour of canvassing costs $16 and one-in-four new registrants votes, each vote costs $64. If one targets community centers, churches, and high schools in these neighborhoods, one may raise the number of registrants per hour to three or more, in which case the cost per vote falls to $21 or less.

As for impersonal tactics, e-mail and untargeted mailings seem to be unproductive for nongovernmental organizations, and the only question is whether direct mail that specifically targets eighteen-year-olds or recent movers pays off. A cautious reading of the experimental evidence suggests that these targeting strategies raise the turnout rate of the average recipient by 0.5 of a percentage point. Mailings sent to eighteen-year-olds are addressed to specific individuals, so it takes 200 mailings to generate one vote. At $0.50 apiece, that comes to $100 per vote. Mailings to movers may be addressed to households, which brings the cost per vote to about $67. This figure is not particularly attractive compared to other GOTV tactics. That said, the people you succeed in registering to vote may as a result be more receptive to your subsequent attempts to mobilize or persuade them.

We close by returning to the debate over whether unregistered people would vote if they were to register. The experimental evidence does not settle the question for the full set of unregistered people, but it does shed light on those who would register if encouraged to do so. The growing body of evidence from site-based registration drives, targeted mailings, and mailings from state agencies suggests that the newly registered do vote. Their voting rates tend to be lower than those who registered on their own, but even in poor neighborhoods one-in-four new registrants votes. In some sense, both sides of this debate are partly right. For many people, registration is not an impediment to voting because they won't vote even if registered; for others, registration leads to turnout.

CHAPTER ELEVEN

Strategies for Effective Messaging

In previous chapters, we organized our discussion around the channels through which your campaign might communicate with voters—door-to-door canvassing, phone calls, mail, and so forth. In this chapter, we consider what you might say to voters once you have reached them. What kinds of appeals get people to vote?

Answers to this question draw inspiration from social psychology and behavioral economics, academic fields in which researchers study the way people process information, take cues from others, and evaluate alternative courses of action. In recent years, the question of how to increase voter turnout has attracted the attention of a growing number of researchers who seek to test their theories in real-world settings.

In this chapter, we discuss several leading theories of how to make GOTV appeals more effective. First, we consider the hypothesis that people are more likely to undertake actions that they have visualized and planned. Next, we review the burgeoning research on social pressure, or the tendency for people to accede to social norms, especially when their behavior is monitored. Finally, we consider other strategies, such as thanking voters for their past participation or reminding them of their pledge to vote. For each hypothesis, we describe the experimental evidence that assesses whether and to what extent each type of message raises voter turnout. Along the way, we reproduce some prototypical messages, which you can adapt to suit your own campaign's needs.

Self-Prophesy and Implementation Intentions

Psychologists have long contended that people are influenced by the pre-
dictions they make about their own behavior.[1] If you ask people about
whether they will do something they know that they ought to do—like
voting, getting a flu shot, or volunteering for a charitable organization—
they become more likely to do so. The so-called self-prophesy effect is
thought to reflect the operation of two psychological processes. First, the
act of making a prediction may subsequently lead a person to think about
the behavior, making it more "cognitively accessible." Putting the question on a person's mental agenda increases the chances that he or she
follows through with the actual behavior. Second, those who predict they
will do the right thing may feel a sense of obligation to follow through,
especially if their self-prediction is recorded by others.[2]

In practice, the self-prophesy hypothesis implies that one could raise
turnout by asking people whether they intend to cast a ballot, something
that is routinely done in the context of opinion surveys or GOTV phone
calls that end by asking respondents whether they "can be counted on to
vote." The appeal of this messaging tactic is that such questions can be
administered easily and inexpensively. But do questions really produce
appreciable increases in turnout?

The experimental literature evaluating the self-prophesy effect started
off with a bang. Prior to the 1984 presidential election, Anthony Greenwald and his colleagues found that asking a few dozen college under-
graduates by phone whether they intended to vote raised turnout by 25
percentage points.[3] Unfortunately, that whopping effect has never been
reproduced in any subsequent study. The original authors later found
much weaker self-prophesy effects in turnout studies conducted in a 1986
Senate election and a 1987 state primary.[4] Subsequent studies by other
scholars have suggested that self-prophesy effects, if they exist at all, have
approximately the same modest effect as a GOTV call from a commercial
phone bank. Jennifer Smith and her colleagues organized a phone bank
to call registered voters in advance of the 2000 presidential primary.[5]
Subjects in the control group were asked if they knew when and where
to vote; subjects in the treatment group were, in addition, asked whether
they expected to vote in Tuesday's election. This control group voted at
a rate of 43.4 percent; the self-prophesy group, at 43.3 percent. Dustin
Cho replicated this experiment on a larger scale in a study conducted
during the 2008 presidential primary and found a 2.2 percentage point
increase in turnout.[6] In the same election, an even larger experiment re-

ported by David Nickerson and Todd Rogers found that those asked to predict whether they would vote turned out at a 2.0 percent higher rate than the control group. Another sizable effect of self-prophesy turned up in a study conducted in the 2010 midterm elections by Alan Gerber, Seth Hill, and Greg Huber.[7] Compared with a control group that was reminded of an upcoming election, the self-prophesy group had 2.0 percentage points higher turnout. Pooled together, these studies suggest that turnout rises when voters are asked to make a prediction.

The apparent effects of questioning people about their vote intentions become weaker, however, when the questions are one small part of a longer conversation. Christopher Mann found that pre-election phone surveys conducted by *Washington Post* pollsters had no effect on turnout.[8] The list of registered voters who were slated for calls asking about their vote intentions and other political attitudes had the same voting rate as a randomly selected control group who were left alone. The same holds for face-to-face conversations. When canvassers go door-to-door and merely ask residents about how they intend to vote, no increase in turnout occurs.[9] Finally, as noted in chapter 6, live calls from commercial phone banks have weak effects, even when the callers ask voters whether they can be counted on to vote. Since urging people to vote and extracting a verbal commitment from them has only a small effect, it would be surprising if one could raise turnout rates appreciably merely by asking people whether they intend to vote.

A related theory stresses the role of priming voters to think about when and where they will vote. The central idea is that getting people to articulate a goal and how they will achieve it raises the salience of the goal and the tendency to follow through with the planned course of action. Typically, this type of intervention is implemented by urging people to fill out a short checklist of items, akin to a reminder card for a dental appointment. In their direct mail experiment in the 2010 midterm election, Todd Rogers and John Ternovski included a checkbox in which voters were told "Voting takes a plan" and were instructed to furnish answers to the questions "What time will you vote?" and "How will you get to your polling place?" When planning is encouraged by phone, callers used the following script: "It sometimes helps citizens remember to vote if they think about when and where they will be before they cast their ballots. What time on Tuesday do you plan to go to your polling location? . . . Where will you be just before you go vote? . . . How will you get to your polling location?"[10] Indeed, Dustin Cho's callers went so far as to cap off the plan-making script with the following:

Please commit yourself to voting by saying the following statement aloud. Can you please repeat after me? "On Tuesday [TIME, for example, "at 4 p.m." or "in the morning"], when I am at [PLACE, for example, "home"], I will [MODE OF TRANSPORTATION, for example, "drive"] to the polling place and cast my vote!"

To what extent does walking people through the planning process increase their turnout rate? Dustin Cho found that questions about implementation intentions led turnout to decline slightly, from 59.1 percent in the control group to 58.9 percent in the treatment group. Conversely, David Nickerson and Todd Rogers found a sizable and statistically significant gain in turnout of 4.1 percentage points. This effect proved more muted (0.6 of a percentage point) when Alan Gerber, Seth Hill, and Greg Huber tested implementation intentions in their study of the 2010 elections. In competitive U.S. House districts in 2010, a nonpartisan mailer that combined plan making with gratitude (see below) elevated turnout by about 0.5 of a percentage point, a statistically significant effect that slightly exceeds that of typical nonpartisan mail.[11] Although some door-to-door canvassing efforts have had success when discussing plan making with voters, it is not clear whether increased turnout stems from planning per se or rather a helpful conversation between canvassers and voters.[12]

An alternative to extracting a plan from respondents is to extract their reasons for voting. Following the lead of psychologists who argue that formulating reasons raises cognitive accessibility and increases motivation, Jennifer Smith and her colleagues asked respondents, "What would you say is the most important single reason for voting?" In some experimental variants this question was asked in conjunction with questions about whether the respondent expected to vote. In neither case did the question raise turnout. Regardless of whether reasons were paired with self-prophesy, the results indicated no gains in turnout.

In sum, turnout does not rise much when people are encouraged to predict whether they will vote, to visualize the process by which they will vote, or to explain why voting is a worthwhile endeavor. These encouragements seem to boost turnout a bit and are probably worthwhile for campaigns that prefer to use benign messaging strategies. Campaigns that are willing to go a bit further out on the edge might consider social pressure messages, which we discuss next.

Social Pressure: Prescriptive versus Descriptive Norms

In electoral systems where bribes and other material inducements are rare, incentives to vote are thought to be social in nature: voters are rewarded by the approbation of others, while nonvoters are criticized or shunned. In other words, people are rewarded or punished according to whether they comply with "social norms," widely shared standards that prescribe how people ought to behave. One such social norm is that citizens ought to vote in elections.[13]

The term social pressure refers to communications that play upon a basic human drive to win praise and avoid chastisement. Social pressure may be exerted by praising those who uphold norms or scorning those who violate them. Social pressure increases with the amount of praise or scorn, which is why social pressure is thought to be amplified when a person's compliance with social norms is disclosed to others. For this reason, social pressure messages typically involve three ingredients: they admonish the receiver to adhere to a social norm, indicate that the receiver's compliance will be monitored, and warn that compliance will be disclosed to others. In practice, social pressure inducements to vote vary from draconian to discreet. At one extreme are policies and programs designed to shame those who fail to vote. At various times and places, governments and newspapers have made a point of chastising nonvoters.[14] At the other end of the spectrum are gentle reminders to do one's civic duty by participating in elections. Somewhere in between are messages that subtly inform recipients that whether they vote is public information by thanking them for participating in a recent election. How much social pressure is needed to induce people to vote? What kinds of social pressure messages are most effective in generating turnout, and why? Although these questions are closely connected to venerable literatures in psychology on compliance with social norms, the creative spark that attracted interest in this subject came from a researcher outside the academy. In search of a cost-effective way to increase turnout, Mark Grebner, a campaign consultant, developed a form of direct mail that presented voters with information about whether they and their neighbors had voted in recent elections. Grebner's intuition was that nonvoters are ashamed of abstaining but believe they can get away with it because no one knows whether they in fact voted:

> While conducting GOTV campaigns, I never met a voter who genuinely needed reminding, since none of them were surprised to be

told it was Election Day. Nor did I meet anyone who resisted the idea that voting was good, normal, important, expected, a duty. But some of them—I later found by checking records—still failed to vote. My attention was drawn to the remarkably large fraction of people who falsely claimed to have voted, as reported by surveys following each November election. Ten days didn't seem like enough time to have genuinely forgotten; it seemed more like intentional lying. This led me to suspect that a substantial number of potential voters believed that voting is essentially a private act, rather than a public one, and it was safe to routinely misreport voting not only to researchers but to friends and family. That would explain why reminding was ineffective; voters weren't unaware of the message, but deliberately evading it. I decided to try to test that model, by seeing if the threat of public exposure would force at least some of them to abandon their pose, and actually vote, by making them think they couldn't continue to get away with it.[15]

Grebner's self-funded research showed promising results: disclosing vote histories increased the effectiveness of direct mail by an order of magnitude.

After reading the first edition of this book, Grebner brought his in-house experiments to our attention, and we collaborated with him on a large mail experiment designed to isolate the active ingredients in his social pressure mailings. Four different mailers were developed for use in a low-salience Michigan primary election. The first mailer scolded recipients to do their civic duty. The second mailer added an element of surveillance: in addition to telling people to do their civic duty, the mailer announced that they were part of an academic study and that their participation in the upcoming election would be monitored. A third "Self" mailer accentuated the level of monitoring and surveillance by reporting whether each voter in the household had voted in recent elections and promising to send an updated mailing to indicate whether ballots were cast in the upcoming election. A final "Neighbors" mailer amplified the level of disclosure by reporting not only whether members of the household voted, but also whether others on the block voted. Turnout in each experimental group was compared with turnout in a large control group, which received no mail.

These mailers, which Grebner designed and distributed to a total of 80,000 households, demonstrated that turnout rises as social pressure increases. When maximal social pressure was applied, a single mailing increased the probability of voting by more than 8 percentage points, which is an astonishingly large effect that eclipses even the effect of face-to-face contact with a canvasser. The mailing that disclosed only the voting record of one's household nevertheless had an effect of between 4 and 5 percentage points. Bear in mind that a single piece of direct mail, partisan or nonpartisan, rarely increases turnout by more than 1 percentage point, and the effect is usually much weaker. Even the mailer that forcefully asserted the norm of civic duty produced a 1.8 percentage point increase in turnout, a result that was replicated in a study of municipal elections a year later.

Like the early airplane, Grebner's invention was both intriguing and hazardous. For the first time, experiments had isolated an enormous effect that could be generated on a large scale at a low unit cost. As a practical matter, however, the use of social pressure messages presents risks for actual political campaigns, which worry that heavy-handed tactics will alienate potential supporters. For this reason, the second edition of this book warned readers against the use of social pressure mailings, predicting that "Your phone will ring off the hook with calls from people demanding an explanation." Indeed, when the "Neighbors" mailing was distributed in the high-profile gubernatorial recall election in Wisconsin in 2012, thousands of complaints were received (roughly one for every 300 households targeted), and journalists swarmed the office of the organization that sent the mail.[16]

The question is whether it is possible to confect a social pressure mailing that is less obnoxious to recipients yet still effective at generating turnout. Many creative approaches have been developed, at least three of which have been tested experimentally. The first approach is to dial back the "we're-gonna-tell-the-neighbors" elements, focusing solely on presenting vote history for the recipient of the mail. As table 11-1 indicates, the "Self" mailing described in box 11-1 has a quite good track record of raising turnout, at least in the low- and medium-salience elections in which it has been tested, and provokes fewer angry responses. Pooling the half-dozen studies that have used the "Self" mailing, we see that the 16 percent (not percentage point) increase in turnout in the original 2006 experiment is replicated in subsequent studies. Variants on the "Self" mailing that do not scold voters for failing to vote or that recast the "Self" mailing in the form of a colorful and upbeat report card produce weaker effects, especially in the context of closely contested elections.[17] For example, a massive experiment conducted in seventeen states prior to the 2014 midterm election replaced the scolding tone with "a

Table 11-1. The Effects of the "Self" Mailer on Voter Turnout across Multiple Studies

Study	Election type	Setting	Softened language?	Control	Self	Percentage increase in turnout
1	2006 August primary	Michigan	No	29.7 (191,243)	34.5 (38,218)	16%*
2	2007 municipal	Michigan	No	27.7 (772,479)	32.4 (27,609)	17%*
3	2007 gubernatorial general (previous nonvoters)	Kentucky	Yes	6.8 (19,561)	8.9 (13,689)	31%*
3	2007 gubernatorial general (previous voters)	Kentucky	Yes	13.2 (25,037)	16.3 (17,731)	23%*
4	2009 municipal special	New York City	No	3.1 (3,445)	4.2 (3,486)	36%*
5	2010 general	Texas	Yes	40.5 (63,531)	43.1 (1,200)	6%
5	2010 general	Wisconsin	Yes	49.0 (43,797)	50.8 (801)	4%
6	2011 municipal	California	No	10.6 (13,482)	12.0 (1,000)	13%
7	2014 midterm	17 states	Yes	31.2 (128,008)	31.9 (1,969,899)	2%

* Statistically significant at p < .01, one-tailed test. Entries are percent voting. In parentheses are the number of voters in the Control or Self conditions. Percentage increase is calculated by subtracting the turnout rate in Control from the turnout rate in Self and dividing by the turnout rate in Control.

Sources:
1. Alan S. Gerber, Donald P. Green, and Christopher W. Larimer, "Social Pressure and Voter Turnout: Evidence from a Large-Scale Field Experiment," *American Political Science Review,* vol. 102 (2008): 33–48.
2. Alan S. Gerber, Donald P. Green, and Christopher W. Larimer, "An Experiment Testing the Relative Effectiveness of Encouraging Voter Participation by Inducing Feelings of Pride or Shame," *Political Behavior,* vol. 32 (2010): 409–22.
3. Christopher B. Mann, "Is There Backlash to Social Pressure? A Large-Scale Field Experiment on Voter Mobilization," *Political Behavior,* vol. 32 (2010): 387–407.
4. Marisa Abrajano and Costas Panagopoulos, "Does Language Matter? The Impact of Spanish versus English-Language GOTV Efforts on Latino Turnout," *American Politics Research,* vol. 39 (2011): 643–63.
5. Richard E. Matland and Gregg R. Murray, "Mobilization Effects Using Mail: Social Pressure, Descriptive Norms, and Timing," *Political Research Quarterly,* vol. 67 (2013): 304–19. The table reports only the results of the "Self" mailer with no additional information about the voting rate of the community.
6. Costas Panagopoulos, Christopher W. Larimer, and Meghan Condon, "Social Pressure, Descriptive Norms, and Voter Mobilization," *Political Behavior,* vol. 36 (2014): 451–69.
7. Alan S. Gerber and others, "The Generalizability of Social Pressure Effects on Turnout Across High-Salience Electoral Contexts: Field Experimental Evidence From 1.96 Million Citizens in 17 States," unpublished manuscript (2016). The results presented are derived from information provided in footnote 16.

Box 11-1. An Example of the "Self" Mailer

Dear Registered Voter:

WHO VOTES IS PUBLIC INFORMATION!

Why do so many people fail to vote? We've been talking about this problem for years, but it only seems to get worse.

This year, we're taking a different approach. We are reminding people that who votes is a matter of public record.

The chart shows your name from the list of registered voters, showing past votes, as well as an empty box which we will fill in to show whether you vote in the November 6 election. We intend to mail you an updated chart when we have that information.

We will note whether you vote or not.

DO YOUR CIVIC DUTY—VOTE!

OAK ST		11/8/05	11/6/07
1234	Homer Simpson	Did Not Vote	_____
1234	Marge Simpson	Voted	_____

Source: Alan S. Gerber, Donald P. Green, and Christopher W. Larimer, "An Experiment Testing the Relative Effectiveness of Encouraging Voter Participation by Inducing Feelings of Pride or Shame," *Political Behavior,* vol. 32 (2010): 409–22.

---

helpful summary of how often you vote and how your participation compares with others in your state"; this mailing raised turnout by just 0.7 of a percentage points, or 2 percent.[18] Alternatively, a "Self" mailing may be reconfigured to confront voters with their lackluster turnout record in past elections but with a twist: instead of scolding, the letter offers a ride to the polls and other forms of assistance.[19] Another version invites feedback: "For this reason, we are asking you to complete and return the attached survey indicating the reason why you are not participating in elections. We have included a return envelope for your response." These "Self"-with-a-twist variants produce sizable and statistically significant effects, but weaker than the stern "Self" mailer. And finally, there is the kind of ominous variant on the "Self" mailer that only Mark Grebner himself could compose:

According to the Secretary of State's records, you DIDN'T vote in the August primary election this year. We want to make sure you remember to vote Tuesday. Because we know you've voted in previous elections, we don't need to tell you how valuable the right to vote is, or how important this election is—you already know. Because we keep track of every individual voter, when you skip an election, we worry that it could become a habit—a bad habit we want you to break. We'll be looking for you at the polls Tuesday.

Like the original "Self" mailer, this version proved effective among Michigan voters, raising turnout in the 2010 midterm election from 24.0 to 28.5 percent.

A second approach is to recast social norms in a positive light—vote to join an honor roll of "perfect voters." An example of this approach was deployed in the 2009 New Jersey gubernatorial election.[20] Large numbers of voters who were identified as unmarried women, African American, or Hispanic were randomly assigned to a mailing that conveyed the following message before presenting the perfect vote history of ten neighbors:

There is no action more important to our democracy than going to the polls to vote. That's why Our Community Votes, a nonprofit organization that encourages voting, is recognizing citizens in your neighborhood who have perfect voting records in the general elections over the past four years. These neighbors deserve our recognition and congratulations for doing their civic duty and making their voices heard. And with New Jersey's election for governor taking place on November 3rd, we hope you will go to the polls and join your neighborhood's Civic Honor Roll of perfect voters. Voting records show that you voted in the presidential election of 2008 but not in the 2005 election for governor. Voting records are public information, so people know when you voted, but never how you voted. By voting on November 3rd, you will join the following voters as perfect voters.

Turnout rose by 2.3 percentage points among African Americans and Hispanics and 1.3 percentage points among women. The former two estimates are statistically distinguishable from zero.

A third approach is to insinuate that nonvoters will be in the awkward position of explaining themselves to others. For example, in their large-scale study of turnout in the 2010 midterm election, Todd Rogers and John Ternovski included a box in the corner of their GOTV mailer that states "You may be called after the election to discuss your experience at the polls." This additional text boosts the effect of the mailer by an extra quarter percentage point, a small but statistically significant effect.[21] Another version of this approach was deployed by Stefano DellaVigna and his colleagues, who distributed door hangers shortly before the 2010 and 2012 general elections. The door hangers informed residents that "researchers will contact you within three weeks of the Election . . . to conduct a survey on your voter participation." They found a 1.4 percentage point increase in turnout in 2010 but no increase in 2012.[22]

The bottom line seems to be that there are plenty of palatable alternatives to the most confrontational social pressure mailings. They may not generate as many votes, but they produce fewer negative side effects. It has become increasingly common to see campaigns spice up a conventional GOTV appeal with a dash of social pressure seasoning, often with positive effects.[23] Still, it is important to recognize the limits of social pressure tactics. First, these appeals generate far fewer votes in the context of high-salience elections. When the "Neighbors" mailing was unleashed in a hotly contested Wisconsin gubernatorial election on a target list of voters whose base rate of turnout averaged 65.4 percent, it increased turnout by just 1 percentage point. The mailing had a 3.3 percentage point effect among those whose base rate of turnout was approximately 30 percent (which was the average rate of turnout in a low-salience election in which the "Neighbors" treatment was originally tested) and essentially no effect on anyone whose baseline rate of turnout was above 60 percent. The implication seems to be that the people who might be moved by the "Neighbors" mailing in a low-salience election are already voting in a high-salience election.

A second limitation is that social pressure tactics are hit or miss when deployed by phone or text. If monitoring were sufficient to boost turnout, one would think that those who had not yet voted by the afternoon of Election Day could be mobilized with a script that emphasized that their failure to vote had been noticed by poll watchers. However, this script fared no better than a conventional GOTV appeal.[24] On the other hand, recorded messages that scold voters for skipping previous elections have tended to work well, as have live calls from commercial phone banks that warned voters that voting is a matter of public record.[25] The results from texting experiments are more uniformly discouraging; as noted in chapter 7, messages that warned "your friends will know whether you voted" were not especially influential.

Finally, social pressure tactics may fall flat when partisan argumentation predominates. For example, a "Self" mailing that produced no apparent increase in turnout presented the recipient's vote history and went on to say: "It is very important for Democrats and Independents to vote in state and local elections! Here are just a few examples of the negative impact Republicans have had since they took control." The remaining paragraphs enumerated these Republican misdeeds.[26] We suspect that the text left recipients thinking that this was just another advocacy mailer rather than a message encouraging them to take seriously their civic obligation to vote.

Gratitude

Like other scholars trying to repackage social pressure messages in a more palatable form, Costas Panagopoulos sought to develop a version of the "Self" mailer that made people aware that their participation in elections was being observed, but in a friendly, nonconfrontational manner. By thanking voters for their participation in a recent election, his mailings subtly reminded voters that voting is a matter of public record and that the sender of the mailer had taken notice, but the tone of the message is altogether different from the scolding "Self" mailer. His thank-you letter is reproduced in box 11-2. His experiments demonstrate that the thank-you mailing increased turnout in three different electoral settings, with effects that are approximately two-thirds as large as the "Self" mailer's effect.[27]

At first glance, these results seem to show that revealing vote history in a friendly way exerts social pressure, albeit less forcefully than the "Self" mailer. However, the details of his experiments reveal something unexpected. It turns out that when a variety of different thank-you mailers are compared head-to-head in the same experiment, they all prove to be effective at raising turnout, even when recipients are praised for being concerned about public affairs, with no mention of their voting record in the past. Evidently, the gratitude effect is distinct from the effects of social pressure, and presenting voters with information about their past votes does not make these gratitude mailers especially effective.

Although further testing is needed, the findings suggest that campaigns seeking an effective, unobjectionable, and inexpensive GOTV

Box 11-2. An Example of the "Gratitude" Mailer

Dear registered voter:

THANK YOU FOR VOTING!

We realize voting takes time and effort, and we just wanted to say "thank you."

Our democracy depends on people like you exercising their right to vote. We appreciate the fact that you made it a priority to cast a ballot in the last midterm election in November 2006.

We also remind you that the primary elections in Georgia will take place on

Tuesday, July 20, 2010. You are eligible to vote.

We hope you will vote on Primary Election Day.

The Vote Georgia Project

Source: Costas Panagopoulos, "Thank You for Voting: Gratitude Expression and Voter Mobilization," *Journal of Politics,* vol. 73 (2013): 707–17.

---

message should consider some version of the thank-you mailer. It does not require the database management and customization of the "Self" mailer, and the sender may even win some points for politely thanking voters for their involvement. Naturally, if everyone starts thanking voters, recipients will quickly become inured to these expressions of gratitude. In the short run, however, this messaging approach seems to be a safe investment, with a respectable track record in low- and medium-salience elections.

Reminding Those Who Pledge to Vote

Upholding one's promise is a powerful social norm. People readily promise to vote when asked. Putting these two ideas together suggests that one could raise turnout by inducing people to pledge to vote and, as the election draws near, remind them to live up to their pledge. The first rigorous experimental tests of this hypothesis were conducted by Mia Costa and her colleagues during the 2016 primary and general elections.[28] Campus organizers for the Environmental Defense Fund devoted their four-hour shifts to one of two randomly selected objectives: encouraging pledges to vote or encouraging people to request a reminder to vote. The organizers attracted approximately the same number of people to comply with each request, and the background attributes of the compliers are quite similar. The pledge group was later mailed their pledge reminder, while the control group was mailed a nonspecific reminder to vote. Among those who were eligible to vote in the primary election, turnout was 4.1 percentage points higher in the pledge group; the comparable effect in the general election was 3.5 percentage points. Taken together, the two estimates make a strong case for the effectiveness of reminding voters not simply of the upcoming election, but of their pledge to vote. One could readily imagine much stronger versions of this effect in settings where people pledge to vote in the context of community gatherings, where the pressure to stand by one's word is much stronger. This line of research deserves special attention from organizations seeking to get more out of their GOTV efforts.

Conclusion

One of the intriguing features of GOTV research is that it sometimes sheds new light on well-known theories that have never been subjected to large-scale experimental tests. Take, for example, the "door-in-the-face" hypothesis, which contends that if you make a demanding request of someone, and they refuse, they become more likely to go along with a more modest request.[29] It's as though your first request softens them up, and they give in to your scaled-back request. Deborah Brown McCabe and Melissa Michelson devised a clever test of this hypothesis.[30] They organized their own phone bank that either made a straight GOTV appeal or, in the treatment condition, prefaced that appeal by inviting the voter to put in an eight-hour shift phoning voters on Election Day. (Just one of the 543 people who were asked to volunteer agreed to do so.) The straight GOTV appeal significantly increased turnout in the next day's local election. The door-in-the-face appeal did not and, in fact, performed significantly worse than the standard GOTV message.

The lesson seems to be that some venerable psychological propositions provide useful inspiration for GOTV messages, while others may be of limited practical value. In the useful category are hypotheses rooted in social norms. Several large experiments have convincingly demonstrated that people are sensitive to widely held notions of appropriate behavior, such as the value of doing one's civic duty. Turnout rises when this norm is asserted forcefully and when compliance with the norm is subject to monitoring and possible disclosure to others. The strong effects of norm-based appeals comport with survey evidence showing that registered voters widely regard voting as something that citizens ought to be doing; indeed, experimental evidence suggests that, all else equal, people who vote are more highly regarded than those who do not.[31] In the limited practical value category are interventions that merely increase the cognitive accessibility of the election, through reminders or whatnot. Somewhere in between are messages that invite people to predict whether they will vote, give reasons for voting, or plan when and where they will vote; experiments testing these tactics sometimes reveal a sizable effect, but the results have been mixed.

A final thought concerning messaging is that too many cooks may spoil the broth. There is a temptation to throw into a single message all of the attractive ingredients from previous experimental tests. A committee of chefs might decide to add a dash of social pressure, a dash of gratitude, and a dash of implementation intentions. The problem is that those on the receiving end of such a mailer or phone call may simply ignore a jumble of messages. Given the difficulty of holding voters' attention for more than a few moments, it may be better to narrow the presentation to a single message that is brief and memorable.

CHAPTER TWELVE

What Works, What Doesn't, and What's Next

The scores of experiments summarized in this book provide a useful reality check for anyone seeking to launch or evaluate a voter mobilization campaign. When we began our experimental research in 1998, we were struck by the fact that even people running very expensive campaigns were operating on little more than their own intuition about what worked. The academic literature in existence at that time was little help. Experimental studies were rare, and the ones that found their way into print reported what we now know to be outlandish findings. One study, based on a few dozen voters, purported to show that partisan mail increased turnout 19 percentage points.[1]

With a mix of optimism and skepticism, researchers in recent years have sought to reproduce these legendary effects. After all, if these enormous effects were truly as the scholarly literature reported, low voter turnout could be cured with a direct mail campaign. Alas, we and other researchers found that an ordinary mailing has a modest effect on turnout, raising it by less than a percentage point.

Looking back, it seems clear that these sensational findings can be attributed to something called "publication bias." Academic journals are reluctant to publish statistically insignificant findings, which means that smaller studies must report larger results if they are to find their way into print. As a result, the experimental studies that appear in academic journals tend to give a misleading picture of what works.[2]

And those are just the experimental studies. If we expand the discussion of unreliable evidence to include nonexperimental research—focus groups, surveys, and case histories that do not involve control groups—the litany of untrustworthy claims becomes vast. These claims are not necessarily false, but the evidence behind them is flimsy and easily trumped by a well-crafted experiment. Take voter guides, for example. Focus group researchers found that people shown a simplified voter guide reported that it increased their enthusiasm about voting.[3] Survey researchers found that people living in areas that provided voter guides and sample ballots were more likely to vote, even after taking their age, education, and other background attributes into account.[4] The effect seemed especially strong among young people and those who never went to college, leading the authors to recommend that states routinely mail voters sample ballots. However, when this proposition was tested experimentally using sample ballots and voter guides distributed through the mail, no effect on turnout was found.[5]

Once the red herrings have been cleared from the path, the experimental results form an intelligible pattern. We begin by summarizing what does *not* work:

✓ Mobilizing voters is not merely a matter of reminding them that Election Day is near. Live calls from commercial phone banks that remind people to vote have weak effects. So do e-mail reminders, Facebook reminders, and reminders sent by direct mail or text message.

✓ Mobilizing voters is not just a matter of putting election-related information in front of them. Leafleting and direct mail campaigns that distribute voter guides have produced disappointing results.

✓ Telling people why they should vote for a particular candidate or cause does not, in itself, lead people to vote at higher rates. Putting a partisan edge on a mailing or a phone call does not seem to enhance its effectiveness.

Having ruled out several widely held notions about how to mobilize voters, we now offer some hypotheses suggested by the experimental results:

✓ To mobilize voters, make them feel wanted at the polls. Mobilizing voters is rather like inviting them to a social occasion. Personal invitations convey the most warmth and work best. Next best are phone calls in which the caller converses with the respondent, as opposed to reading a canned script. Mailed invitations typically don't work very well.

✓ Building on voters' preexisting level of motivation to vote is also important. Calling back a voter who has previously expressed an intention to vote appears to be an effective mobilization tactic.

✓ Many nonvoters nevertheless think of themselves as voters and feel that voting is a civic obligation. They will vote if urged to do their civic duty and shown that whether they vote is a matter of public record.

All three of these hypotheses share a common theme: the decision to vote is strongly shaped by one's social environment. One may be able to nudge turnout upward slightly by making voting more convenient, supplying voters with information, and reminding them about an imminent election; these effects, however, are small in comparison to what happens when voters are placed in a social milieu that urges their participation. That said, providing social inducements to vote is neither easy nor cheap. So a natural question is whether, when cost is taken into account, effective GOTV tactics are also cost-effective.

Summarizing the Cost-Effectiveness of GOTV Tactics

Table 12-1 summarizes our assessment of the bottom line. What does it cost to make a voter out of someone who would otherwise abstain? Each of the GOTV tactics is characterized in terms of costs and benefits. In constructing our dollars-per-vote estimates, we err on the side of caution and provide figures only for those tactics that have been shown to work. In other words, table 12-1 reports the cost-effectiveness of tactics whose average impact has been demonstrated to be greater than zero. Tactics such as television advertising, whose average mobilizing effect has yet to be distinguished statistically from zero, are excluded from this segment of the table. Interested readers may look back at previous chapters for our speculations about the cost-effectiveness of these unproven tactics.

As you examine this table, remember that the attractiveness of any GOTV tactic depends on the resources available to your campaign and the constraints within which it must operate. If your campaign is long on enthusiastic volunteers but short on money, you might consider canvassing or conducting a volunteer phone bank. If your campaign has money but lacks volunteers, you might invest your money in carefully supervised commercial phone banks or perhaps direct mail.

One of the most important lessons to draw from table 12-1 is that conventional GOTV campaigns seldom work miracles. Canvassing 100 registered voters at their doorstep will not generate 100 votes. A more realistic estimate is six additional votes among those you speak to and perhaps an extra one or two if word spreads to others in the household. Even this figure may be high if the canvassing targets are very likely or very unlikely voters. Similarly, sending a piece of conventional GOTV mail to 10,000 registered voters will not bring 10,000 people to the polls. The number of additional voters you should expect from this type of direct mail campaign is around thirty-five. We are not saying that GOTV work is fruitless. Our point is rather that an ambitious GOTV campaign requires a serious investment of time and resources.

Another approach is to place even greater emphasis on the quality of the GOTV work. A call or visit by a charismatic candidate, as opposed to a volunteer canvasser, might well produce larger effects. The same goes for most any GOTV tactic. With rigorous testing and targeting, your mail or phone calls may become far more effective than the average results reported in table 12-1. It is not uncommon to see field tests in which the most effective mailing or phone script repeatedly proves to be two or three times as effective as what the group had been using previously.

If you are contemplating a campaign that emphasizes high-quality communications and optimal targeting, keep things in perspective. The scale of your outreach effort still determines your likely impact. For example, even if your efforts were twice as effective as the most effective door-to-door canvassing campaign, you would still need to contact several thousand registered voters to produce 1,000 votes. To sway election outcomes, high-quality campaigns must also be high-quantity campaigns.

Further Thoughts on Cost-Effectiveness: Mobilizing Voters over the Long Haul

Voter turnout campaigns tend to focus on the here and now. They work to generate votes during the waning days of the campaign, and when the polls close, the campaign closes shop as well. Apart from influencing the outcome of an election, what lasting effects do GOTV campaigns have?

One of the most interesting findings to emerge from GOTV research is that voter mobilization campaigns have enduring effects. The New Haven residents who were randomly assigned to receive direct mail or face-to-face canvassing in 1998 were more likely to vote in both the election held in November 1998 and the mayoral election held in November 1999.[6] This type of persistent effect has since been replicated many times over.[7] For example, the voters assigned to receive mailings in the Michigan social pressure experiment not only voted at higher rates in the August 2006 primary, they were also significantly more likely to vote in August primaries in 2008, 2010, and 2012. The "Self" mailing generated approximately 1,850 votes in August 2006, plus an additional 900 votes over the next three August primaries.[8] This pattern of persistence over time holds for other large social pressure studies and for the array of experiments that Lisa García Bedolla and Melissa Michelson report in their multielection study of minority mobilization.[9]

How many votes carry over from one election to the next? The answer appears to depend on the elections in question. For example, it seems to be the case that boosting turnout in primary elections has a bigger effect on subsequent primary elections than on subsequent general elections, suggesting that voters get into the habit of voting in particular types of elections or at certain times of the year.

The enduring impact of voter mobilization has profound implications. First, it suggests that voting is a habit-forming activity. Someone who votes in this election is more likely to vote in the next election. Someone who skips an election is less likely to vote in the future. America's low turnout rates may reflect the fact that we have the most frequent elections on earth. One might liken sleepy municipal elections to gateway drugs: by enticing so many people to abstain from voting, they weaken voting habits.

Second, this finding casts a different light on the usual way of evaluating the costs and benefits of a GOTV campaign. The typical approach is to think only in terms of votes produced in the current election. A more realistic calculation would take into account the future effects of this year's voter mobilization drive. If your campaign generates 1,000 additional votes at a cost of $40,000, this price amounts to $40 per vote for the current election. But if your campaign generates an extra 400 votes in future elections, the price falls to $40,000/1,400 = $29 per vote. This added efficiency is an important consideration for political parties and other organizations that have a long-term interest in producing votes, especially if the alternative is to spend money on persuasive messages that may have no long-term impact once the current slate of candidates has moved on.

Table 12-1. Cost-Effectiveness of Get-Out-the-Vote Tactics[a]

GOTV effort	Start-up and overhead costs	Ongoing management	Effectiveness per contact[b]	Is effect statistically reliable?	Dollar cost per vote (excluding start-up and management costs)
Door-to-door	Recruit, prepare walk lists	Substantial ongoing training and supervision	One vote per 16 contacts plus effects of spillover on housemates	Yes	At $16 per hour and 6 contacts per hour, one vote costs $33
Leafleting	Recruit, prepare walk lists and leaflets	Monitor walkers, check work	One vote per 189 voters reached by leaflets	Not significantly greater than zero	*
Direct mail, advocacy	Design, print, distribute	Intensive during start-up, then postal service takes over	No detectable effect	Yes, large number of studies	*
Direct mail, nonpartisan (conventional message)[c]	Design, print, distribute	Intensive during start-up, then postal service takes over	One vote per 282 recipients (unconventional messages tend to be more productive)	Yes, large number of studies	At $0.50 per piece, one vote costs $94
Phone, volunteer	Recruit enthusiastic callers	Ongoing training and supervision	One vote per 36 contacts	Yes, large number of studies	At $16 an hour and 16 contacts per hour, one vote costs $36
Commercial live calls	Obtain phone list	Requires monitoring to ensure quality	One vote per 106 contacts	Yes, large number of studies	At $0.50 per contact, one vote costs $53
Robocalls	Obtain phone list, recording talent	Due diligence to check legal requirements	One vote per 430 landlines targeted	Experimental literature is divided	At $0.15 per targeted number for a series of three calls, one vote costs $64
E-mail	Amass e-mail list, compose message(s), distribute	Most of the work is in the start-up	No detectable effects, except when sent by registrar	Large number of studies show average effect cannot be large	*

GOTV effort	Start-up and overhead costs	Ongoing management	Effectiveness per contact[b]	Is effect statistically reliable?	Dollar cost per vote (excluding start-up and management costs)
Text messages	Amass target list, compose message(s), distribute	One-to-one messaging requires large staff of volunteers	One vote per 312 voters targeted	Yes, several large studies, including five in presidential elections	Lists and texting services average $0.35 per target number, implying $109 per vote
Election Day festivals	Find site, organize event, advertise	Requires staff on hand to host and supervise events	Raises precinct-wide turnout by 0.1–3.8 percentage points	Yes, five experiments suggest an average precinct-wide increase of 1 percentage point	Ranges from $33 to $200 per vote
Television GOTV	Produce and place ads	None	Raises turnout by 0.5 of a percentage point	Not significantly greater than zero	*
Radio GOTV	Produce and place ads	None	Raises turnout by 1 percentage point	Not significantly greater than zero	*

a. Costs may vary due to local circumstances and market conditions.

b. "Contact" is defined as follows: for door-to-door canvassing, talking to target voter; for commercial and volunteer phone calls, talking to target voter; for robocalls, attempting to reach a target voter (since robocalls typically leave voice mail); for mail, mail sent; for leaflets, leaflet dropped at door. For direct mail, leafleting, and door-to-door canvassing, calculations assume that the average household has 1.5 voters. For canvassing, it is assumed that nonpartisan messaging is directed at voters whose baseline probability of voting is between 30 and 50 percent and that 60 percent of the effect on the directly contacted spills over to housemates. Across all canvassing studies, the average cost per vote is approximately $52, including spillovers. See appendix A.

c. Unconventional messages, such as those that apply social pressure, are often substantially more effective. See chapter 11.

* Cost-effectiveness is not calculated for tactics that are not proven to raise turnout.

Synergy?

One common refrain among those who design campaigns is the importance of "touching" voters with a steady stream of campaign communication. Touch them first with a mailer, then with a live call, then with another mailer, a robocall, and so forth. When thinking about the cost-effectiveness of this approach, it is important to be clear about exactly what is being claimed. A GOTV campaign consisting of a mailer and a phone call probably will produce more votes than a campaign consisting of just a phone call or just a mailer. The notion that "more is better" is not really at issue here. When consultants speak of an "integrated" campaign in which the whole is greater than the sum of the parts, they are suggesting that those who receive mail are especially responsive to the ensuing phone call (or vice versa). Suppose that mail increases turnout 1 percentage point and phone contact increases it 2 percentage points. The claim is that mail and phone together increase turnout more than 3 percentage points because the mailing warms voters up to the message that they receive via phone.

This claim has been tested in several large experiments, and the results decisively reject the synergy hypothesis. To cite just a few examples, in the 1998 New Haven study, mail did not increase the effectiveness of phone calls, and phone calls did not enhance the effects of door-to-door canvassing. The 2002 NALEO experiment failed to support the hypothesis that robocalls enhance the effectiveness of direct mail or vice versa. Neither direct mail nor robocalls amplified the effects of live calls. The same may be said of nonpartisan live calls and direct mail sent by groups mobilizing Asian Americans in 2006 and of live calls, robocalls, mail, and canvassing directed at predominantly Latino neighborhoods in California. Three studies of mail, robotic calls, and live calls by environmental organizations in the 2004 and 2006 elections showed no synergy. Emily Cardy's study of direct mail and phone calls on behalf of a gubernatorial candidate did show some (albeit statistically insignificant) signs of synergy, raising the possibility that the hypothesis applies to partisan messages. Some hints of synergy also turn up in a 2014 study of phone calls and direct mail targeting Republican women, but a much larger 2005 study of partisan mail, phone calls, and canvassing in another gubernatorial contest found no evidence that combinations of different treatments had especially strong effects.[10] In sum, experimental researchers searched long and hard for the El Dorado of synergy only to conclude that combinations of GOTV appeals do not appear to deliver a bonus of votes.

Perhaps the reason for the lack of synergy has to do with the mechanisms by which GOTV campaigns work. Getting a piece of direct mail rarely creates a personal sense of belonging, so the subsequent phone call does not build on a growing predisposition to vote. Conversely, for those who have received a phone call, the ensuing mailer does not have special resonance. Although it is possible to imagine a situation in which one GOTV tactic amplifies the effect of another (for example, follow-up phone calls with those who pledge to vote), experiments have rarely detected these synergies, which explains why this book is organized into chapters that look at GOTV tactics one at a time rather than in special combinations.

Frontiers of GOTV Research

Although the science of voter mobilization has come a long way in recent years, unanswered questions abound. These open questions fall into two broad categories: when and who. The "when" question has to do with the optimal timing of messages: How early should one start? Given scarce resources, should one strive to contact voters early in the campaign to encourage them to pay attention to the upcoming election or late in the campaign to give them a big push right before Election Day? Several experiments have attempted to shed light on the "when" question, but the results have been murky. The reason is that it takes a very large experiment to differentiate the effects of early and late GOTV work. For example, Costas Panagopoulos conducted an experiment in advance of the 2005 municipal elections in Rochester in which nonpartisan GOTV calls were made four weeks, two weeks, or three days before Election Day. Each of the treatments raised turnout slightly, but because only 2,000 people were assigned to each treatment group, the apparent variation in treatment effects does not provide much guidance.[11] Two much larger nonpartisan experiments were conducted in 2008 and 2010, each with 15,000 households assigned to early calls (a week before Election Day) and 15,000 to late calls (one to two days before) from a commercial phone bank. The 2008 study gave a slight edge to late calls, but both had weak effects that were statistically indistinguishable from one another. The 2010 study found both early and late calls to be (equally) ineffective.[12] The large study conducted in 2014 gave an edge to early calls.[13] Two further studies randomly varied the timing of direct mail. Gregg Murray and Richard Matland conducted an experiment in which social pressure mailings were distributed eight days or four days prior to Election Day in 2010. The results suggest that mail sent later was more effective, although the difference in effectiveness falls just shy of conventional standards of statistical significance.[14] Prior to the 2014 elections in California, David Broockman and Donald Green evaluated a labor union's direct mail campaign and found that mail sent four weeks before Election Day was ineffective but that mail sent nineteen days before was slightly more effective than mail sent twelve days before. This pattern holds even after excluding permanent absentee voters, but as with previous studies, one cannot rule out the possibility that the variation in treatment effects is simply due to chance. Text messaging experiments suggest that early messages are almost as effective as late messages, and there is no special payoff to urgent messages on Election Day itself. Taken together, these experiments hint that late communications tend to work better, but the many exceptions to this rule suggest that the role of timing is subtle or context dependent.

The "who" question is as follows: Which voters should a campaign target for its GOTV appeals? In previous chapters, we noted that it tends to be easier to generate votes when targeting those whose baseline probability of voting falls roughly between 20 and 80 percent. This rule of thumb is a reasonable starting point, but to really squeeze more efficiency from one's targeting requires a more systematic investigation stretching over multiple elections. In recent years, a growing number of researchers have applied "data mining" methods to the analysis of large-scale experiments in an effort to figure out which types of voters are most responsive to various forms of GOTV tactics and messages.[15] These algorithms are able to sift through a vast number of subgroups to identify the combinations of background attributes that predict whether a voter will respond to a GOTV intervention. Moreover, these algorithms have become increasingly sophisticated in the way that they learn from the data, continually testing whether the generalizations drawn from one part of the subject pool correctly predict what happens in another part. This process of cross-validation makes the search for highly responsive subgroups less prone to false discoveries. Of course, there is no guarantee that any subjects are especially responsive to a GOTV tactic; some tactics simply do not work, period. But as the cost of high-performance computing declines and data-mining software becomes more user-friendly, data mining makes increasing sense for organizations that want to optimize their targeting over a series of elections.

To illustrate the potential advantages of data-driven targeting, suppose that the 2007 Michigan social pressure experiment involving the "Self" mailer had been used to optimize the targeting of voters in the 2009 Illinois study using the same mailer.[16] A data-mining program called BART was used to predict treatment effects in 2007 based on variables that are common to both data sets: gender, age, household size, and turnout in the 2004 and 2006 primary and general elections. The algorithm was used to partition the 2009 subject pool into those who were predicted to be above average or below average in terms of their responsiveness to the "Self" mailer. Had the 2009 mailer gone only to those predicted to be especially responsive, the average lift in turnout would have been 5.5 percentage points, as compared with just 2.0 percentage points among those predicted to be less responsive.[17] Since the cost of mailing the two groups is the same in this instance, proper targeting has a profound effect on the cost per vote. For organizations that are planning to conduct GOTV campaigns in a series of elections, data mining and optimized targeting make good economic sense.

In Search of Supertreatments

One of the most exciting challenges in GOTV research is to use intuitions about why certain GOTV tactics work to aid the search for unusually powerful methods of increasing turnout. The literature on synergy suggests that supertreatments are not likely to be found in special elixirs that combine conventional treatments. Instead, recent experiments imply that supertreatments are likely to turn up when powerful social-psychological forces are harnessed. For example, the strong tendency for people to respond to social norms is illustrated in the striking finding that a single mailing can produce an increase of 8 percentage points in turnout by revealing a person's past voting record to the neighbors.

On the frontier of GOTV research lies the investigation of other social influences, such as the effects of friends and family members communicating the importance of voting, expressing interest in the electoral process, and intimating their disdain for those who fail to fulfill this civic obligation. A related topic is the study of how social networks can be used as mobilizing agents. Can workplaces, religious groups, online communities, and other social ties be used to bind people together into blocs of voters? In the heyday of machine politics, it was common for "block captains" to mobilize a specific list of voters. The idea of recruiting people to be responsible for turning out a small group of friends, neighbors, parishioners, or coworkers is essentially an attempt to harness the formidable social influence that peers exert on each other. Experiments discussed in chapter 7 suggest that Facebook social networks have the potential to operate in this way. This highly personalized style of mobilization is sometimes called "relational organizing," and recent experiments suggest that it has the potential to be quite effective, even when the mobilizers are acquaintances. For example, organizers for the nonpartisan group PICO compiled a list of voters with whom they had some prior interaction (for example, when registering them to vote). These names were then divided randomly into three groups: a group that was called by the organizer, who had a personal connection to the group; a group that was called by a paid staff member within the organization; and a control group. Both sets of calls (relational calls and live calls) were made during the final days of the 2016 presidential election. Researchers found that those assigned to the relational calls voted at a rate of 4.2 percentage points above the control group and 2.0 percentage points above the more conventional live calls.[18] Perhaps the influence of social ties could be further enhanced by linking other forces, such as the feeling of obligation to honor a commitment to vote expressed to a friend.[19] The question for researchers is whether these social influences, separately or in combination, reliably produce large increases in turnout. Once these effects are discovered and confirmed, the next line of research is whether the effects can be reproduced inexpensively on a large scale, perhaps using new communication technologies.

Conducting Your Own Experiment

The experiments described in this book have only begun to scratch the surface of all that can be learned about making GOTV campaigns more efficient. While reading this book, you may have thought of some experiments of your own. You may be running for office, wondering how you can use the lessons learned from your upcoming campaign to improve the efficiency of subsequent campaigns. Or perhaps you remain unpersuaded by the experimental results presented in this book and want to see for yourself whether they hold up.

With a bit of thought and planning, you should be able to put a meaningful experiment into place. You do not need an advanced degree in social science, but it is important to proceed methodically so as to guard against the problems that sometimes confront this type of research.[20] Here is a brief overview of how experiments are designed, conducted, and analyzed.

Spell Out Your Hypothesis

A useful first step in any experimental project is to write, in a single sentence, the claim that you will be testing. This will force you to clarify what the treatment is and who the subjects are. For example, "Among voters with Latino surnames, Spanish-language mailers increase turnout more than English-language mailers," or "Candidates are better able to mobilize voters through door-to-door canvassing than are the activists who work for candidates," or "Election Day rides increase voter turnout among those who live more than a mile from their polling place."

Define Your Target List

Create a list of voters who will be targeted for the GOTV intervention you are evaluating. Depending on how your campaign is organized, the lists of targets may be individual people or places (such as voting precincts or media markets). For example, your list may consist of Latino voters in Fresno County. If there are some areas or people that your campaign absolutely must treat, exclude them from the list to be randomized. These must-treat observations are outside your experiment.

Determine How Many People (or Places) You Wish to Assign to the Treatment and Control Categories

The larger the numbers in each category, the more precise your results will be. However, do not assign more people to the treatment group than you have the resources to treat. Apportion your experimental groups so that your contact rate in the treatment group will be as high as possible.

Divide the List into Treatment and Control Groups

Creating random treatment and control groups is easy to do with a spreadsheet program. Box 12-1 walks you through the steps of randomly sorting and subdividing your target list.

Random sorting is useful even if you are apprehensive about excluding a control group. Suppose you are conducting a phone canvass. Sort your phone list so that it is in random order. Call names on the randomly sorted list, starting from the top and working your way down. When your campaign is over, any names that you did not attempt to call represent your control group. The names that you did attempt to call represent the treatment group.[21] Nothing about the campaign's execution has changed, but now it becomes amenable to rigorous evaluation in the event that you were unable to call all of the names on your target list. This approach is ideal for evaluating campaigns whose goals outstrip their resources.

Box 12-1. Random Assignment

Random assignment to treatment and control groups is easily accomplished with a spreadsheet program, such as the freeware available at OpenOffice.org. First, open the spreadsheet containing the list of voters. Second, place your cursor on an empty cell in the spreadsheet and click the equal sign in order to call up the equation editor. Enter the formula RAND() and hit enter. A random number between 0 and 1 should appear in the cell. Third, copy and paste this random number into a column beside the columns in your data set. Now every row in your data set should contain a different random number. Fourth, highlight all of the columns in your data set and click DATA > SORT. A box should appear asking you to indicate which column(s) to sort by. Choose the column that corresponds to the column of random numbers just generated. Click OK. Fifth, having sorted the data in random order, add a new column to your data set. This new column will indicate whether each person is assigned to the treatment group. If you want 500 people in your treatment group, put the number 1 into the first 500 rows and the number 0 into the remaining rows.

Check the Randomization

Random assignment should, in principle, create treatment and control groups that have similar background characteristics. To ensure that you have conducted the randomization properly, check to see that the treatment and control groups have approximately the same rate of voter turnout in some recent election (before your intervention). If this information is not available, check to see that the average age in the treatment group is approximately the same as the average age in the control group. If the treatment and control groups differ appreciably, you may have made a computer error. Check your work, and redo your randomization.

Administer the Treatment to the Treatment Group Only

Be vigilant about adhering to the treatment and control assignments. Do not contact anyone on the control list! The easiest way to keep the experiment from going awry is to release only the treatment names to the phone bank or direct mail vendor. Send leafleteers and door-to-door canvassers out with the names of people in the treatment group only and remind them not to knock blindly on every door.

Maintain Records of Who Was Contacted

Maintain records of who was contacted, even if that person is someone in the control group who was contacted by mistake. You will need this information to calculate the effect of actually receiving your intervention.

Archive Your Campaign Materials

Once you have successfully carried out this protocol, archive your campaign materials and write a brief description of the experimental procedures. While you wait for registrars to furnish voter turnout information, and before you forget the details, write up the description of the experiment and how it was conducted. Create a physical or electronic archive of your campaign materials—your scripts, recorded messages, mailings, and so forth. Be sure to collect whatever data you need from canvassers (for example, walk sheets with contact information) and callers before these materials disappear.

Calculate Turnout Rates

When voter turnout data become available, calculate the turnout rates of the people in the treatment and control groups. Remember, your treatment group consists of those individuals assigned at the outset to the treatment group, regardless of whether you were able to contact them.

Analyze the Results

Analyze the experimental results. The difference in turnout between the original treatment and control groups—ignoring for the moment whether persons in the treatment group were actually treated—tells you quite a lot. (Note: Do not discard people in the treatment group who weren't home or were found to have moved.) If the turnout rate in the assigned treatment group is higher, your intervention seems to have worked. This difference is known as the intent-to-treat effect, because it compares those you intended to treat with those you intended to leave alone.

Next, calculate the contact rate. Divide the number contacted in the treatment group by the number assigned to the treatment group. If your contact rate is less than 100 percent, divide the intent-to-treat effect by the contact rate. This number indicates the effect of the treatment on those who were contactable. Consider the following example. Your control group votes at a rate of 42 percent. Your treatment group votes at a rate of 47 percent. Your contact rate is 50 percent. So the effect of the treatment on contactable subjects is estimated to be $(47 - 42)/0.5 = 10$ percentage points.

Perform a Statistical Analysis

A bit of statistical analysis can indicate how likely it is that the difference you are seeing was produced by chance. Why worry about chance? Sometimes just by luck of the draw you may underestimate or overestimate the effectiveness of the treatment. We have developed some (free) web tools to walk you through this process as painlessly as possible and to give you some pointers about how to interpret the numbers (see box 12-2).

Crafting an experiment requires planning and supervision, yet experience has shown that any energetic and well-organized researcher can learn to do it. For decades we have taught courses and workshops on experimental design. Many of the participants have gone on to conduct clever and well-executed voter mobilization studies. One got a team of friends together to make GOTV calls on behalf of a candidate for governor; another designed and distributed nonpartisan direct mail; another organized a large-scale precinct walking campaign; another mobilized her Facebook friends. One of the most gratifying aspects of writing a book like this is hearing about the imaginative experiments that readers have conducted.

Experimental research requires a fair amount of effort, but the biggest hurdle in conducting a successful experiment is conceptual. To design and execute a randomized experiment, you must first understand why a randomly assigned control group is essential. At every stage in the process of executing an experiment, people will whine about your insistence on a control group. They will propose instead that you simply consider the people the campaign happened to treat as the treatment group and that you consider the people the campaign failed to contact as the control group. In other words, they will propose that you forget about random assignment and just let them treat whomever they please. You will have to convince them that a randomly assigned control group is indispensable.

When you balk at their alternative research proposal, its advocates may try to reassure you by suggesting that you can make the research design serviceable by comparing a select group of people who did or did not receive the call. The select group they have in mind are people who are similar in age, party attachment, and voter turnout rate in previous elections. Do not give in. What they are suggesting is a flawed research design. Here's why. Even if the people who were treated have the same observed attributes as the people who were not treated, there is no guarantee that their unobserved attributes are the same. Learning that a person is home when you call reveals something about his or her likelihood of voting (that is, the person has not moved, is not dead, is willing to pick up the phone when a stranger calls). Even if your phone calls had no effect on turnout, the people you reached will vote at higher rates than the folks you could not or did not reach.

To drive this point home to our academic colleagues, we conducted an experiment a couple of days before the November 2004 election. We called 15,000 registered voters in Illinois and urged them to buckle their seat belt when driving during the holiday season.[22] Not a word was said about voting or politics. Just seat belts. Obviously, the true effect of this call on voter turnout was zero. But sure enough, the people who actually received the buckle-up message voted at a rate that was 5 percentage points higher than that of the people who were not called, even though the two groups shared exactly the same pattern of voter turnout dur-

Box 12-2. Simplified Web Software for Analyzing Experimental Data

For the convenience of first-time experimenters, we helped to create a free application that reads in experimental results and generates a statistical analysis. Go to https://egap.shinyapps.io/gotv-app or google "GOTV shiny app." You supply six numbers: the number of people that you (1) assigned to the treatment group, (2) assigned to the control group, (3) successfully treated in the treatment group, (4) inadvertently treated in the control group, (5) found to have voted in the treatment group, and (6) found to have voted in the control group.

To see how the program works, suppose you wish to analyze results from Melissa Michelson's door-to-door canvassing experiment in Dos Palos, California. Prior to the 2001 election, she assigned 466 people with Latino surnames to the treatment group and 297 Latinos to the control group. Of the people in the treatment group, 342 were successfully contacted. No one in the control group was contacted. In the treatment group, 86 people voted, whereas 41 people voted in the control group. The six inputs are, therefore, 466, 297, 342, 0, 86, and 41.

After entering these numbers in the appropriate boxes, you will see output that summarizes the research findings and estimates the size and precision of the treatment effects. Check the statistical summary that appears in the middle of the page to ensure that you have entered the data correctly. The computer will summarize the voting rates and contact rates based on the numbers you provided. Next, examine the intent-to-treat estimate. This number is calculated by subtracting the voting rate in the control group from the voting rate in the treatment group. In this example, the intent-to-treat estimate is 4.7, suggesting that assignment to the treatment group raised turnout 4.7 percentage points. Beneath this

ing the previous decade. Why? Because this comparison excluded the dead, the moved, and the unfriendly from the treatment group but did not exclude them from the control group. The point here is that if your research design is flawed, you risk generating deeply misleading conclusions. Don't get fooled into thinking that you can patch up a flawed design by focusing on people who share the same observed characteristics.

What is the right way to test the mobilizing effects of a phone call? Randomly assign voters to receive a call or not. Keep track of the frac-

figure is the standard error of the estimated intent-to-treat effect. The larger this number, the more uncertainty surrounds the intent-to-treat estimate. The average treatment effect among those who were reachable by canvassers is estimated by dividing the intent-to-treat estimate (4.7) by the contact rate (0.73), which produces the number 6.3. Door answerers who received the treatment became 6.3 percentage points more likely to vote. The uncertainty of this estimate is measured by its standard error, 3.7.

Finally, the statistical software makes three useful calculations. The first is the 95 percent confidence interval, which spans from −0.9 to 13.5. This type of interval has a 95 percent chance of bracketing the true average treatment effect among door answerers. The second calculation is the one-tailed significance of the estimated treatment effect. When conducting GOTV experiments, it is conventional to expect turnout to rise as a result of the treatment. The so-called null hypothesis is that the treatment failed to increase turnout. The one-tailed significance level states the probability of obtaining an estimate as large as the observed intent-to-treat effect simply by chance. When this probability is below 0.05, as is the case here, the estimate is conventionally dubbed "statistically significant." Naturally, if the experiment were repeated, the results might come out differently. The "power" of an experiment describes the probability that it would produce a statistically significant estimate assuming the observed intent-to-treat effect were the true effect of assignment. In this case, Michelson's experimental design has a 51 percent probability of rejecting the null hypothesis given that the intent-to-treat effect is 4.7 percentage points.

tion of the treatment group that actually received the calls. Compare the voting rates among those originally assigned to the treatment and control groups and divide by the fraction of the treatment group that received the calls. (Or just use the web-based software described in box 12-2.) Because you are comparing the randomly assigned treatment and control groups, the groups have the same expected voting rate, and there is no bias in favor of finding that phone calls work (or don't work).

Another common concern among those who resist experimental research is that a campaign cannot risk extracting a control group from its list of targeted voters. This concern is often based on an unrealistic sense of how effective their mobilization campaign is likely to be (or how close the election is likely to be). If, for example, a state legislative campaign has resources to target 15,000 voters and you remove a control group of 1,500, two things happen. First, the campaign can reallocate its resources to the 13,500 and treat some of them more intensively. Second, your control group will cost the campaign votes in proportion to its effectiveness. Suppose the campaign does an outstanding job of mobilizing and persuading its base of supporters. If left untreated, suppose the control group votes at a rate of 45 percent and votes four to one in favor of your candidate. Had the control group been treated, this group would have voted at a rate of 50 percent and supported your candidate by a five-to-one margin. In the worst-case scenario, the campaign reaps no additional votes from the extra resources it reallocates to the treatment group and loses ninety-five votes. That is probably a much smaller number than the campaign envisioned when it worried about extracting a control group. These kinds of calculations help campaign managers to see that the small short-term risks associated with an experiment are outweighed by the long-term benefits of acquiring knowledge.

Present Your Results

Once you have conducted your experiment, try to present it in a manner that enables it to contribute to the accumulation of scientific knowledge about campaigns. Here is a brief checklist of what to report to your audience.

✓ Describe the experimental setting. When and where was the campaign conducted? What other kinds of campaign activity or public debate might voters have been exposed to?

✓ Describe the experimental treatments. What were the interventions? When were they deployed and by whom? Present the phone or canvassing scripts. Show pictures of the mailings or e-mails.

✓ What were the experimental groups, and from what population were they drawn? Describe the randomization procedure used to assign the groups. Describe the number of observations assigned to each experimental group.[23] Show whether, as expected, the treatment and control groups have similar background attributes, such as average age or past voting rates.

✓ Were the treatments successfully administered to all of the people who were supposed to receive them? If not, what proportion of the treatment group actually received the treatment? Did the control group inadvertently receive your treatment? If so, what proportion of the control group was inadvertently treated?

✓ Briefly explain the source of your voter turnout information and how you dealt with cases in which people in the original treatment groups were not found on the rolls of voters. (Sometimes those not found are classified as nonvoters, and sometimes they are excluded from the analysis altogether.) Check whether the treatment and control groups have similar rates of being found on the voter rolls. Present the voting rates for each experimental group, including the number of observations used to calculate each voting rate.

These are the essential ingredients of any experimental write-up. Obviously, if you have the statistical skills, you can go into much more detail, but do not skip directly to a complex statistical analysis without first walking the reader through the simple facts of the experiment mentioned above. One of the most attractive features of experimentation is that it lends itself to a straightforward and transparent style of presentation.

Strategies for Increasing Electoral Participation

Although much of this book is directed to those who seek to sway elections, it also speaks to those whose larger purpose is to remedy low rates of voter participation. Nowadays about three-fifths of the eligible electorate votes in U.S. presidential elections, and roughly half do so in federal midterm elections. Municipal and special elections sometimes spark voter interest, but more often than not they attract less than one-third of eligible voters.

The question is what can be done to raise turnout in the United States. Proposals abound (see box 12-3). For simplicity, we group them into three categories. The first is a massive constitutional overhaul. Institute a new electoral system that encourages minor parties so that voters will be able to choose from a wide spectrum of candidates. Introduce a system of direct electoral control over policy. Consolidate elections at all levels of government so that voters have to vote only once every two years.

Although these ideas make wonderful discussion topics for college seminars, they cannot be considered serious proposals for policy reform. Even if one were convinced that proportional representation does

---

Box 12-3. Further Reading on Voter Turnout in the United States

The following books span a range of perspectives on why American voter turnout is low or declining. Diagnoses range from the media-centered campaigns to restrictive registration laws to the lack of vigorous party competition. Prescriptions range from civic education to changes in electoral rules.

Adam J. Berinsky, "The Perverse Consequences of Electoral Reform in the United States," *American Politics Research*, vol. 33 (2005): 471–91.

David E. Campbell, *Why We Vote: How Schools and Communities Shape Our Civic Life* (Princeton University Press, 2006).

Benjamin Highton, "Voter Registration and Turnout in the United States," *Perspectives on Politics*, vol. 2 (2004): 507–15.

Jan E. Leighley and Jonathan Nagler, *Who Votes Now? Demographics, Issues, Inequality, and Turnout in the United States* (Princeton University Press, 2013).

Frances Fox Piven and Richard A. Cloward, *Why Americans Still Don't Vote and Why Politicians Want It That Way* (Boston: Beacon Press, 2000).

Stephen J. Rosenstone and John Mark Hansen, *Mobilization, Participation, and Democracy in America* (New York: Macmillan, 1993).

---

a better job of attracting voter participation than other electoral systems (turnout patterns in countries like New Zealand, which have switched to a proportional representation system, call this assumption into question[24]), the chances that the United States will adopt such constitutional reforms are, as it were, statistically indistinguishable from zero. As for direct democracy, it is doubtful whether states that regularly present ballot initiatives and referenda to their citizens enjoy higher voter turnout as a result. And introducing direct democracy at the federal level would require a constitutional revision that fundamentally alters the dual system of representation that currently accords power on a per capita basis in the House of Representatives and on a per state basis in the Senate. Such constitutional revisions are not likely to occur any time soon.

Somewhat more realistic, if only because it is more concrete, is the idea of consolidating the election calendar. Compared with constitutional revisions, this one poses fewer risks of unintended consequences. Consolidating the election calendar might increase voter turnout rates. Parties and candidates would channel their GOTV efforts toward a single campaign, the gravity of which would attract greater interest. The problem is generating the political will to impose uniformity on municipal, county, state, and federal election calendars. It is no accident that some jurisdictions choose to hold their elections at odd times; this is a calculated move by parties and interest groups seeking to diminish the influence of national election tides on their local or state elections.[25]

A second group of proposals involves more modest policy changes related to voting procedures. Allow voters to cast ballots online. Allow ballots to be cast over a three-week period. Permit everyone who so desires to vote by mail. Create a national database that automatically registers people when they turn eighteen or change addresses. Or institute same-day registration nationwide. One might reasonably anticipate that each of these ideas will be adopted one day, but the track record of this kind of tinkering is mixed. Those who have examined the effects of changing balloting and registration rules on patterns of state turnout over time find that the introduction of same-day registration rules in Idaho, Maine, Minnesota, New Hampshire, Wisconsin, and Wyoming was associated with only modest gains in turnout.[26] Permitting voting by mail and early in-person voting also boosted turnout, but again only to a small extent. The Motor Voter Law, which made the registration process easier and more widely accessible, also had small positive effects. These innovations seem to nudge turnout upward, but not markedly so.

The last category of proposals involves some form of voter education. Create hotlines and websites that provide free information about where to vote and what choices will appear on the ballot. Convene public debates among candidates so that voters can learn about where they stand on the issues. Encourage journalists to devote more attention to issues and less to the horse race competition between candidates. These well-intentioned proposals may be worthwhile for a host of reasons, but they seem unlikely to increase voter turnout appreciably. Candidate debates, like Sunday morning talk shows with politicians, typically attract appreciative but tiny audiences. Public interest websites attract little traffic. Journalists who write about policy debates rather than the vicissitudes of electoral fortunes find their work ignored by all but a small constituency of readers. Politics does not interest most people. It is noble but unrealistic to expect nonvoters to seek out edifying news stories, websites, or public events.

Our perspective on how to raise voter turnout is rather different. Examine a range of GOTV tactics and figure out which ones are effective and cost-efficient. By demonstrating what works (and what does not), this systematic inductive approach provides an important signal to those engaged in electoral competition. If the market for campaign services learns from a reliable source that a particular GOTV tactic is a more cost-effective way of garnering votes, we eventually will see campaigns allocate more resources to this tactic.

We should emphasize the word *eventually* in the previous sentence. Findings from scientific studies are not likely to win converts overnight. People who run political campaigns are justifiably skeptical of what passes for research. And even if some of this skepticism could be put to rest by blue-ribbon panels executing studies of the highest quality, the problem of conflicting economic interests remains. Big money is at stake in the market for campaign services, and those who earn their livelihood in this line of work are unlikely to sit still as their product or domain of expertise is threatened. On the one hand, campaign managers sometimes profit from the services they sell, either because they hold a financial stake in firms with which the campaign subcontracts or because they expect to have an ongoing business relationship with the subcontractors. On the other hand, managers also have a financial incentive to win elections, so as to burnish their reputation en route to future consulting work. The tension between these two economic incentives comes into play when campaign managers are able to protect their reputation by employing well-accepted, profitable, but inefficient campaign tactics. In this case, they can have their cake and eat it too, by running "credible" campaigns whose activities make for handsome profits.

If we are correct in our suspicions concerning the cost-inefficiency of campaigns that rely heavily on mass media, digital ads, and automated phone calls, scientific evidence will hasten a gradual evolutionary process. Managers who run inefficient campaigns eventually will be pushed aside by those who prove more successful in electoral competition. Admittedly, the process of natural selection could take a long time to unfold. After all, there are many reasons why elections are won and lost, and the market may have difficulty identifying which tactics are truly associated with success. Perhaps that is how capital-intensive campaigning came to prominence in the first place. Nevertheless, the recent shift in campaign tactics toward more personal interaction with voters increases our confidence that political campaigns are attentive to and influenced by scientific findings.[27]

The Cost-Effectiveness of Turnout versus Persuasion

A great many research questions must be answered before those seeking to sway elections will have reason to embrace GOTV activity as an attractive way to invest campaign dollars. The experimental research reported in this book examines only whether people vote, not how they vote. Before we can say whether cost-effective voter mobilization tactics are also cost-effective vote-generation tactics, we need to see how they compare with persuasive communication. As explained in box 12-4, a persuasion campaign that convinces a voter who would otherwise vote against a ballot measure to vote for it changes the vote margin by two votes, whereas convincing a nonvoter who supports the ballot measure to vote changes the vote margin by one vote. The gains from mobilization are watered down even further if the campaign is unsure whether the nonvoter truly supports the ballot measure. In other words, if persuasion were half as easy as mobilization, it might be more attractive to a political campaign. To what extent do phone calls, direct mail, and other campaign tactics affect voters' preferences?

By comparison to the immense field experimental literature on voter turnout, relatively few rigorous studies have assessed the persuasive effects of campaign communications. Due to the constraints of the secret ballot, it is harder to study vote choice than voter turnout. Experimental researchers must either randomly assign their treatments at the level of the voting precinct, where vote choice can be counted in the aggregate, or gather individual-level data using a postelection survey.[28] Many campaigns are unwilling or unable to randomize their interventions at the precinct level or pay for a large survey. As a result, the literature on persuasion (much of it unpublished) has lagged behind the literature on voter mobilization.

Previous editions of *Get Out the Vote* described every persuasion experiment, but the literature has now grown to a point where a study-by-study summary would be tedious. A comprehensive systematic review of this literature may be found in an essay by Joshua Kalla and David Broockman, who summarized prior research as well as a large number of original studies they conducted in collaboration with door-to-door canvassing campaigns.[29] Kalla and Broockman's reading of the literature is very much in line with ours, and we would call readers' attention to three key points from their review.

First, notwithstanding the enormous resources that campaigns invest in persuading voters during the final two months before a general elec-

Box 12-4. Generating Votes: Mobilization versus Persuasion

In order to see how GOTV fits into crafting a winning campaign, imagine that you are a Republican candidate running for local office. There are 8,000 registered voters, and Election Day is approaching. The 2,000 registered Republicans favor you 80 versus 20 percent, but ordinarily only half of them vote. The remaining 6,000 people in the electorate favor your opponent 67.5 versus 32.5 percent; one-third of them can be expected to vote. So, with 800 votes from registered Republicans and 650 from the rest of the electorate, you are in danger of losing 1,450 to 1,550:

	Voters		Nonvoters	
Intent	Registered Republicans	Others	Registered Republicans	Others
Intend to vote for you	800	650	800	1,300
Intend to vote for your opponent	200	1,350	200	2,700

Thinking about how to win in this situation is really a matter of thinking about where to find at least 100 additional votes. All of the factors that got you those 1,450 votes—your good looks, your record in office, and so forth—are important in shaping the eventual outcome of the election, but the strategic decisions from this point forward must focus on what you will do now to change the expected outcome.

A GOTV strategy aims to transform nonvoters into voters. If you can identify the 2,100 abstainers who would vote for you, try to get at least 100 of them to the polls. Voter identification (ID) programs use brief polls to identify these potential supporters, who will later be targeted for mobilization.

Voter ID programs require planning and money, however. A simpler approach is to focus GOTV attention solely on Republicans. Bear in mind that if you attempt to mobilize some of the 1,000 Republicans who otherwise would not vote, you will need to get at least 167 to the polls because you only gain 60 net votes for every 100 Republicans you mobilize.

Alternatively, a persuasion strategy attempts to convert some of the 1,550 opposing voters into your supporters. Conversions rapidly close the margin of votes between you and your opponent. Just fifty successes would make the race a dead heat. It is also possible to blend persuasion and mobilization strategies, for example, by appealing to the 2,000 Republicans in ways that both mobilize and persuade them.

tion, the experimental evidence suggests that the average effect on candidate choice is very close to zero. In other words, when Republicans and Democrats square off in a general election, efforts to persuade voters about the merits of one candidate or another tend to fall flat. This conclusion holds for TV ads, digital ads, direct mail, and so forth. Even messages that have been shown to work early in the campaign season cease to work down the stretch.

Second, persuasive communication does affect vote preference on ballot measures and choices where party labels are absent. The reason may be that voters know less about ballot measures and primary candidates; that is, in the absence of party cues, information and arguments help them form their vote preferences.

Third, it is possible to amplify persuasive effects through careful field testing before the launch of a persuasive effort, although campaigns seldom try to do so. Typically, they defer to campaign consultants for guidance about what messages to deploy and which audiences should be targeted. Campaign consultants rarely conduct rigorous field tests before rolling out their communications.

In sum, the experimental evidence on persuasion suggests that it is much more difficult than one might think, especially in advance of general elections. Although much research remains to be done, the emerging literature on persuasion is encouraging to those who think that GOTV efforts are the most cost-effective ways of producing votes. It turns out that minds are often difficult and expensive to change, particularly in the closing days of an election involving well-known candidates from major parties. It is hard for a campaign to know in advance whether its persuasive messages will resonate with voters. Although by no means cheap or easy, mobilizing supporters may turn out to be the most dependable and cost-effective way to influence elections, especially when one takes into account the fact that each additional voter will cast votes for many offices and ballot measures.

Scientific Frontiers

Many of the major advances in the history of science have occurred in the wake of the discovery of new measurement technologies. The telescope and the microscope are but two examples of instruments that accelerated the pace of scientific discovery.

The experimental approach to the study of voter mobilization is not only changing the way in which campaign tactics are evaluated, but also changing the way in which social science is practiced. For the first time, social scientists have at their disposal a method for measuring the causal effect of a treatment in a real-world setting. And as field experimentation spreads, social scientists accumulate a diverse set of increasingly reliable measurements of what interventions work and under what conditions. These measurements, in turn, help to guide and refine the theoretical understanding of human behavior. In an earlier era, social scientists were able to speculate in a manner that was largely unconstrained by hard facts, because causal measurements were unreliable. As field experiments usher in hard facts, theorizing necessarily becomes more challenging. Theories must account not only for today's well-established facts, but also for the facts that experiments will soon unearth.

The field experimental movement has brought social scientists into the world and forced them to grapple with the practical problems that political campaigns routinely confront. Social science is replete with theories of action, but how do they measure up when put to the challenge of urging people to vote? Theories of persuasion and opinion change abound, but what happens when these theories are forced to shoulder the burden of persuading voters to support a candidate or cause?

Consider this parting example. In recent years, the hypothesis that "liberals and conservatives rely on different sets of moral foundations" has captured the imaginations of many thinkers on both the right and left.[30] Moral foundations are said to be profoundly important for voter turnout. Survey research suggests that "the higher the salience of care and fairness concerns, the higher the level of voter turnout *among liberals*, while the higher the levels of support for the binding foundations—loyalty, authority, and sanctity—the greater the turnout *among conservatives*."[31] The implication is that GOTV arguments that stress care and fairness concerns will mobilize liberals, while appeals to "binding" foundations will mobilize conservatives. Yet when Gregg Murray and Richard Matland conducted direct mail experiments in Texas and Wisconsin that did just that, they found no support whatsoever for the claim that moral arguments work especially well when they are tailored to specific ideological groups. Moral arguments worked equally well, or badly, regardless of who received them. Is the theory wrong? Or are moral arguments diluted when communicated by mail? Or did the mail reach the wrong targets due to the difficulty of identifying liberals and conservatives based on the information available in the voter file? When tests are conducted under real-world conditions, politics is a humbling laboratory from which few theories emerge unscathed. The challenge is to continually innovate and test until the right blend of theoretical inspiration and practical application produces reliable results.

Meta-Analysis of Door-to-Door Canvassing Experiments

This technical appendix describes how we assembled and analyzed the results from randomized experiments on door-to-door canvassing. Table A-1 lists the results from each distinct study in which door-to-door canvassing was evaluated experimentally. Table entries were in most cases gleaned from the results presented by the research teams, whether published or unpublished; in some cases, we updated the analysis to take account of various methodological nuances, such as clustered assignment. By "distinct study" we mean a study in a given election year involving a single organization. For example, in their book *Mobilizing Inclusion,* Lisa García Bedolla and Melissa Michelson report dozens of canvassing experiments that People Improving Communities through Organizing (PICO) conducted in the weeks leading up to the November 2008 general elections. Rather than list each of these experiments individually, table A-1 combines the estimates from this family of studies into a single weighted average, where the weights are the inverse of each experiment's squared standard error. In cases where the experiment tested two or more versions of canvassing (for example, with different scripts), we have combined the results from all of the treatment arms into a single treatment.

The estimates reported in table A-1 are of the treatment effect among

Table A-1. Results of Door-to-Door Canvassing Experiments

Context	Study	CACE	SE	Control turnout	Advocacy?
1998G	Gerber & Green (New Haven)	8.4	2.6	30% to 50%	
2000G	Green & Gerber (OR)	8.4	4.5	50% to 70%	
2001G	Green et al. (Bridgeport)	14.4	5.3	Under 30%	
2001G	Green et al. (Columbus)	9.7	7.9	Under 30%	
2001G	Green et al. (Detroit)	7.8	4.5	30% to 50%	
2001G	Green et al. (Minneapolis)	10.1	8.7	Under 30%	
2001G	Green et al. (Raleigh)	0.2	3.2	Under 30%	
2001G	Green et al. (St. Paul)	14.4	6.4	30% to 50%	
2001G	Michelson (Dos Palos)	4.1	2.2	Under 30%	
2002G	Bennion (IN)	0.6	5.1	30% to 50%	
2002G	Gillespie (St. Louis)	0.8	1.0	Under 30%	
2002G	Michelson (Fresno)	3.5	1.6	Under 30%	
2002G	Nickerson et al. (MI)	16.8	15.9	30% to 50%	X
2002M	Gillespie (Newark)	−7.9	27.9	30% to 50%	X
2002P	Nickerson (Denver)	8.6	4.2	30% to 50%	
2002P	Nickerson (Minneapolis)	10.9	4.1	Under 30%	
2002R	Gillespie (Newark)	1.2	7.3	Under 30%	X
2003G	Arceneaux (Kansas City)	7.0	3.9	Under 30%	X
2003G	Michelson (Phoenix)	12.9	1.8	Under 30%	X
2004G	LeVan (Bakersfield)	24.2	7.5	30% to 50%	
2004G	Matland & Murray (TX)	7.4	4.3	30% to 50%	
2005G	Anonymous (VA)	3.5	2.4	30% to 50%	X
2005G	Nickerson (VA)	27	15.4	Under 30%	X
2006G	Bedolla & Michelson (AACU)	−3.4	8.1	30% to 50%	
2006G	Bedolla & Michelson (CARECEN)	−0.5	2.9	50% to 70%	
2006G	Bedolla & Michelson (CCAEJ)	4.4	5.9	50% to 70%	
2006G	Bedolla & Michelson (PICO)	3.1	3.9	30% to 50%	
2006G	Bedolla & Michelson (SCOPE)	6.6	2.1	30% to 50%	
2006G	Nickerson (Dearborn)	8.7	3.8	30% to 50%	
2006G	Nickerson (Grand Rapids)	−0.4	4.3	Under 30%	X
2006P	Bedolla & Michelson (CARECEN)	2.2	1.8	Under 30%	
2006P	Bedolla & Michelson (CCAEJ)	43.1	12.5	Under 30%	
2006P	Bedolla & Michelson (SCOPE)	2.6	3.3	Under 30%	

Context	Study	CACE	SE	Control turnout	Advocacy?
2007G	Davenport (Boston)	13.4	7.0	Under 30%	
2007P	Bedolla & Michelson (AACU)	−1.4	2	Under 30%	
2008G	Arceneaux et al. (CA)	10.7	10.2	Above 70%	
2008G	Bedolla & Michelson (CARECEN)	0.7	6.0	50% to 70%	
2008G	Bedolla & Michelson (CCAEJ)	0.3	4.5	50% to 70%	
2008G	Bedolla & Michelson (PICO)	1.2	1.7	50% to 70%	
2008G	Bedolla & Michelson (SCOPE)	0.5	1.1	Above 70%	
2008P	Bedolla & Michelson (CARECEN)	4.0	2.6	Under 30%	
2008P	Bedolla & Michelson (CCAEJ)	3.9	2.8	Under 30%	
2008P	Bedolla & Michelson (PICO)	1.0	1.3	Under 30%	
2008PP	Bedolla & Michelson (CARECEN)	0.9	3.2	50% to 70%	
2008PP	Bedolla & Michelson (PICO)	9.0	3.4	30% to 50%	
2008PP	Bedolla & Michelson (SCOPE)	3.4	2.3	50% to 70%	
2008P	Bailey et al. (WI)	1.5	2.0	50% to 70%	X
2010G	Barton et al. (Midwest)	−7.7	3.8	50% to 70%	X
2010G	Bryant (San Francisco)	−32.9	21.6	50% to 70%	
2010G	Cann et al. (UT)	8.2	4.6	50% to 70%	
2010G	Hill & Lachelier (FL)	1.8	9.3	Under 30%	
2014R	Green et al. (TX)	3.1	1.8	30% to 50%	
2015M	Michelson (WA)	11.0	5.6	Under 30%	X
2016P	Michelson (WA)	1.0	2.9	Above 70%	X
2016P	Kalla & Broockman (NC)	2.3	1.0	50% to 70%	X
2016P	Broockman & Green (AZ)	2.6	1.7	50% to 70%	

Notes: Context refers to the election year and type, where G = general; M = municipal; P = primary; PP = presidential primary; R = runoff. CACE = the estimated complier average causal effect (that is, the average treatment effect among compliers); SE = standard error of the estimated CACE. Advocacy refers to appeals that urge support for candidates or causes. AACU = African-American Churches United; CARECEN = Central American Resource Center; CCAEJ = Center for Community Action and Environmental Justice; PICO = People Improving Communities through Organizing; SCOPE = Strategic Concepts in Organizing and Policy Education.

compliers—that is, those who are reachable if assigned to the treatment group. In the statistics literature, this quantity is termed the CACE, for complier average causal effect. Since these experiments encountered one-sided noncompliance (some of those who are assigned to the treatment go untreated, but no one in the control group inadvertently receives treatment), these estimates also tell us about the average treatment effect among those who receive treatment.

The estimated CACEs were obtained by (1) computing the difference between the voting rate in the assigned treatment group and the assigned control group and (2) dividing this number by the proportion of the treatment group that was contacted by canvassers. No control variables were used in this analysis (except, in some instances, indicator variables marking each block within which random assignment occurred). This approach provides the most straightforward reading of the results and avoids the possible biases that may be introduced through post hoc adjustment.

We exclude from this list a few studies that assign the treatment group to a package of treatments that includes canvassing. For example, Michael Alvarez and his colleagues evaluated a voter mobilization campaign that included phone calls, e-mail, and direct mail in addition to canvassing.[1] We also eliminated a handful of early studies that did not measure contact rates. For example, Joel Middleton conducted an evaluation of Election Day canvassing in urban areas in battleground states during the 2004 presidential election.[2]

This collection of estimated CACEs is summarized using a random effects model, which allows for treatment effects to vary according to the type of canvasser, target population, or electoral context. For all studies combined, we obtain an average estimate of 4.0, with a 95 percent confidence interval that ranges from 2.8 to 5.2. That estimate implies one vote per 25 contacts.

As we noted in previous editions of this book, there is reason to suppose that mobilization effects are weaker when turnout is especially low or high. Table A-2 displays the average CACEs according to the vote propensity of the target population, as gauged by the turnout rate in the control group. These estimates are calculated using random effects meta-analysis. When turnout in the control group was below 30 percent, the average CACE is 4.8. This figure climbs to 6.2 when turnout in the control group is between 30 and 50 percent and falls sharply thereafter. This pattern is also apparent when we restrict our attention to canvassing efforts that were nonpartisan in nature. Here, the average CACE is

Table A-2. Meta-Analysis Results, by Base Rate of Turnout

Turnout rate in the control group	All canvassing: Average CACE	Nonadvocacy canvassing only: Average CACE
Under 30%	4.8 [2.6, 7.0] (23)	3.3 [1.4, 5.2] (17)
30% to 50%	6.2 [4.2, 8.2] (16)	6.7 [4.4, 9.0] (13)
50% to 70%	1.8 [0.4, 3.3] (14)	2.2 [0.5, 3.9] (11)
70% and higher	0.7 [−1.3, 2.7] (3)	0.6 [−1.5, 2.8] (2)

Notes: Estimates were obtained through random effects meta-analysis; 95 percent confidence intervals are in brackets. The number of distinct experiments is in parentheses.

6.7 percentage points among the thirteen studies that evaluated canvassing drives directed at populations whose turnout was between 30 and 50 percent. The estimated CACEs are less than half as large when we consider the thirty studies in which nonpartisan efforts were directed at populations with higher or lower turnout.

The implied number of contacts needed to produce one vote varies depending on the vote propensity of the target group. A CACE of 6.7 implies that fifteen contacts are required to produce one vote. Note that this contact-per-vote figure does not take into account possible within-household spillovers.

Meta-Analysis of Direct Mail Experiments

This technical appendix describes how we assembled and analyzed the results from randomized experiments on direct mail. Table B-1 lists the results from each distinct study in which direct mail was evaluated experimentally. Table entries were in most cases gleaned from the results presented by the research teams, whether published or unpublished; in some cases, we updated the analysis to take account of various methodological nuances, such as clustered assignment. By "distinct study" we mean a study in a given election year involving a single organization. For example, in their book *Mobilizing Inclusion*, Lisa García Bedolla and Melissa Michelson report eight mail experiments that the PICO organization conducted in the weeks leading up to the November 2006 elections. Rather than list each of these experiments individually, table B-1 combines the estimates from this family of studies into a single weighted average, where the weights are the inverse of each experiment's squared standard error. In cases where the experimental treatment comprised multiple mailings, the entry in the table reflects the increase in turnout per mailer.

We exclude from this list a few studies that assign the treatment group to a package of treatments that includes direct mail. For example, Michael Alvarez and his colleagues evaluated a voter mobilization campaign that included phone calls, e-mail, and canvassing in addition to direct mail.[1]

No control variables were used when calculating the effect size for each study (except, in some instances, indicator variables marking each block within which random assignment occurred). This approach provides the most straightforward reading of the results, without danger of post hoc adjustment.

Table B-1 categorizes the mailers according to whether they convey a conventional or social pressure message. Social pressure messages (see chapter 11) urge turnout through some combination of the forceful assertion of social norms, presentation of a voter's record of turnout in past elections, or promise to monitor and disclose this information in the future. The category of conventional mailings is subdivided according to whether the message is nonpartisan or advocates on behalf of an issue or candidate.

A total of 104 distinct studies provides the database for our meta-analysis. For each category of mail—social pressure, nonsocial-pressure advocacy, and nonsocial-pressure nonpartisan—the collection of estimated effects is summarized using random effects meta-analysis, which allows for treatment effects to vary according to the type of canvasser, target population, or electoral context. For nonpartisan mailers that do not invoke social pressure, we find an average effect on turnout of 0.468 of a percentage point per mailer with a 95 percent confidence interval ranging from 0.228 to 0.708. When we extract from this set of fifty-nine distinct studies the forty-nine studies that invoke neither gratitude, nor reminders of past pledges to vote, nor the soft social pressure tactics of the 2006 or 2007 Michigan studies' "Civic Duty" mailer, the estimate drops to 0.296 with a confidence interval ranging from 0.138 to 0.454. Advocacy mailers that do not invoke social pressure have an average effect on turnout of 0.078 with a confidence interval ranging from –0.072 to 0.229. Social pressure mailers are a disparate category with widely varying effects (see chapter 11), but when pooled have an average effect on turnout of 2.146 with a confidence interval ranging from 1.443 to 2.859.

Table B-1. Results of Direct Mailing Experiments

Context	Study	Average treatment effect	SE	Advocacy?	Social pressure?
1998G	Gerber & Green (New Haven)	0.5	0.3		
1999G	Gerber & Green (New Haven)	0.3	0.2		
1999G	Gerber et al. (CT and NJ)	0	0.1	X	
2000G	Green (NAACP)	0	0.5	X	
2002G	Ramirez (NALEO)	0.1	0.1		
2002G	Wong (Los Angeles County)	1.3	1		
2002M	Gillespie (Newark)	−1.1	2.5	X	
2002P	Cardy (PA)	−0.2	0.5	X	
2002P	Gerber (PA)	−0.1	0.3	X	
2002S	Gillespie (Newark)	−1.6	2	X	
2003M	Niven (West Palm Beach)	1.4	2.1		
2004G	Anonymous (MN)	−0.9	0.7		
2004G	Matland & Murray (Brownsville)	2.9	1.1		
2004G	Trivedi (Queens County)	1.1	1.7		
2005G	Anonymous (VA)	0	0.1	X	
2006G	Barabas et al. (FL)	0.3	0.6		
2006G	Bedolla & Michelson (APALC)	1.1	0.5		
2006G	Bedolla & Michelson (OCAPICA)	−0.5	0.8		
2006G	Bedolla & Michelson (PICO)	−3.2	1		
2006G	Gray & Potter (Franklin County)	−2.9	2.7	X	
2006G	Mann (MO)	−0.1	0	X	
2006G	Anonymous (MD)	−0.4	0.3	X	
2006P	Bedolla & Michelson (APALC)	0	0.3		
2006P	Bedolla & Michelson (PICO)	1.1	0.8		
2006P	Gerber et al. (MI)	1.8	0.3		
2006P	Gerber et al. (MI)	5.2	0.2		X
2007G	Gerber et al. (MI)	1.8	0.9		
2007G	Gerber et al. (MI)	5.1	0.5		X
2007G	Mann (KY)	2.7	0.2		X
2007G	Panagopoulos (Gilroy)	−0.3	1.4		
2007G	Panagopoulos (IA and MI)	2.2	0.8		X
2008G	Keane & Nickerson (CO)	−0.7	0.3		
2008G	Nickerson (APIAVote)	−1.2	0.6		
2008G	Nickerson (FRESC)	−0.2	0.7		
2008G	Nickerson (Latina Initiative)	0.2	0.3		
2008G	Nickerson (NCL)	1.5	0.6		
2008G	Nickerson (Voto Latino)	−0.6	0.3		
2008G	Rogers & Middleton (OR)	−0.1	0.5	X	
2008P	Enos (Los Angeles County)	2	1.1		
2008PP	Barabas et al. (FL)	−2.7	0.6		
2008PP	Nickerson & White (NC)	0.8	0.7		
2008PP	Nickerson & White (NC)	1	0.3		X
2009G	Larimer & Condon (Cedar Falls)	0.7	2.4		X
2009G	Mann (Houston)	1.2	0.6		
2009G	Panagopoulos (NJ)	2.5	0.5		
2009G	Panagopoulos (NJ)	2	0.5		X
2009S	Abrajano & Panagopoulos (Queens)	1.1	0.4		X
2009S	Mann (Houston)	1.1	0.5		
2009S	Panagopoulos (Staten Island)	2	1		

Context	Study	Average treatment effect	SE	Advocacy?	Social pressure?
2009S	Sinclair et al. (Chicago)	4.4	0.6		X
2010G	Anonymous (NV)	0.2	0.5		X
2010G	Barton et al. (unknown state)	−2.2	1.6	X	
2010G	Bryant (San Francisco)	1.7	2		
2010G	Gerber et al. (CT)	2	0.5	X	
2010G	Gerber et al. (CT)	0.4	0.6		
2010G	Gerber et al. (CT)	0.9	0.2		
2010G	Mann & Mayhew (ID, MD, NC, and OH)	2	0.4		
2010G	Murray & Matland (TX and WI)	1.7	0.7		
2010G	Murray & Matland (TX and WI)	1.5	0.7		X
2010G	Rogers et al. (17 states)	0.6	0.1		
2010M	Panagopoulos (Lancaster)	−1.1	1		
2010P	Binder et al. (San Bernardino County)	−0.1	0.5	X	
2010P	Binder et al. (CA)	−0.1	0.5		
2010P	Panagopoulos (GA)	2.5	0.6		
2011G	Mann & Kalla (ME)	2.4	0.6		
2011G	Panagopoulos (Lexington)	1	0.8		
2011G	Panagopoulos et al. (Hawthorne)	−0.4	0.7		
2011G	Panagopoulos et al. (Hawthorne)	2.2	0.6		X
2011M	Panagopoulos (Key West)	1.1	0.5		X
2011M	Panagopoulos (Key West)	−0.1	0.4		
2011S	Mann (NV)	0.9	0.3		
2011S	Panagopoulos (Charlestown)	−0.3	0.5		
2012G	Citrin et al. (VA and TN)	0.7	0.4		
2012G	Doherty & Adler (battleground state)	0.1	0.2	X	
2012G	Levine & Mann (GA and OH)	0.2	0.3		
2012G	Mann et al. (FL)	0.0	0.0		
2012M	Panagopoulos (VA)	0	0.6		
2012P	Condon et al. (IA)	2.8	0.6		X
2012P	Condon et al. (IA)	0.4	0.9	X	
2012P	Condon et al. (IA)	2.7	0.9		
2012P	Shi (NC)	−0.7	0.5	X	
2012R	Gerber et al. (WI)	1.1	0.7		
2012R	Rogers et al. (WI)	1	0.3		X
2013G	Biggers (VA)	0.1	0.2		
2013G	Matland & Murray (MN, OH, TX, and VA)	0.4	0.3		
2013M	Matland & Murray (El Paso)	0.1	0.4		
2013M	Murray & Matland (WI and TX)	0.4	0.2		
2014G	Broockman & Green (CA)	0.3	0.1	X	
2014G	Cubbison (NC)	−0.1	0.1	X	
2014G	Gerber et al. (17 states)	0.7	0.1		X
2014G	Gerber et al. (MS)	3.4	0.4		X
2014G	Gerber et al. (AR, FL, GA, KS, MA, MI, and WI)	0.4	0.1		
2014G	Gerber et al. (AK, GA, LA, MI, NC, and TX)	0.8	0.2		X
2014P	Green et al. (TX)	0.1	0.5	X	
2014P	Hill & Kousser (CA)	0.5	0.1		
2014P	Hughes et al. (CA [information])	0.5	0.1		
2014P	Hughes et al. (CA [partisan])	0.5	0.1	X	
2015G	Mann et al. (NJ, VA)	2.2	0.1		X
2015M	Michelson (WA)	6.4	1.6	X	
2016G	Mann & Fischer (NC)	1.3	0.5		X

Context	Study	Average treatment effect	SE	Advocacy?	Social pressure?
2016G	Mann et al. (NC)	1.0	0.4		X
2016G	Costa et al. (CO)	3.5	1.3		
2016P	Sweeney (IL)	1.7	1.1		X
2016P	Costa et al. (PA)	4.5	2.2		
2016S	Hassell (MI)	0.4	0.8	X	
2017G	Endres & Panagopoulos (VA)	0.0	0.5		

Notes: Context refers to the election year and type, where G = general; M = municipal; P = primary; PP = presidential primary; R = runoff. SE = standard error of the estimated CACE. Advocacy refers to appeals that urge support for candidates or causes. Social pressure refers to appeals that emphasize compliance with the social norm of civic participation. APALC = Asian Pacific American Legal Center; APIAVote = Asian and Pacific Islander American Vote; FRESC = Front Range Economic Strategy Center; NAACP = National Association for the Advancement of Colored People; NALEO = National Association of Latino Elected Officials; NCL = National Council of La Raza; OCAPICA = Orange County Asian and Pacific Islander Community Alliance; PICO = People Improving Communities through Organizing; SEIU = Service Employees International Union.

Meta-Analysis of Phone-Call Experiments

his technical appendix describes how we assembled and analyzed the results from randomized experiments on phone calls. Table C-1 lists the results from each distinct study in which phone calls were evaluated experimentally. Table entries were in most cases gleaned from the results presented in published or unpublished reports; in some cases, we updated the analysis to take account of various methodological nuances, such as clustered assignment. By "distinct study" we mean a study in a given election year involving a single organization. For example, in their book *Mobilizing Inclusion*, Lisa García Bedolla and Melissa Michelson report six experiments that the Orange County Asian and Pacific Islander Community Alliance (OCAPICA) conducted in the weeks leading up to the November 2006 elections. Rather than list each of these experiments individually, table C-1 combines the estimates from this family of studies into a single weighted average, where the weights are the inverse of each experiment's squared standard error.

For phone bank studies involving live callers, the estimates reported in table C-1 gauge the treatment effect among compliers (that is, those who are reachable if assigned to the treatment group). In the statistics literature, this quantity is termed the CACE, for complier average causal effect. Since these experiments encountered one-sided noncompliance

Table C-1. Results of Phone-Call Experiments

Context	Study	CACE for Live Calls, ITT for Robo	SE	Robo	Volunteer	Professional
1998G	Gerber & Green (New Haven)	−1.9	2.4			X
1998G	Gerber & Green (West Haven)	−0.5	2			X
2000G	Green (NAACP)	2.3	2.3			X
2000G	Green & Gerber (Youth Vote 2000)	4.9	1.7		X	
2000G	Nickerson (Youth Vote)	2.3	2.5		X	
2001G	Nickerson (Seattle)	−0.6	0.9	X		
2002G	Gerber & Green (IA and MI)	0.4	0.5			X
2002G	McNulty (Cal Dems)	−8.5	6		X	
2002G	McNulty (No on D)	0.5	2.6			X
2002G	McNulty (Youth Vote)	12.9	5.5		X	
2002G	Nickerson (Youth Vote Coalition)	0.5	0.6		X	
2002G	Nickerson (Youth Vote Coalition)	3.2	0.7			X
2002G	Nickerson et al. (MI)	3.2	1.7		X	
2002G	Ramirez (NALEO)	4.6	1.8		X	
2002G	Ramirez (NALEO)	0	0.2	X		
2002G	Wong (Los Angeles County)	2.3	2.4		X	
2002P	Green (PA)	−0.1	5.5			X
2003G	Michelson et al. (NJ)	10.5	3.6		X	
2003G	Nickerson (MI)	1.4	0.9		X	
2003S	McNulty (Cal Dems)	−5.3	6.2		X	
2004G	Arceneaux et al. (IL)	2	1.2			X
2004G	Green & Karlan (MO and NC)	0	0.3	X		
2004G	Ha & Karlan (MO and NC)	0.8	0.6			X
2005G	Panagopoulos (Albany)	0.1	1.3			X
2005G	Panagopoulos (Rochester)	0.9	1.1			X
2006G	Barabas et al. (FL)	−3	8		X	
2006G	Bedolla & Michelson (APALC)	5.3	2.4		X	
2006G	Bedolla & Michelson (APALC)	3.4	1.7		X	
2006G	Bedolla & Michelson (NALEO)	0.7	1.5		X	
2006G	Bedolla & Michelson (OCAPICA)	2.8	1.9		X	
2006G	Bedolla & Michelson (PICO)	−1	2.7		X	
2006G	Michelson et al. (Los Angeles County)	9.3	3.2		X	
2006P	Bedolla & Michelson (APALC)	2.7	1.5		X	
2006P	Bedolla & Michelson (NALEO)	2.1	2.4		X	
2006P	Shaw et al. (TX)	0.4	0.3	X		
2006S	Middleton (CA)	3.9	1.2		X	
2008G	Bedolla & Michelson (NALEO)	−1.2	2.2		X	
2008G	Gerber et al. (ME, MO, and NJ)	0.1	0.6			X
2008P	Bedolla & Michelson (OCAPICA)	11.1	2.1		X	
2008P	Bedolla & Michelson (PICO)	−1.9	3		X	
2008P,G	Green (MI)	1.9	0.5	X*		
2008PP	Nickerson & Rogers (PA)	2.8	1.3			X
2009G	Green et al. (IA and MI)	−0.1	1.7		X	
2010G	Bryant (San Francisco)	−7	8.5		X	
2010G	Gerber et al. (CA, IA, and NV)	0.1	0.6			X
2010G	Gerber et al. (CO, CT, and FL)	1.3	0.7			X
2010G	Mann & Klofstad (IL, MI, NY, and PA)	0.4	0.3			X
2010G	Mann & Klofstad (FL, IA, IL, ME, MI, MN, NM, NY, OH, PA, and SC)	0.6	0.2			X

Context	Study	CACE for Live Calls, ITT for Robo	SE	Robo	Volunteer	Professional
2011G	Mann & Kalla (ME)	7	5.8			X
2011G	McCabe & Michelson (San Mateo County)	8.4	5.1		X	
2013G	Collins et al. (VA)	7.8	4.3		X	
2013G	Mann & Lebron (WA)	1.7	1.7			X
2013S	Pringle et al. (Palo Alto)	4.4	2.2		X	
2014P	Gerber et al. (MI, MO, TN)	2.3	0.7			X
2014P	Gerber et al. (MI, MO, TN)	1.4	0.7			X
2014P	Zelizer (TX)	0.6	0.3	X		
2014G	Gerber et al. (CO)	1.2	1.4			X
2014P	Kling & Stratmann (GA, NE, NM, OH, PA, VA)	0.3	0.2	X		
2014G	Bedolla et al. (NALEO)	1.2	0.5		X	
2014G	Bedolla et al. (CoCo)	14.3	9.1		X	
2014G	Bedolla et al. (AAAJ)	2.2	4.6		X	

Notes: * This robocall used the social pressure script described in chapter 6. Context refers to the election year and type, where G = general; M = municipal; P = primary; PP = presidential primary; R = runoff. CACE = the estimated complier average causal effect (that is, the average treatment effect among compliers); SE = standard error of the estimated CACE. Advocacy refers to appeals that urge support for candidates or causes. For experiments involving robocalls, the estimate is the average intent-to-treat effect, which ignores contact rates. APALC =Asian Pacific American Legal Center; NAACP = National Association for the Advancement of Colored People; NALEO = National Association of Latino Elected Officials; OCAPICA = Orange County Asian and Pacific Islander Community Alliance; PICO = People Improving Communities through Organizing.

(some of those who are assigned to the treatment go untreated, but no one in the control group inadvertently receives treatment), these estimates also tell us about the average treatment effect among those who receive treatment. The estimated CACEs were obtained by (1) computing the difference between the voting rate in the assigned treatment group and the assigned control group and (2) dividing this number by the proportion of the treatment group that was contacted by callers. For studies involving robocalls, table entries represent intent-to-treat estimates, and no adjustment is made for contact rates (which tend to be very high, as they comprise both direct contacts and voicemail).

We exclude from this list a few studies that assign the treatment group to a package of treatments that includes phone calls. For example, Michael Alvarez and his colleagues evaluated a voter mobilization campaign that included canvassing, e-mail, and direct mail in addition to phone calls.[1]

No control variables were used when calculating the effect size for each study (except, in some instances, indicator variables marking each block within which random assignment occurred). This approach provides the most straightforward reading of the results and avoids the possible biases that may be introduced through post hoc adjustment.

Table C-1 categorizes the phone calls according to whether they were conducted by volunteer phone banks using live callers, commercial phone banks using live callers, or commercial phone banks using prerecorded messages. We exclude the one study of prerecorded social pressure messages, as the large effects found in that study are uncharacteristic of prerecorded messages generally (see chapter 6).

The estimates from these studies provide the database for our meta-analysis. For each category of call—volunteer, commercial, or prerecorded—the collection of estimated effects is summarized using random effects meta-analysis, which allows for treatment effects to vary according to the type of caller, target population, or electoral context.

Volunteer calls have been the subject of thirty-two distinct experiments. Random effects meta-analysis of the estimated CACEs indicates that contact with volunteer callers raises turnout by 2.800 percentage points, with a 95 percent confidence interval ranging from 1.756 to 3.844.

Commercial phone banks have been the subject of twenty-two distinct experiments. Random effects meta-analysis of the estimated CACEs from these studies renders an estimated effect of 0.947 of a percentage point, with a 95 percent confidence interval ranging from 0.528 to 1.366.

Across six distinct studies of robocalls, meta-analysis produces an average intent-to-treat effect of 0.234 of a percentage point, with a 95 percent confidence interval ranging from 0.039 to 0.430. It should be noted, however, that this estimate becomes small and statistically insignificant when we score the treatment according to the number of calls made, as the two most recent studies find that heavy dosages of robocalls achieve nothing beyond small dosages.

Notes

Chapter One

1. Louis-Philippe Beland and Sara Oloomi, "Party Affiliation and Public Spending: Evidence from U.S. Governors." *Economic Inquiry,* vol. 55, no. 2 (2017): 982–95.

2. Justin de Benedictis-Kessner and Christopher Warshaw, "Mayoral Partisanship and Municipal Fiscal Policy," *The Journal of Politics,* vol. 78, no. 4 (October 2016): 1124–38.

3. Bernard L. Fraga and Eitan D. Hersh, "Are Americans Stuck in Uncompetitive Enclaves? An Appraisal of U.S. Electoral Competition." *Quarterly Journal of Political Science,* vol. 13, no. 3 (2018): 291-311.

4. Hal Malchow, *The New Political Targeting* (Washington, D.C.: *Campaigns & Elections Magazine,* 2003), pp. 281–82.

Chapter Two

1. Kevin Arceneaux, Alan S. Gerber, and Donald P. Green, "A Cautionary Note on the Use of Matching to Estimate Causal Effects: An Empirical Example Comparing Matching Estimates to an Experimental Benchmark," *Sociological Methods and Research,* vol. 39 (2010): 256–82.

2. For more discussion of this and other issues related to experimental design and analysis, see Alan S. Gerber and Donald P. Green, *Field Experiments: Design, Analysis, and Interpretation* (New York: W. W. Norton, 2012).

3. Alan S. Gerber and Donald P. Green, "The Effects of Canvassing, Direct Mail, and Telephone Contact on Voter Turnout: A Field Experiment," *American Political Science Review,* vol. 94 (2000): 653–63; Alan S. Gerber and Donald P.

Green, "Correction to Gerber and Green (2000), Replication of Disputed Findings, and Reply to Imai (2005)," *American Political Science Review,* vol. 99 (2005): 301–13.

4. Daron R. Shaw, Donald P. Green, James G. Gimpel, and Alan S. Gerber, "Do Robotic Calls from Credible Sources Influence Voter Turnout or Vote Choice? Evidence from a Randomized Field Experiment," *Journal of Political Marketing,* vol. 11 (2012): 231–45.

5. Neil Malhotra, Melissa R. Michelson, and Ali Adam Valenzuela, "Emails from Official Sources Can Increase Turnout," *Quarterly Journal of Political Science,* vol. 7 (2012): 321–32.

6. Donald P. Green and Oliver McClellan, "The Effects of Election Festivals on Voter Turnout: A Field Experiment Conducted During a Presidential Election" (July 9, 2017). Available at SSRN (http://dx.doi.org/10.2139/ssrn.2999305).

Chapter Three

1. See "More Outside Spending in Senate Races Goes to Digital," spending on general election races through October 10, 2014, Federal Election Commission (www.nytimes.com/interactive/2014/10/16/upshot/100000003177162 .embedded.html?_r=0), suggesting that less than 5 percent of all expenditures by senatorial campaigns go to fieldwork.

2. Ryan D. Enos and Eitan D. Hersh, "Party Activists as Campaign Advertisers: The Ground Campaign as a Principal-Agent Problem," *American Political Science Review,* vol. 109 (2015): 252–78.

3. In the first edition of this book, we defined contact to include speaking to a voter's housemate. Thus, if a canvasser spoke to eight people at different addresses and each household contained an average of 1.5 voters, we counted that as twelve contacts. Because recent experiments have measured contact with the targeted individual (as opposed to household members), we distinguish between direct contact (speaking with the targeted individual) and indirect contact (speaking with the target's housemate).

4. On instructions to canvassers, see Ann Beaudry and Bob Schaeffer, *Winning Local and State Elections: The Guide to Organizing Your Campaign* (New York: Free Press, 1986); Catherine Shaw, *The Campaign Manager: Running and Winning Local Elections,* 5th ed. (Boulder, Colo.: Westview Press, 2014). Shaw (p. 132) advises, "When training canvassers, I tell them never to talk about the issues. That is for the candidate or the campaign team. No canvasser, I don't care how closely related to the campaign, can possibly know how a candidate stands on all the issues. So what do canvassers say when asked a question at the door? They can say, 'That is a good question. Why don't you give [the candidate] a call and ask him or her?' The only thing canvassers can truthfully say is why they are out working for the candidate."

5. Melissa R. Michelson, "Getting Out the Latino Vote: How Door-to-Door Canvassing Influences Voter Turnout in Rural Central California," *Political Behavior,* vol. 25 (2003): 247–63.

6. Melissa R. Michelson, "Meeting the Challenge of Latino Voter Mobilization," *Annals of the American Academy of Political and Social Science,* vol. 601 (2005): 85–101.

7. Alan S. Gerber and Donald P. Green, "The Effects of Canvassing, Direct Mail, and Telephone Contact on Voter Turnout: A Field Experiment," *American Political Science Review,* vol. 94 (2000): 653–63; Alan S. Gerber and Donald P. Green, "Correction to Gerber and Green (2000), Replication of Disputed Findings, and Reply to Imai (2005)," *American Political Science Review,* vol. 99, no. 2 (2005): 301–13.

8. Elizabeth A. Bennion, "Caught in the Ground Wars: Mobilizing Voters during a Competitive Congressional Campaign," *Annals of the American Academy of Political and Social Science,* vol. 601 (2005): 123–41.

9. Gregg R. Murray and Richard E. Matland, "An Experimental Test of Mobilization Effects in a Latino Community," *Political Research Quarterly,* vol. 65 (2012): 192–205.

10. Damon M. Cann and others, "Incentives and Voter Turnout: A Field Experiment," paper presented at the Annual Meeting of the Midwest Political Science Association, Chicago, April 1, 2010.

11. Donald P. Green and Alan S. Gerber, "Getting Out the Youth Vote: Results from Randomized Field Experiments," unpublished manuscript (Yale University, Institution for Social and Policy Studies, 2001).

12. Kevin Arceneaux, "Using Cluster Randomized Field Experiments to Study Voting Behavior," *Annals of the American Academy of Political and Social Science,* vol. 601 (2005): 169–79; Donald P. Green and Melissa R. Michelson, "ACORN Experiments in Minority Voter Mobilization," in *The People Shall Rule: ACORN, Community Organizing, and the Struggle for Economic Justice,* edited by Robert Fisher (Vanderbilt University Press, 2009), pp. 235–48.

13. Betsy Sinclair, Margaret A. McConnell, Melissa R. Michelson, and Lisa García Bedolla, "Local Canvassing: The Efficacy of Grassroots Voter Mobilization," *Political Communication,* vol. 30 (2013): 42–57.

14. Melissa R. Michelson, Margaret A. McConnell, and Lisa García Bedolla, "Heeding the Call: The Effect of Targeted Two-Round Phone Banks on Voter Turnout," *Journal of Politics,* vol. 71 (2009): 1549–63.

15. Donald P. Green, Alan S. Gerber, and David W. Nickerson, "Getting Out the Vote in Local Elections: Results from Six Door-to-Door Canvassing Experiments," *Journal of Politics,* vol. 65 (2003): 1083–96.

16. Green and Gerber, "Getting Out the Youth Vote."

17. Michelson, "Meeting the Challenge of Latino Voter Mobilization."

18. Lisa García Bedolla and Melissa Michelson, *Mobilizing Inclusion: Transforming the Electorate through Get-Out-the-Vote Campaigns* (Yale University Press, 2012). Lisa García Bedolla, Marisa Abrajano, and Jane Junn, "Testing New Technologies in Mobilizing Voters of Color: An Analysis from the November 2014 Elections" (The James Irvine Foundation, 2015).

19. Joshua L. Kalla and David E. Broockman. "The Minimal Persuasive Effects of Campaign Contact in General Elections: Evidence from 49 Field Experiments." *American Political Science Review,* vol. 112, no. 1 (2018): 148–66.

20. David E. Broockman and Donald P. Green. "Results of Text Messaging and Door-to-Door Canvassing Experiments, November 2016," unpublished memo (One Arizona, 2017).

21. Daniel E. Ho, Alison Morantz, Cassandra Handan-Nader, and Tom A. Rutter, "The Effectiveness of a Hyper-Localized Get-Out-the-Vote Program: Ev-

idence from the 2017 Virginia State Elections," unpublished manuscript (Stanford University, 2018).

22. David W. Nickerson, Ryan D. Friedrichs, and David C. King, "Partisan Mobilization Campaigns in the Field: Results of a Statewide Turnout Experiment in Michigan," *Political Research Quarterly,* vol. 59 (2006): 85–97.

23. Joel A. Middleton, "Voting Is Power 2004 Mobilization Effort," unpublished manuscript (University of California, Berkeley, Travers Department of Political Science, 2015).

24. David W. Nickerson, "Forget Me Not? The Importance of Timing and Frequency in Voter Mobilization," paper presented at the Annual Meeting of the American Political Science Association, Philadelphia, August 31–September 3, 2006.

25. Julia Gray and Philip Potter, "Does Signaling Matter in Elections? Evidence from a Field Experiment," paper presented at the Annual Meeting of the American Political Science Association, Chicago, August 30–September 2, 2007.

26. Kevin Arceneaux, "I'm Asking for Your Support: The Effects of Personally Delivered Campaign Messages on Voting Decisions and Opinion Formation," *Quarterly Journal of Political Science,* vol. 2 (2007): 43–65.

27. Jared Barton, Marco Castillo, and Ragan Petrie, "What Persuades Voters? A Field Experiment on Political Campaigning," *Economic Journal,* vol. 124 (2014): F293–F326.

28. Brandon Lenoir and Donald P. Green, "The Effects of Multiple Canvassing Visits on Voter Turnout: A Field Experiment in Competitive Electoral Settings," paper presented at the Annual Meeting of the Midwest Political Science Association (Chicago, 2015).

29. Kevin Arceneaux and David W. Nickerson, "Who Is Mobilized to Vote? A Re-Analysis of 11 Field Experiments," *American Journal of Political Science,* vol. 53 (2009): 1–16.

30. Middleton, "Voting Is Power 2004 Mobilization Effort."

31. Sinclair and others, "Local Canvassing."

32. Kevin Arceneaux and David Nickerson, "Comparing Negative and Positive Campaign Messages: Evidence from Two Field Experiments," *American Politics Research,* vol. 38 (2010): 54–83.

33. Kalla and Broockman, 2017. Michael A. Bailey, Daniel J. Hopkins, and Todd Rogers. "Unresponsive and unpersuaded: The unintended consequences of a voter persuasion effort." *Political Behavior,* vol. 38, no. 3 (2016): 713–46.

34. One canvassing tactic that seems to produce large effects is to present voters with their record of past turnout; see Tiffany C. Davenport, "Public Accountability and Political Participation: Effects of a Face-to-Face Feedback Intervention on Voter Turnout of Public Housing Residents," *Political Behavior,* vol. 32 (2010): 337–68. See chapter 11 for the pros and cons of this approach.

35. David W. Nickerson, "Is Voting Contagious? Evidence from Two Field Experiments," *American Political Science Review,* vol. 102 (2008): 49–57.

36. We are aware of no comparable experiments that assess the spillover effects of phone calls to others in the household. For spillover effects of mail, see Betsy Sinclair, Margaret McConnell, and Donald P. Green, "Detecting Spillover

Effects: Design and Analysis of Multi-Level Experiments," *American Journal of Political Science,* vol. 56 (2012): 1055–69.

37. Personal communication, January 12, 2015.

38. Beaudry and Schaeffer, *Winning Local and State Elections,* p. 91. This quotation is italicized in the original.

Chapter Four

1. For another take on conceptualizing and designing leaflets, see Ann Beaudry and Bob Schaeffer, *Winning Local and State Elections: The Guide to Organizing Your Campaign* (New York: Free Press, 1986); Catherine Shaw, *The Campaign Manager: Running and Winning Local Elections,* 2d ed. (Boulder, Colo.: Westview Press, 2000), p. 156. They advise, for instance, "When in doubt about leaflet design, keep it simple! Too many candidates fall into the trap of: 'I paid for this piece of paper, and I'm going to print on every square inch of it.' "

2. Alan S. Gerber and Donald P. Green, "The Effect of a Nonpartisan Get-Out-the-Vote Drive: An Experimental Study of Leafleting," *Journal of Politics,* vol. 62 (2000): 846–57.

3. David W. Nickerson, Ryan D. Friedrichs, and David C. King, "Partisan Mobilization Campaigns in the Field: Results of a Statewide Turnout Experiment in Michigan," *Political Research Quarterly,* vol. 59, no. 1 (2006): 85–97.

4. Julia Azari and Ebonya Washington, "Results from a 2004 Leafleting Field Experiment in Miami-Dade and Duval Counties, Florida," unpublished manuscript (Yale University, Institution for Social and Policy Studies, 2006).

5. Valerie A. Frey and Santiago Suárez, "Mobilización Efectiva de Votantes! Analyzing the Effects of Bilingual Mobilization and Notification of Bilingual Ballots on Latino Turnout," unpublished manuscript (Yale University, Institution for Social and Policy Studies, 2006).

6. Lisa García Bedolla and Melissa Michelson, *Mobilizing Inclusion: Transforming the Electorate through Get-Out-the-Vote Campaigns* (Yale University Press, 2012).

7. Donald P. Green, Jonathan S. Krasno, Alexander Coppock, Benjamin D. Farrer, Brandon Lenoir, and Joshua N. Zingher. "The effects of lawn signs on vote outcomes: Results from four randomized field experiments." *Electoral Studies,* vol. 41 (2016): 143–50.

8. Green and others, "The Effects of Lawn Signs on Vote Outcomes."

9. Amy White and Alex Coppock, "The Effects of MoveOn's 2018 GOTV Lawn Signs," unpublished manuscript, 2019.

10. Green and others, "The Effects of Lawn Signs on Vote Outcomes."

11. Costas Panagopoulos, "Street Fight: The Impact of a Street Sign Campaign on Voter Turnout," *Electoral Studies,* vol. 28 (2009): 309–13.

12. David W. Nickerson, Ryan D. Friedrichs, and David C. King, "Partisan Mobilization Campaigns in the Field: Results of a Statewide Turnout Experiment in Michigan," *Political Research Quarterly,* vol. 59, no. 1 (2006): 85–97. Lisa García Bedolla and Melissa Michelson, *Mobilizing Inclusion: Transforming the Electorate through Get-Out-the-Vote Campaigns* (Yale University Press, 2012).

Chapter Five

1. Because state laws are complex, varied, and subject to interpretation by local officials, make a point of investigating state and local laws before your mail is designed and sent out.

2. Microtargeting is a topic that warrants experimental evaluation in its own right. In brief, microtargeting databases are constructed by conducting an opinion survey with registered voters. The information on the voter file, augmented with consumer information, is used to forecast the survey responses. These forecasts are then imputed to other (nonsurveyed) people on the voter file. The predictive accuracy of these forecasts may be poor, which is why we use the word "ostensible" in the text to describe what microtargeters take to be groups of like-minded voters. A long-overdue experiment is one that tests whether individuals are more strongly influenced when they receive microtargeted rather than generic mail.

3. Megan Moore, "Briefing on Laws Related to Campaign Advertising Disclaimers in Other States for the State Administration and Veterans' Affairs Interim Committee" (http://leg.mt.gov/content/Committees/Interim/2011-2012/State-Administration-and-Veterans-Affairs/Meeting-Documents/April%202012/OTHER%20STATES%20ANON.pdf).

4. The U.S. Postal Service website (www.usps.gov) presents a complete rundown on mailing sizes and weights.

5. Catherine Shaw, *The Campaign Manager: Running and Winning Local Elections,* 5th ed. (Boulder, Colo.: Westview Press, 2014).

6. Lawrence Grey, *How to Win a Local Election* (New York: M. Evans and Company, 1999).

7. Grey, *How to Win a Local Election,* p. 163.

8. See Lisa García Bedolla and Melissa Michelson, *Mobilizing Inclusion: Transforming the Electorate through Get-Out-the-Vote Campaigns* (Yale University Press, 2012). For a journalistic account of letter-writing efforts and evaluations, see also Shumita Basu, "Grassroots GOTV Campaign Sends 283,000 Handwritten Postcards To New Yorkers Ahead Of State Primary" (http://gothamist.com/2018/09/12/postcards_to_voters_2018.php), and David W. Nickerson, "Memo on Several Field Experiments Testing the Effects of Handwritten Postcards on Voter Turnout among Young Voters, Working Women, and Minorities in 2010," unpublished correspondence, May 22, 2019.

9. Donald P. Green and Adam Zelizer, "How Much GOTV Mail Is Too Much? Results from a Large-Scale Field Experiment," *Journal of Experimental Political Science,* vol. 4 (2019): 107–18.

10. See Christopher B. Mann, Matt Davis, and Melissa R. Michelson, "Are Two Better than One? Bilingual vs. English Communication in Mobilization of Latino Voters," unpublished manuscript, 2017.

11. David Doherty and E. Scott Adler, "The Persuasive Effects of Partisan Campaign Mailers," *Political Research Quarterly,* vol. 67 (2014): 562–73.

12. Ricardo Ramírez, "Giving Voice to Latino Voters: A Field Experiment on the Effectiveness of a National Nonpartisan Mobilization Effort," *Annals of the American Academy of Political and Social Science,* vol. 601 (2005): 66–84.

13. Bedolla and Michelson, *Mobilizing Inclusion.*

14. Daniel R. Biggers, "Can the Backlash against Voter ID Laws Mobilize

Low-Propensity Voters? A Field Experiment Examining Voter Mobilization through Psychological Reactance," paper presented at the Annual Meeting of the American Political Science Association, Washington, D.C., August 31, 2014.

15. Betsy Sinclair, Margaret McConnell, and Donald P. Green, "Detecting Spillover Effects: Design and Analysis of Multi-Level Experiments," *American Journal of Political Science*, vol. 56 (2012): 1055–69, table A-2.

16. Alan S. Gerber, Gregory A. Huber, Daniel R. Biggers, and David J. Hendry, "Ballot Secrecy Concerns and Voter Mobilization," *American Politics Research*, vol. 42 (2014): 896–923; Alan S. Gerber and others, "Who Wants to Discuss Vote Choices with Others? Polarization in Preferences for Deliberation," *Public Opinion Quarterly*, vol. 77 (2013): 474–96. Alan S. Gerber, Gregory A. Huber, Albert H. Fang, and Andrew A. Gooch, "Non-Governmental Campaign Communication Providing Ballot Secrecy Assurances Increases Turnout: Results from Two Large-Scale Experiments," unpublished manuscript (Yale University, 2016).

17. Lisa A. Bryant and Michael Hanmer, "A Field Experiment to Examine States' Efforts to Increase Registration & Turnout," prepared for the Election Sciences, Reform, and Administration Conference (Madison, WI, July 26–27, 2018). Christopher B. Mann and Lisa A. Bryant, "If You Ask, They Will Come (to Register and Vote): Field Experiments with State Election Agencies on Encouraging Voter Registration," unpublished manuscript (Skidmore College, 2015).

18. William Cubbison, "The Marginal Effects of Direct Mail on Vote Choice," paper presented at the Annual Meeting of the Midwest Political Science Association, Chicago, April 17, 2015.

19. For example, labor unions have successfully increased turnout among their members with advocacy mailings that emphasize turnout with effects that are similar to nonpartisan GOTV mailings. David Broockman and Donald Green, "SEIU 2014 Latino Member Mail Program Evaluation," unpublished manuscript (2015).

20. Peter Miller, Rebecca Reynolds, and Matthew Singer, "Mobilizing the Young Vote: Direct Mail Voter Guides in the 2015 Chicago Mayoral Election," *Research & Politics*, vol. 4, no. 4 (2017).

21. See Christopher B. Mann, Matt Davis, and Melissa R. Michelson, "Are Two Better than One? Bilingual vs. English Communication in Mobilization of Latino Voters," unpublished manuscript, 2017; Marisa Abrajano and Costas Panagopoulos, "Does Language Matter? The Impact of Spanish versus English-Language GOTV Efforts on Latino Turnout," *American Politics Research*, vol. 39 (2011): 643–63.

22. Alan S. Gerber and Donald P. Green, "The Effects of Canvassing, Direct Mail, and Telephone Contact on Voter Turnout: A Field Experiment," *American Political Science Review*, vol. 94 (2000): 653–63; Neema Trivedi, "The Effect of Identity-Based GOTV Direct Mail Appeals on the Turnout of Indian Americans," *Annals of the American Academy of Political and Social Science*, vol. 601 (2005): 115–22; Costas Panagopoulos, "Raising Hope: Hope Inducement and Voter Turnout," *Basic and Applied Social Psychology*, vol. 36 (2014): 494–501.

23. Seth J. Hill and Thad Kousser, "Turning Out Unlikely Voters? A Field Experiment in the Top-Two Primary," *Political Behavior*, vol. 38, no. 2 (2016): 413–432.

24. Alan S. Gerber, Donald P. Green, and Christopher W. Larimer, "Social Pressure and Voter Turnout: Evidence from a Large-Scale Field Experiment," *American Political Science Review*, vol. 102 (2008): 33–48.

25. Todd Rogers and others, "Social Pressure and Voting: A Field Experiment Conducted in a High-Salience Election," *Electoral Studies,* vol. 46 (2017): 87–100.

26. Costas Panagopoulos, "Thank You for Voting: Gratitude Expression and Voter Mobilization," *Journal of Politics,* vol. 73 (2013): 707–17.

27. We also exclude experiments that test whether financial inducements increase turnout. We include studies that test mailings featuring a photo of eyes, as it remains unclear whether "watchful eyes" are a significant source of social pressure. See Costas Panagopoulos, "I've Got My Eyes on You: Implicit Social Pressure Cues and Prosocial Behavior," *Political Psychology,* vol. 35 (2014): 23–33; Costas Panagopoulos, "Watchful Eyes: Implicit Observability Cues and Voting," *Evolution and Human Behavior,* vol. 35 (2014): 279–84; and Richard E. Matland and Gregg R. Murray, "I Only Have Eyes for You: Does Implicit Social Pressure Increase Voter Turnout?" *Political Psychology,* vol. 37, no. 4 (2016).

28. Mia Costa, Brian F. Schaffner, and Alicia Prevost, "Walking the Walk? Experiments on the Effect of Pledging to Vote on Youth Turnout," *PLOS ONE,* vol. 13, no. 5 (2018).

29. Richard E. Matland and Gregg R. Murray, "An Experimental Test for 'Backlash' against Social Pressure Techniques Used to Mobilize Voters," *American Politics Research,* vol. 41 (2013): 359–86.

30. Rogers and others, "Social Pressure and Voting."

Chapter Six

1. Lawrence Grey, in *How to Win a Local Election,* states, "Some people think using phone banks to call registered voters and solicit their votes is a good idea. We don't. While the phone banks might make it easier for the volunteers and may have had some success in the past, telemarketers have killed off the usefulness of this technique. People no longer want to get unsolicited phone calls trying to sell them something, even if the something is a political candidate." Lawrence Grey, *How to Win a Local Election* (New York: M. Evans and Company, 1999). For a much more optimistic assessment of the impact of phone calls, see Janet Grenzke and Mark Watts, "Hold the Phones: Taking Issue with a Get-Out-the-Vote Strategy," *Campaigns & Elections* (December/January 2005): 81–83.

2. Federal Communications Commission, "Enforcement Advisory—Robo Calls" (www.fcc.gov/document/political-campaigns-restrictions-autodialed-prerecorded-calls) [Accessed June 25, 2015].

3. Federal Communications Commission, "Enforcement Advisory—Robo Calls."

4. Stephen J. Blumberg and Julian V. Luke, "Wireless Substitution: Early Release of Estimates from the National Health Interview Survey, January–June 2018" (www.cdc.gov/nchs/data/nhis/earlyrelease/wireless201812.pdf).

5. This figure assumes an up-to-date calling list, something that should not be taken for granted if the numbers were obtained from official lists of registered voters.

6. A recent study of millions of calls by predictive dialers in the 2016 presidential election found that 12 percent of targeted voters were successfully contacted. See Abrajano and others, "When campaigns call, who answers? Using

observational data to enrich our understanding of phone mobilization," *Electoral Studies,* in press (https://doi.org/10.1016/j.electstud.2019.03.001).

7. For other discussions of the goals and mechanics of GOTV phone calls, see, for example, Catherine Shaw, *The Campaign Manager: Running and Winning Local Elections,* 5th ed. (Boulder, Colo.: Westview Press, 2014); Grey, *How to Win a Local Election.*

8. David W. Nickerson, "Memo on the Effects of Phone-Banking Campaigns during the 2001 Election," unpublished manuscript (Yale University, Institution for Social and Policy Studies, 2002).

9. Ricardo Ramírez, "Giving Voice to Latino Voters: A Field Experiment on the Effectiveness of a National Nonpartisan Mobilization Effort," *Annals of the American Academy of Political and Social Science,* vol. 601 (2005): 66–84.

10. Shang E. Ha and Dean S. Karlan, "Get-Out-the-Vote Phone Calls: Does Quality Matter?" *American Politics Research,* vol. 37 (2009): 353–69.

11. Lisa García Bedolla and Melissa Michelson, *Mobilizing Inclusion: Transforming the Electorate through Get-Out-the-Vote Campaigns* (Yale University Press, 2012).

12. Daron R. Shaw, Donald P. Green, James G. Gimpel, and Alan S. Gerber, "Do Robotic Calls from Credible Sources Influence Voter Turnout or Vote Choice? Evidence from a Randomized Field Experiment," *Journal of Political Marketing,* vol. 11 (2012): 231–45.

13. Daniel Kling and Thomas Stratmann, "Repeated Treatment in a GOTV Field Experiment: Distinguishing between Intensive and Extensive Margin Effects," Journal of Economic Behavior (2018).

14. Alan S. Gerber, Donald P. Green, and Holger L. Kern, "Baseline, Placebo, and Treatment: Efficient Estimation for Three-Group Experiments," *Political Analysis,* vol. 18 (2010): 297–315.

15. Adam Zelizer, "How Many Robocalls Are Too Many? Results from a Large-Scale Field Experiment," Journal of Political Marketing, forthcoming (2019).

16. Alan S. Gerber and Donald P. Green, "The Effects of Canvassing, Direct Mail, and Telephone Contact on Voter Turnout: A Field Experiment," *American Political Science Review,* vol. 94 (2000): 653–63; Alan S. Gerber and Donald P. Green, "Do Phone Calls Increase Voter Turnout? A Field Experiment," *Public Opinion Quarterly,* vol. 65 (2001): 75–85; Alan S. Gerber and Donald P. Green, "Do Phone Calls Increase Turnout? An Update," *Annals of the American Academy of Political and Social Science,* vol. 601 (2005): 142–54; Alan S. Gerber and Donald P. Green, "Correction to Gerber and Green (2000), Replication of Disputed Findings, and Reply to Imai (2005)," *American Political Science Review,* vol. 99 (2005): 301–13.

17. Kevin Arceneaux, Alan S. Gerber, and Donald P. Green, "Comparing Experimental and Matching Methods Using a Large-Scale Voter Mobilization Experiment," *Political Analysis,* vol. 14 (2006): 1–36.

18. Kevin Arceneaux, Alan S. Gerber, and Donald P. Green, "A Cautionary Note on the Use of Matching to Estimate Causal Effects: An Empirical Example Comparing Matching Estimates to an Experimental Benchmark," *Sociological Methods and Research,* vol. 39 (2010): 256–82.

19. Ha and Karlan, "Get-Out-the-Vote Phone Calls."

20. David W. Nickerson, "Quality Is Job One: Professional and Volunteer

Voter Mobilization Calls," *American Journal of Political Science,* vol. 51 (2007): 269–82.

21. Alan S. Gerber and others, "A Field Experiment Shows that Subtle Linguistic Cues Might Not Affect Voter Behavior," *Proceedings of the National Academy of Sciences of the United States of America*, vol. 113 (2016): 7112–7117.

22. Ha and Karlan, "Get-Out-the-Vote Phone Calls."

23. Christopher B. Mann and Casey A. Klofstad, "The Role of Call Quality in Voter Mobilization: Implications for Electoral Outcomes and Experimental Design," *Political Behavior,* vol. 37 (2015): 135–54.

24. Alan S. Gerber and others, "When Does Increasing Mobilization Effort Increase Turnout? New Theory and Evidence from a Field Experiment on Reminder Calls," unpublished manuscript (2016).

25. Grenzke and Watts, "Hold the Phones."

26. John E. McNulty, "Phone-Based GOTV: What's on the Line? Field Experiments with Varied Partisan Components, 2002–2003," *Annals of the American Academy of Political and Social Science,* vol. 601 (2005): 41–65.

27. Christopher Mann, "Field Experimentation in Political Communication for Mobilization," Ph.D. dissertation, Yale University, Department of Political Science, 2008.

28. Emily Arthur Cardy, "An Experimental Field Study of the GOTV and Persuasion Effects of Partisan Direct Mail and Phone Calls," *Annals of the American Academy of Political and Social Science,* vol. 601 (2005): 28–40.

29. Costas Panagopoulos, "Partisan and Nonpartisan Message Content and Voter Mobilization: Field Experimental Evidence," *Political Research Quarterly,* vol. 62 (2009): 70–77. 30. David Nickerson, "Volunteer Phone Calls Can Increase Turnout," *American Politics Research,* vol. 34, no. 3 (2006): 271–92.

31. Nickerson, "Quality Is Job One."

32. David W. Nickerson, Ryan D. Friedrichs, and David C. King, "Partisan Mobilization Campaigns in the Field: Results from a Statewide Turnout Experiment in Michigan," *Political Research Quarterly,* vol. 59 (2006): 85–97.

33. Ramírez, "Giving Voice to Latino Voters."

34. Lisa García Bedolla, Marisa Abrajano, and Jane Junn, "Testing New Technologies in Mobilizing Voters of Color: An Analysis from the November 2014 Elections" (The James Irvine Foundation, 2015). Interestingly, the calls did not seem to increase turnout among the high-propensity voters who are targeted. This finding is corroborated by a study of a special election in Palo Alto, California, in 2013, which found that a "mobilize your neighbors" script was no better than a conventional GOTV script. See Lisa Pringle and others, "Calling All Neighbors: Mobilizing Turnout for a Local Housing Referendum," *Journal of Political Marketing,* vol. 17, no. 4 (2016): 418–41.

35. Ali A. Valenzuela and Melissa R. Michelson, "Turnout, Status, and Identity: Mobilizing Latinos to Vote with Group Appeals," *American Political Science Review,* vol. 110 (2016): 615–30.

36. Melissa R. Michelson, Margaret A. McConnell, and Lisa García Bedolla, "Heeding the Call: The Effect of Targeted Two-Round Phone Banks on Voter Turnout," *Journal of Politics,* vol. 71 (2009): 1549–63.

37. Mann and Klofstad, "The Role of Call Quality in Voter Mobilization."

38. For evidence suggesting that volunteer callers had similar effects on turn-

out in the 2004 presidential election regardless of whether the scripts focused on policy gains or losses, see study 1 in Kevin Arceneaux and David W. Nickerson, "Comparing Negative and Positive Campaign Messages: Evidence from Two Field Experiments," *American Politics Research,* vol. 38 (2010): 54–83.

39. Alan S. Gerber and others, "When Does Increasing Mobilization Effort Increase Turnout? New Theory and Evidence from a Field Experiment on Reminder Calls," unpublished manuscript (2016).

Chapter Seven

1. Pew Research Center, "Internet Use over Time" (www.pewinternet.org/data-trend/internet-use/internet-use-over-time/) [Accessed May 10, 2019].

2. Pew Research Center, "Social Media Use over Time" (www.pewinternet.org/data-trend/social-media/social-media-use-all-users/) [Accessed May 10, 2019].

3. Holly Teresi, "Wired for Influence: A Series of Experiments Evaluating the Ability of Peer Interaction through Social Network Sites to Influence Political Knowledge, Attitudes, and Behavior," Ph.D. dissertation (Georgia State University, Department of Political Science, 2012). Holly Teresi and Melissa R. Michelson, "Wired to Mobilize: The Effect of Social Networking Messages on Voter Turnout," *Social Science Journal,* vol. 52 (2015): 195–204.

4. Michael J. Hanmer, Paul S. Herrnson, and Claire M. Smith, "The Impact of E-mail on the Use of New Convenience Voting Methods and Turnout by Overseas Voters: A Field Experiment to Address Their Challenges with New Technology," *Election Law Journal,* vol. 14 (2015): 97–110.

5. David W. Nickerson, "Does Email Boost Turnout?" *Quarterly Journal of Political Science,* vol. 2 (2008): 369–79.

6. Nickerson, "Does Email Boost Turnout?"

7. Alissa Stollwerk, "Does Partisan E-mail Affect Voter Turnout? An Examination of Two Field Experiments in New York City," unpublished manuscript (Columbia University, Department of Political Science, 2015).

8. Stollwerk, "Does Partisan E-mail Affect Voter Turnout?"

9. While similar in many ways, 501(c)(4) organizations differ from 501(c)(3)s in their range of political activity. Only 501(c)(4)s are permitted to engage in political campaign activity, and that activity must be consistent with the organization's mission, but cannot be its primary purpose.

10. Note that 7.9 percent of the control group also recalled receiving this e-mail, which attests to the low reliability of survey-based measures of campaign exposure.

11. Lisa García Bedolla, Marisa Abrajano, and Jane Junn, "Testing New Technologies in Mobilizing Voters of Color: An Analysis from the November 2014 Elections" (The James Irvine Foundation, 2015).

12. Nikhil Bontha and others, "Vote.org SMS and Email GOTV Test Results," unpublished manuscript (Analyst Institute, 2017), public version accessed at www.vote.org/research/.

13. Neil Malhotra, Melissa R. Michelson, and Ali Adam Valenzuela, "Emails from Official Sources Can Increase Turnout," *Quarterly Journal of Political Science,* vol. 7 (2012): 321–32.

14. Allison Dale and Aaron Strauss, "Don't Forget to Vote: Text Message

Reminders as a Mobilization Tool," *American Journal of Political Science,* vol. 53 (2009): 787–804.

15. Two prior text-messaging experiments were smaller in scope and generated less precise estimates. Ryan Friedrichs, "Young Voter Mobilization in 2004: Analysis of Outreach, Persuasion, and Turnout of 18–29-Year-Old Progressive Voters," unpublished manuscript (Skyline Public Works, 2006); Costas Panagopoulos, "The Impact of SMS Text Messages on Voter Turnout," unpublished manuscript (Fordham University, Department of Political Science, 2007).

16. Neil Malhotra and others, "Text Messages as Mobilization Tools: The Conditional Effect of Habitual Voting and Election Salience," *American Politics Research,* vol. 39 (2011): 664–81.

17. John Ternovski, Josh Kalla, and Lauren Keane, "Election Day 2012 Text Message GOTV Experiments" (Analyst Institute, 2013); cited in Green and Gerber, *Get Out the Vote: How to Increase Voter Turnout,* Third Edition (2015), with permission from Rock the Vote.

18. David Broockman and Donald Green, "Results of Text Messaging and Door-to-Door Canvassing Experiments, November 2016," unpublished manuscript (2017).

19. David E. Broockman, Donald P. Green, and Joseph L. Sutherland, "Are Social Pressure Text Messages Effective GOTV? Voter Mobilization in the 2016 Presidential Election," unpublished manuscript (2017).

20. Nikhil Bontha and others, "Vote.org SMS and Email GOTV Test Results," unpublished manuscript (Analyst Institute, 2017); public version accessed at www.vote.org/research/.

21. Joshua Kalla. "Results from 2016 Illinois Text Message Experiment," unpublished manuscript (2017). Used by permission.

22. Alex Gold and others, "VOTE.org Hustle SMS GOTV Test Results Memo," unpublished manuscript (Analyst Institute, 2017); public version accessed at www.vote.org/research/.

23. Alan Yan and Joshua Kalla. "Results from 2017 Virginia Text Message Experiment," unpublished manuscript (2017). Used by permission.

24. Rani Molla and Kurt Wagner, "People Spend Almost as Much Time on Facebook as They Do on Instagram," *recode,* June 25, 2018 (www.recode.net/2018/6/25/17501224/instagram-facebook-snapchat-time-spent-growth-data).

25. David E. Broockman and Donald P. Green, "Do Online Advertisements Increase Political Candidates' Name Recognition or Favorability? Evidence from Randomized Field Experiments," *Political Behavior,* vol. 36 (2013): 263–89.

26. Robert M. Bond and others, "A 61-Million-Person Experiment in Social Influence and Political Mobilization," *Nature,* vol. 489 (2012): 295–98.

27. Jason J. Jones and others, "Social Influence and Political Mobilization: Further Evidence from a Randomized Experiment in the 2012 U.S. Presidential Election," *PLOS ONE* (2017).

28. Kevin Collins, Lauren Keane, and Joshua Kalla, "Youth Voter Mobilization through Online Advertising: Evidence from Two GOTV Field Experiments," paper presented at the Annual Meeting of the American Political Science Association (Washington, D.C., August 30, 2014).

29. Lisa García Bedolla, Marisa Abrajano, and Jane Junn, "Testing New Technologies in Mobilizing Voters of Color."

30. Katherine Haenschen and Jay Jennings, "Mobilizing Millennial Voters with Targeted Internet Advertisements: A Field Experiment," *Political Communication* (2019) (https://doi.org/10.1080/10584609.2018.1548530).

31. Joshua Kalla, "Results from 2016 Online Ad Voter Turnout Experiment," unpublished manuscript (2017).

32. Teresi and Michelson, "Wired to Mobilize."

33. Solomon Messing, Eytan Bakshy, and Andrew Fiore, "Friends that Matter: How Exposure to News via Social Media Increases Civic Engagement," unpublished manuscript (University of Massachusetts Amherst, College of Social and Behavioral Sciences, 2014).

34. Katherine Haenschen, "Social Pressure on Social Media: Using Facebook Status Updates to Increase Voter Turnout," *Journal of Communication*, vol. 66 (2016): 542–63.

35. Tiffany C. Davenport, "Unsubscribe: New Evidence that E-mail Mobilization Can Be Effective after All; Results from a Randomized Field Experiment Comparing the Effects of Peer-to-Peer and Mass E-mail Messages on Voter Turnout," unpublished manuscript (Yale University, Institution for Social and Policy Studies, 2007).

Chapter Eight

1. Elizabeth M. Addonizio, Donald P. Green, and James M. Glaser, "Putting the Party Back into Politics: An Experiment Testing Whether Election Day Festivals Increase Voter Turnout," *PS: Political Science and Politics*, vol. 40 (2007): 721–27; Richard Franklin Bensel, *The American Ballot Box in the Mid-Nineteenth Century* (Cambridge University Press, 2004).

2. Jac C. Heckelman, "The Effect of the Secret Ballot on Voter Turnout," *Public Choice*, vol. 82 (1995): 107–24.

3. "Parade in the Eighth Ward," *Hartford Daily Courant*, October 28, 1884, p. 3.

4. Addonizio, Green, and Glaser, "Putting the Party Back into Politics."

5. One important exception is a remarkable series of experiments that test whether paying people to vote (in states where such payments are allowed) increases turnout. Offers of up to $25 increased turnout by a few percentage points in off-year elections. Costas Panagopoulos, "Extrinsic Rewards, Intrinsic Motivation and Voting." *Journal of Politics*, vol. 75, no. 1 (2012): 266–80.

6. Donald P. Green and Oliver A. McClellan. "The Effects of Election Festivals on Voter Turnout: A Field Experiment Conducted During a Presidential Election," unpublished manuscript (2017).

7. Green and McClellan. "The Effects of Election Festivals on Voter Turnout."

8. Green and McClellan. "The Effects of Election Festivals on Voter Turnout."

9. Adria Lawrence and Bethany Albertson, "How Does Television Change Us? An Analysis of Three Field Experiments," paper presented at the Annual Meeting of the American Association of Public Opinion Research, Miami, May 12–15, 2005.

10. Sendhil Mullainathan, Ebonya Washington, and Julia Azari, "The Impact

of Electoral Debate on Public Opinions: An Experimental Investigation of the 2005 New York City Mayoral Election," in *Political Representation*, edited by Ian Shapiro and others (Cambridge University Press, 2009), pp. 324–41.

11. David W. Nickerson, "Results from the Spring 2006 Candidates Gone Wild Experiment," unpublished manuscript (Notre Dame University, Department of Political Science, 2007).

12. Lisa García Bedolla, Marisa Abrajano, and Jane Junn, "Testing New Technologies in Mobilizing Voters of Color: An Analysis from the November 2014 Elections" (The James Irvine Foundation, 2015).

Chapter Nine

1. For one discussion of mass media and media consultants for smaller campaigns, see, for example, J. Sherie Strachan, *High-Tech Grass Roots: The Professionalization of Local Elections* (New York: Rowman and Littlefield, 2003). For a discussion of targeting and media, see, for example, Daniel M. Shea and Michael John Burton, *Campaign Craft: The Strategies, Tactics, and Art of Political Campaign Management* (Westport, Conn.: Praeger, 2001).

2. Jonathan Krasno and Donald Green, "Do Televised Presidential Ads Increase Voter Turnout? Evidence from a Natural Experiment," *Journal of Politics,* vol. 70 (2008): 245–61.

3. Scott Ashworth and Joshua D. Clinton, "Does Advertising Exposure Affect Turnout?" *Quarterly Journal of Political Science,* vol. 2 (2007): 27–41.

4. An alternative hypothesis is that ads mobilize voters of the same party and demobilize those in the opposite party, producing no net effect when both sides air roughly the same amount of TV advertising. See Jowei Chen and Kyle A. Dropp, "Televised Political Ads and Voter Turnout: A Theory of Asymmetric Partisan Mobilization," unpublished manuscript (University of Michigan, Center for Political Studies, 2014).

5. Joshua D. Clinton and John S. Lapinski, "'Targeted' Advertising and Voter Turnout: An Experimental Study of the 2000 Presidential Election," *Journal of Politics,* vol. 66 (2004): 69–96.

6. Lynn Vavreck and Donald P. Green, "Do Public Service Announcements Increase Voter Turnout? Results from a Randomized Field Experiment," paper presented at the Annual Meeting of the American Political Science Association, Chicago, September 2–5, 2004.

7. Donald P. Green and Lynn Vavreck, "Analysis of Cluster-Randomized Experiments: A Comparison of Alternative Estimation Approaches," *Political Analysis,* vol. 16 (2008): 138–52.

8. Rock the Vote does not pay television stations to air its material; rather, it relies on its corporate partners to place its ads for free, as public service announcements. As a result, the ads were seldom shown in smaller media markets, where Rock the Vote's corporate partners had little control over television programming.

9. Eline A. de Rooij and Donald P. Green, "Radio Public Service Announcements and Voter Participation Among Native Americans: Evidence from Two Field Experiments," *Political Behavior,* vol. 39 (2017): 327–46.

10. Costas Panagopoulos and Donald P. Green, "Field Experiments Testing the Impact of Radio Advertisements on Electoral Competition," *American Journal of Political Science*, vol. 52 (2008): 156–68.

11. Costas Panagopoulos and Donald P. Green, "Spanish-Language Radio Advertisements and Latino Voter Turnout in the 2006 Congressional Elections: Field Experimental Evidence," *Political Research Quarterly*, vol. 64 (2011): 588–99.

12. Panagopoulos and Green, "Spanish-Language Radio Advertisements and Latino Voter Turnout in the 2006 Congressional Elections."

13. Matthew Gentzkow, "Television and Voter Turnout," *Quarterly Journal of Economics*, vol. 121 (2006): 931–72.

14. Alan Gerber, Dean S. Karlan, and Daniel Bergan, "Does the Media Matter? A Field Experiment Measuring the Effect of Newspapers on Voting Behavior and Political Opinions," *American Economic Journal: Applied Economics*, vol. 1 (2009): 35–52.

15. Panagopoulos and Green, "Field Experiments Testing the Impact of Radio Advertisements on Electoral Competition."

16. Jay Newell, Charles T. Salmon, and Susan Chang, "The Hidden History of Product Placement," *Journal of Broadcasting & Electronic Media*, vol. 50 (2006): 575–94.

17. Elizabeth Levy Paluck and others, "Does Product Placement Change Television Viewers' Social Behavior?" *PLOS ONE*, vol. 10 (2015).

Chapter Ten

1. For a review of the scholarly debate, see David Nickerson, "Do Voter Registration Drives Increase Participation? For Whom and When?" *Journal of Politics*, vol. 77 (2015): 88–101.

2. Frances Fox Piven and Richard A. Cloward, *Why Americans Still Don't Vote and Why Politicians Want It That Way* (Boston: Beacon Press, 2000).

3. Steven J. Rosenstone and Raymond E. Wolfinger, "The Effect of Registration Laws on Voter Turnout," *American Political Science Review*, vol. 72 (1978): 22–45.

4. Michael D. Martinez and David Hill, "Did Motor Voter Work?" *American Politics Quarterly*, vol. 27 (1999): 296–315.

5. For exceptions, see Harold F. Gosnell, *Getting-Out-the-Vote: An Experiment in the Stimulation of Voting* (University of Chicago Press, 1927); and Irwin N. Gertzog, "The Electoral Consequences of a Local Party Organization's Registration Campaign: The San Diego Experiment," *Polity*, vol. 3 (1970): 247–64.

6. U.S. Census Bureau, "Voting and Registration in the Election of November 2016" (www.census.gov/data/tables/time-series/demo/voting-and-registration/p20-580.html); United States Election Project, "2016 November General Election Turnout Rates" (www.electproject.org/2016g).

7. Stephen Ansolabehere, Eitan Hersh, and Kenneth Shepsle, "Movers, Stayers, and Registration: Why Age Is Correlated with Registration in the U.S.," *Quarterly Journal of Political Science*, vol. 7 (2012): 333–63.

8. Claudine Gay, "Moving to Opportunity: The Political Effects of a Housing Mobility Experiment," *Urban Affairs Review*, vol. 48 (2012): 147–79.

9. Elizabeth M. Addonizio, "The Fourth of July Vote: A Social Approach to Voter Mobilization and Election Day," Ph.D. dissertation, Yale University, 2012.

10. Addonizio, "The Fourth of July Vote."

11. Elizabeth A. Bennion and David W. Nickerson, "I Will Register and Vote, If You Teach Me How: A Field Experiment Testing Voter Registration in College Classrooms," *PS: Political Science & Politics*, vol. 49, no. 4 (2016): 867–71.

12. David W. Nickerson, "Does Email Boost Turnout?" *Quarterly Journal of Political Science*, vol. 2 (2008): 369–79.

13. Elizabeth A. Bennion and David W. Nickerson, "The Cost of Convenience: An Experiment Showing E-Mail Outreach Decreases Voter Registration," *Political Research Quarterly*, vol. 64 (2011): 858–69.

14. Bennion and Nickerson, "The Cost of Convenience."

15. Nickerson, "Do Voter Registration Drives Increase Participation?"

16. Alan Gerber and others, "Evidence-Based Campaign Strategy: Results from 2005," unpublished presentation to the Texans for Rick Perry campaign (Austin, TX, January 27, 2006).

17. Christopher B. Mann and Lisa A. Bryant, "If You Ask, They Will Come (to Register and Vote): Field Experiment with State Election Agencies on Encouraging Voter Registration," unpublished manuscript (Skidmore College, Department of Government, 2015). This manuscript reports only two of the six experiments conducted from 2012 through 2014. The Oregon study took place prior to the state's enactment of a law mandating automatic registration of people who obtain a driver's license.

18. Lisa A. Bryant and Michael Hanmer, "A Field Experiment to Examine States' Efforts to Increase Registration & Turnout," paper presented at the Annual Meeting of the American Political Science Association, Boston, August 30–September 2, 2018.

19. Jeff Ferguson, Leo Liu, Josh Rosmarin, Lena Tom, and Miya Woolfalk, "Vote.org SMS Voter Registration Test Results," unpublished manuscript (Analyst Institute, 2017); public version accessed at www.vote.org/research/.

Chapter Eleven

1. S. J. Sherman, "On the Self-Erasing Nature of Errors of Prediction," *Journal of Personality and Social Psychology,* vol. 39 (1980): 211–21.

2. The first of these two mechanisms requires only that people have their attention drawn to an activity such as voting, regardless of whether they actually make a prediction. If cognitive accessibility alone were sufficient to generate higher turnout, the "mere mention" of an upcoming election should produce higher turnout. We have seen ample evidence in previous chapters that no such effect exists.

3. Anthony G. Greenwald and others, "Increasing Voting Behavior by Asking People if They Expect to Vote," *Journal of Applied Psychology,* vol. 72 (1987): 315–18.

4. Anthony G. Greenwald and others, "The Self-Prophecy Effect: Increasing Voter Turnout by Vanity-Assisted Consciousness Raising," unpublished manuscript (University of Washington, Department of Psychology, 1988).

5. Jennifer K. Smith, Alan S. Gerber, and Anton Orlich, "Self-Prophecy Effects and Voter Turnout: An Experimental Replication," *Political Psychology,* vol. 24 (2003): 593–604.

6. Dustin Cho, "Acting on the Intent to Vote: A Voter Turnout Experiment," unpublished manuscript (Yale University, Department of Political Science, 2008).

7. Alan S. Gerber, Seth J. Hill, and Gregory A. Huber, "Small Cues and Large Effect: The Results from a Collection of Simultaneous Field Experiments," paper presented at the Annual Meeting of the Midwest Political Science Association, Chicago, April 17, 2015.

8. Christopher B. Mann, "Unintentional Voter Mobilization: Does Participation in Preelection Surveys Increase Voter Turnout?" *Annals of the American Academy of Political and Social Science,* vol. 601 (2005): 155–68.

9. Donald P. Green, Adam Zelizer, and David Kirby, "Testing the Effects of Mail, Phone, and Canvassing Treatments in Partisan Primary Runoff Elections," unpublished manuscript (Columbia University, Department of Political Science, 2014).

10. David Nickerson and Todd Rogers, "Do You Have a Voting Plan? Implementation Intentions, Voter Turnout, and Organic Plan Making," *Psychological Science,* vol. 21 (2010): 194–99.

11. Todd Rogers and John Ternovski, "'We May Ask if You Voted'": Accountability and a Behavior's Importance to the Self," unpublished manuscript (Harvard University, Kennedy School of Government, 2015).

12. Joshua L. Kalla and David E. Broockman, "The Minimal Persuasive Effects of Campaign Contact in General Elections: Evidence from 49 Field Experiments," American Political Science Review, vol. 112 (2018): 148–66.

13. Alan S. Gerber and others, "Why People Vote: Estimating the Social Returns to Voting," *British Journal of Political Science* (forthcoming).

14. See Alan S. Gerber, Donald P. Green, and Christopher W. Larimer, "Social Pressure and Voter Turnout: Evidence from a Large-Scale Field Experiment," *American Political Science Review,* vol. 102 (2008): 33–48; and Costas Panagopoulos, "Affect, Social Pressure and Prosocial Motivation: Field Experimental Evidence of the Mobilizing Effects of Pride, Shame and Publicizing Voting Behavior," *Political Behavior,* vol. 32 (2010): 369–86.

15. Quoted in Donald P. Green and Alan S. Gerber, "Introduction to Social Pressure and Voting: New Experimental Evidence," *Political Behavior,* vol. 32 (2010): 331–36.

16. Todd Rogers and others, "Social Pressure and Voting: A Field Experiment Conducted in a High-Salience Election," unpublished manuscript (Harvard University, Kennedy School of Government, 2014).

17. The Murray and Matland mailer does not scold voters. See Gregg R. Murray and Richard E. Matland, "Mobilization Effects Using Mail: Social Pressure, Descriptive Norms, and Timing," *Political Research Quarterly,* vol. 67 (2013): 304–19. The MoveOn mailer is a colorful, upbeat report card. A description of the MoveOn study and its results may be found in Sasha Issenberg, "The 'Voter Report Card' That MoveOn Hopes Will Shame Slackers," *Slate,* October 31, 2012 (www.slate.com/blogs/victory_lab/2012/10/31/moveon_can_its_voter_report_card_shame_slackers_into_turning_out.html).

18. Alan S. Gerber and others, "The Generalizability of Social Pressure Effects on Turnout Across High-Salience Electoral Contexts: Field Experimental Evidence From 1.96 Million Citizens in 17 States," unpublished manuscript (2016).

19. Christopher B. Mann, "Is There Backlash to Social Pressure? A Large-Scale Field Experiment on Voter Mobilization," *Political Behavior,* vol. 32 (2010): 387–407.

20. Costas Panagopoulos, "Positive Social Pressure and Prosocial Motivation: Evidence from a Large-Scale Field Experiment on Voter Mobilization," *Political Psychology,* vol. 34 (2013): 265–75.

21. Rogers and Ternovski, "'We May Ask if You Voted.'"

22. Stefano DellaVigna and others, "Voting to Tell Others," *The Review of Economic Studies,* vol. 84 (2017): 143–181.

23. Ali Adam Valenzuela and Melissa R. Michelson, "Turnout, Status, and Identity: Mobilizing Latinos to Vote with Group Appeals," *American Political Science Review,* vol. 110 (2016): 615–30.

24. Donald P. Green, Christopher W. Larimer, and Celia Paris, "When Social Pressure Fails: The Untold Story of Null Findings," paper presented at the 68th Annual Meeting of the Midwest Political Science Association, Chicago, April 22–25, 2010.

25. Alan S. Gerber, Donald P. Green, and Holger L. Kern, "Baseline, Placebo, and Treatment: Efficient Estimation for Three-Group Experiments," *Political Analysis,* vol. 18 (2010): 297–315. Alex DeGolia, Michael Schwam-Baird, and Nathaniel Olin, "PICO Relational Organizing Test Results Memo," unpublished manuscript, 2017. We thank Hahrie Han and PICO for sharing a public-facing version.

26. Jaime E. Settle and Margaret J. Schwenzfeier, "When Social Pressure Fails: Evidence from Two Direct Mail Experiments," unpublished manuscript (College of William and Mary, Government Department, 2014).

27. Costas Panagopoulos, "Thank You for Voting: Gratitude Expression and Voter Mobilization," *Journal of Politics,* vol. 73 (2013): 707–17.

28. Mia Costa, Brian F. Schaffner, and Alicia Prevost, "Walking the Walk? Experiments on the Effect of Pledging to Vote on Youth Turnout," PLOS ONE (2018).

29. Robert B. Cialdini and others, "Reciprocal Concessions Procedure for Inducing Compliance: The Door-in-the-Face Technique," *Journal of Personality and Social Psychology,* vol. 31 (1975): 206–15.

30. Deborah Brown McCabe and Melissa R. Michelson, "Pushing Too Hard: Using Door-in-the-Face to Get Voters out the Door," *Journal of Political Marketing,* vol. 14 (2015): 316–32.

31. Gerber and others, "Why People Vote: Estimating the Social Returns to Voting."

Chapter Twelve

1. Roy E. Miller, David A. Bositis, and Denise L. Baer, "Stimulating Voter Turnout in a Primary: Field Experiment with a Precinct Committeeman," *International Political Science Review,* vol. 2 (1981): 445–59, table 1.

2. For further discussion and evidence on this point, see Alan S. Gerber, Donald P. Green, and David Nickerson, "Testing for Publication Bias in Political Science," *Political Analysis,* vol. 9 (2001): 385–92.

3. (https://cavotes.org/research/increasing-voter-turnout) [Accessed June 26, 2015].

4. Raymond E. Wolfinger, Benjamin Highton, and Megan Mullin, "How Postregistration Laws Affect the Turnout of Registrants," CIRCLE Working Paper 15 (University of Maryland, School of Public Policy, 2004).

5. Lisa García Bedolla and Melissa R. Michelson, "What Do Voters Need to Know? Testing the Role of Cognitive Information in Asian American Voter Mobilization," *American Politics Research,* vol. 37 (2009): 254–74.

6. Alan S. Gerber, Donald P. Green, and Ron Shachar, "Voting May Be Habit Forming: Evidence from a Randomized Field Experiment," *American Journal of Political Science,* vol. 47 (2003): 540–50.

7. Melissa R. Michelson, "Dos Palos Revisited: Testing the Lasting Effects of Voter Mobilization," paper presented at the Annual Meeting of the Midwest Political Science Association, April 3–6, 2003; David W. Nickerson, "Habit Formation from the 2001 Youth Vote Experiments," ISPS Working Paper (Yale University, Institution for Social and Policy Studies, December 15, 2003); David W. Nickerson, "Habit Formation from 2002 Placebo Controlled Experiments," ISPS Working Paper (Yale University, Institution for Social and Policy Studies, December 16, 2003). Taken together, these studies imply that each 100 votes in the current election generates an additional 32.5 votes in the subsequent election ($SE = 12.4$). This pattern of persistence has also been demonstrated on an even larger scale using the social pressure mailings discussed in chapter 11. See Tiffany C. Davenport and others, "The Enduring Effects of Social Pressure: Tracking Campaign Experiments over a Series of Elections," *Political Behavior,* vol. 32 (2010): 423–30.

8. Alexander Coppock and Donald P. Green, "Is Voting Habit Forming? New Evidence from Experiments and Regression Discontinuities," *American Journal of Political Science,* vol. 60 (2016): 1044–62.

9. Davenport and others, "The Enduring Effects of Social Pressure," *Political Behavior,* vol. 32 (2010): 423–30; Todd Rogers and others, "Social Pressure and Voting: A Field Experiment Conducted in a High-Salience Election," *Electoral Studies,* vol. 46 (2017): 87–100; Lisa García Bedolla and Melissa Michelson, *Mobilizing Inclusion: Transforming the Electorate through Get-Out-the-Vote Campaigns* (Yale University Press, 2012).

10. A corollary point is that throwing the kitchen sink at a low-turnout group often produces disappointing results. In 2017, Look Ahead American sought to mobilize 6,000 microtargeted law-and-order voters who failed to vote in several recent elections prior to a Virginia state election, but a suite of email, direct mail, robocalls, and paid calls was unable to raise turnout. Turnout in the treatment group was 1.5 percent, as compared to 1.7 percent in the control group.

11. Costas Panagopoulos, "Timing Is Everything? Primacy and Recency Effects in Voter Mobilization Campaigns," *Political Behavior,* vol. 33 (2012): 79–93.

12. Donald P. Green and Shang Ha, "Follow-up Phone Calls from Commercial Phone Banks: Results from Two Multi-State Field Experiments," unpub-

lished manuscript (Columbia University, Department of Political Science, 2015).

13. Alan S. Gerber and others, "When Does Increasing Mobilization Effort Increase Turnout? New Theory and Evidence from a Field Experiment on Reminder Calls," unpublished manuscript (2016).

14. Gregg R. Murray and Richard E. Matland, "Mobilization Effects Using Mail: Social Pressure, Descriptive Norms, and Timing," *Political Research Quarterly*, vol. 67 (2014): 304–19.

15. See Kosuke Imai and Aaron Strauss, "Estimation of Heterogeneous Treatment Effects from Randomized Experiments, with Application to the Optimal Planning of the Get-Out-the-Vote Campaign," *Political Analysis*, vol. 19 (2011): 1–19; and Donald P. Green and Holger L. Kern, "Modeling Heterogeneous Treatment Effects in Survey Experiments with Bayesian Additive Regression Trees," *Public Opinion Quarterly*, vol. 76 (2012): 491–511.

16. See Alan S. Gerber, Donald P. Green, and Christopher W. Larimer, "An Experiment Testing the Relative Effectiveness of Encouraging Voter Participation by Inducing Feelings of Pride or Shame," *Political Behavior*, vol. 32 (2010): 409–22; Betsy Sinclair, Margaret McConnell, and Donald P. Green, "Detecting Spillover Effects: Design and Analysis of Multilevel Experiments," *American Journal of Political Science*, vol. 54 (2012): 1055–69.

17 Alexander Coppock, "Targeting GOTV Efforts with BART," unpublished manuscript (Columbia University, Department of Political Science, 2015). The standard errors for the high- and low-responsiveness groups, respectively, are 0.6 and 0.9, implying that the two estimated effects differ much more than would be expected by chance.

18. Alex DeGolia, Michael Schwam-Baird, and Nathaniel Olin, "PICO Relational Organizing Test Results Memo," 2017; public version shared with PICO's permission by Hahrie Han.

19. For a study in which canvassing by a local organization included presentation of voters' past turnout records, see Tiffany Davenport, "Public Accountability and Political Participation: Effects of a Face-to-Face Feedback Intervention on Voter Turnout of Public Housing Residents," *Political Behavior*, vol. 32 (2010): 337–68.

20. If you already have a research background, you might glean some design ideas from our textbook: Alan S. Gerber and Donald P. Green, *Field Experiments: Design, Analysis, and Interpretation* (New York: W. W. Norton, 2012).

21. Note that all the names you attempted to call belong in the treatment group, even those who could not be reached when called. For a discussion of how to implement this procedure, see David W. Nickerson, "Scalable Protocols Offer Efficient Design for Field Experiments," *Political Analysis*, vol. 13 (2005): 233–52.

22. Kevin Arceneaux, Alan S. Gerber, and Donald P. Green, "A Cautionary Note on the Use of Matching to Estimate Causal Effects: An Empirical Example Comparing Matching Estimates to an Experimental Benchmark," *Sociological Methods and Research*, vol. 39 (2010): 256–82.

23. If you took out a set of observations before random assignment, you should note this.

24. Jeffrey A. Karp and Susan A. Banducci, "The Impact of Proportional Representation on Turnout: Evidence from New Zealand," *Australian Journal of Political Science*, vol. 34 (1999): 363–77.

25. Sarah F. Anzia, *Timing and Turnout: How Off-Cycle Elections Favor Organized Groups* (University of Chicago Press, 2014).

26. Matthew R. Knee and Donald P. Green, "The Effects of Registration Laws on Voter Turnout: An Updated Assessment," in *The Democratic Experiment: Explorations in the Analysis of Public Opinion and Political Participation,* edited by Paul M. Sniderman and Benjamin Highton (Princeton University Press, 2011), pp. 312–28.

27. For reports that campaigns on both the right and left were attentive to experimental studies of GOTV tactics, see David Frum, "Bush's Secret Canadian Weapon," *National Post,* August 2, 2005, p. A12; Matt Bai, "Who Lost Ohio?" *New York Times Magazine,* November 21, 2004, p. 67; and Sasha Issenberg, *The Victory Lab: The Secret Science of Winning Campaigns* (New York: Crown, 2012).

28. The allure of randomizing at the precinct level is that results can be gathered quickly, inexpensively, and without problems of attrition.

29. Joshua L. Kalla and David E. Broockman, "The Minimal Persuasive Effects of Campaign Contact in General Elections: Evidence from 49 Field Experiments," American Political Science Review, vol. 112 (2018): 148–66.

30. Jesse Graham, Jonathan Haidt, and Brian A. Nosek, "Liberals and Conservatives Rely on Different Sets of Moral Foundations," *Journal of Personality and Social Psychology,* vol. 96, no. 5 (2019): 1029–46.

31. Quotation from Gregg R. Murray and Richard E. Matland, "Testing Moral Foundations Theory as a Tool for Mobilizing Voters," unpublished manuscript, 2017 (p. 8), summarizing Kate M. Johnson and others, "Ideology-Specific Patterns of Moral Indifference Predict Intentions Not to Vote," *Analyses of Social Issues and Public Policy,* vol. 14, no. 1 (2014): 61–77.

Appendix A

1. R. Michael Alvarez, Asa Hopkins, and Betsy Sinclair, "Mobilizing Pasadena Democrats: Measuring the Effects of Partisan Campaign Contacts," *Journal of Politics,* vol. 72 (2010): 31–44.

2. Joel A. Middleton, "Voting Is Power 2004 Mobilization Effort," unpublished manuscript (University of California, Berkeley, Travers Department of Political Science, 2015).

Appendix B

1. R. Michael Alvarez, Asa Hopkins, and Betsy Sinclair, "Mobilizing Pasadena Democrats: Measuring the Effects of Partisan Campaign Contacts," *Journal of Politics,* vol. 72 (2010): 31–44.

Appendix C

1. R. Michael Alvarez, Asa Hopkins, and Betsy Sinclair, "Mobilizing Pasadena Democrats: Measuring the Effects of Partisan Campaign Contacts," *Journal of Politics,* vol. 72 (2010): 31–44.

Index